MORE CLOAK THAN DAGGER

One Woman's Career in Secret Intelligence

MORE CLOAK THAN DAGGER

ONE WOMAN'S CAREER IN SECRET INTELLIGENCE

Molly J. Sasson

Foreword by Peter Coleman AO

Connor Court Publishing

Connor Court Publishing Pty Ltd

Copyright © Molly J. Sasson 2015

ALL RIGHTS RESERVED. This book contains material protected under International and Federal Copyright Laws and Treaties. Any unauthorised reprint or use of this material is prohibited. No part of this book may be reproduced or transmitted in any form or by any means, electronic or mechanical, including photocopying, recording, or by any information storage and retrieval system without express written permission from the publisher.

PO Box 224W
Ballarat VIC 3350
sales@connorcourt.com
www.connorcourt.com

ISBN: 9781925138726 (pbk)

Cover design by Ian James

Printed in Australia

DEDICATION

This book is dedicated, with gratitude, to the memory of Brigadier Sir Charles Spry, CBE, DSO, who served his country, Australia, with great distinction not only in World War II, but afterwards as the second Director-General of the Australian Security Intelligence Organisation (ASIO), from 1950 to 1970.

Contents

Foreword by Peter Coleman AO	ix
Abbreviations and acronyms	xiii
Author's note	xv
Acknowledgements	xvi
Introduction	xvii
1 Growing up between the wars	1
2 War service in the RAF	20
3 In the ruins of Hitler's Reich	26
4 A different sort of engagement	36
5 On assignment for British secret intelligence	44
6 Britain rocked by treachery of the Cambridge spies	59
7 Air photographic intelligence during the Cold War	92
8 Working with Dutch counter-espionage	102
9 Dancing with the enemy	114
10 A special invitation from an eminent Australian	126
11 A cool reception in Canberra	135
12 Heroes, has-beens, bunglers, spies	142
13 ASIO's national headquarters in Melbourne	162
14 Soviet penetration of Australian security: the evidence	172
15 The last secrets of the Cold War	204
16 MI5's Roger Hollis and the founding of ASIO	215
17 Looking to the future	236
18 Judging cat shows from Melbourne to Moscow	239

19	Coffee and cake with my interrogator	251
20	The Most Ancient Republic of San Marino	262
21	Destiny turns up trumps again	267
	Notes and references	274
	Bibliography	298
	Index	309

Foreword by Peter Coleman AO

More Cloak Than Dagger is Molly J. Sasson's personal story of her 40 years in the secret services, monitoring Nazism and communism in Britain, Holland and Australia. (She retired in 1983 before the era of terrorism.) But it is her cool appraisal of the Australian Security Intelligence Organisation (ASIO) that will command most attention and raises still unanswered questions of great importance.

Despite ASIO's historic success in managing the defection of the Petrovs in 1954, it remains Sasson's conviction that 'a number' of ASIO officers betrayed Australian, British and U.S. secrets to the Soviet Union over many decades. She relies largely on the testimony of Soviet defectors Major-General Oleg Kalugin and Colonel Oleg Gordievsky, both senior officers of the KGB. But she believes that the most significant disclosures of the KGB's 'penetration' of ASIO came from Major Vasili Mitrokhin, a former senior archivist of the KGB.

In 1972 the KGB gave him sole responsibility for supervising the moving of 300,000 top-secret files from the overcrowded Lubyanka in Moscow to a new location. It took him twelve years. But the more he examined the archives the more horrified he became. 'I could not believe such evil,' he said. Like the Stasi officer in the great German film *The Lives of Others*, he could no longer control or suppress his conscience. He carefully made notes of the files and smuggled them home in his shoes or trousers, and buried them at weekends in tins and milk churns under the floor of his dacha. He hoped in due course to publicise his records; but there was no possibility of this until after the collapse of the Soviet Union in 1991.

In 1992 he was able to take a holiday in Latvia where he asked the American embassy in Riga to allow him to defect to the United

States, with his archive. But the CIA officials decided the sample files that Mitrokhin showed them were fakes. He did not have original documents, only copies and notes. They turned him away. But the British Embassy quickly recognised his importance. The problem was that most of Mitrokhin's files were still buried in his dacha outside Moscow. Six MI6 officers dressed as workmen unearthed six trunks of files and loaded them into a van. They then 'exfiltrated' Mitrokhin, his family and files to Britain where they finally arrived on September 7, 1992. The American FBI described the files as 'the most complete and extensive intelligence ever received from any source'. Mitrokhin lived under police protection, and under a false name, for the rest of his life. He died in January 2004.

But soon after settling in Britain he began collaborating with Professor Christopher Andrew of Cambridge to publish two volumes based on his archives. The first appeared in 1999 and the second in 2005. They examined most countries in the world, but not Australia –although MI6 had almost immediately passed to Australian authorities the Mitrokhin material about the KGB operations in Australia and, in particular, in ASIO. The Keating government thereupon ordered two inquiries into ASIO. The first, by the Australian Federal Police, was codenamed Operation Liver. Its findings remain secret, but, according to Sasson, were 'so sensational' that the Keating government appointed Michael Cook AO, a former Director-General of the Office of National Assessments and Australian ambassador to Washington, to write a full report on suspected Russian penetration of ASIO. The Cook Report also remains secret.

Sasson concludes: 'Surely the Australian people have a right to know if real spies were operating, and for how long, in our government departments, instrumentalities and intelligence agencies.' They should have been exposed and prosecuted, but they were allowed to retire with full pension rights. She calls for the publication of Mitrokhin's revelations, the results of Operation Liver and the contents of the Cook Report.

We need not worry, she says, about what our American and British allies might think. 'They would know this already! They have lived with our "problem" for far too long.' There may conceivably be a good explanation for the silence of the authorities. If there is, it should be made public. It is extraordinary that Mitrokhin's revelations about almost every country in the world have been made public but not Australia with no reason given. Small wonder that Sasson asks: 'Why the cover-up?'

She asks the same question about a number of other issues in the history of ASIO and of the British and Dutch intelligence services in which she has served. (She devotes a chapter to the allegation that Roger Hollis, a former Director-General of MI5, was a Soviet agent. She leaves the question open.) Scholars are now writing a three-volume official history of ASIO. Volume One, *The Spy Catchers* by David Horner, was published in 2014. In *More Cloak than Dagger* Sasson contributes her experience, ideas and doubts to the official story.

It is noteworthy that she pays a special tribute to Sir Charles Spry, the Director-General of ASIO from 1950 to 1970, who recruited her in 1967 to help him in dealing with suspected moles in the intelligence services – 'a task I was, sadly, prevented from completing due to lack of support, deliberate or otherwise, displayed by my colleagues and others in the organisation at that time'. Referring to an ABC documentary of 2010 that smeared Spry's good name and character, she writes: 'What greatly surprises me is that the government of the day never intervened to refute the unfair attacks on this great man who had put the security of his country uppermost against the heavy odds he had to face.... May he always be remembered as a great Australian.'

In the report of the royal commission into ASIO (1986) Justice Robert Hope judiciously concluded: 'ASIO may be, or may have been, penetrated by a hostile intelligence service'. Spry had, and Sasson has, no doubt about it. *More Cloak Than Dagger* gives much of the evidence.

It is now surely time that a biography of Brigadier Sir Charles Spry was written to complement the official history of ASIO. Sasson dedicates her book to him.

Author and former parliamentarian Peter Coleman AO was editor of *The Bulletin* **and** *Quadrant* **during the Cold War and has published 16 books on political, biographical and cultural subjects.**

Abbreviations and Acronyms

ASIO	Australian Security Intelligence Organisation, responsible for domestic security and counter-intelligence.
ASIS	Australian Secret Intelligence Service, responsible for supplying the Australian government with foreign intelligence, and for undertaking counter-intelligence activities and co-operation with other intelligence agencies overseas.
AVH	*Államvédelmi Hatóság*, communist Hungary's secret police.
BVD	*Binnenlandse Veiligheidsdienst* the Dutch Domestic Security Service.
DPs	Displaced Persons.
GRU	*Glavnoye Razvedyvatel'noye Upravleniye*, Soviet Military Intelligence.
JAPIC	Joint Air Photographic Intelligence Centre (UK).
KGB	*Komitet Gosudarstvennoy Bezopasnosti*, Soviet Committee for State Security.
MI5	Britain's Security Service, responsible for domestic security and counter-intelligence. (MI5 originally stood for 'Military Intelligence, Section 5').
MI6	alternative name for the UK Secret Intelligence Service. (MI6 originally stood for 'Military Intelligence, Section 6').
NATO	North Atlantic Treaty Organisation, a military alliance established by the North Atlantic Treaty (also called the Washington Treaty) of April 4, 1949, which sought to create a counterweight to Soviet armies stationed in the 'Iron Curtain' countries of central and eastern Europe after World War II.

ONA	Office of National Assessments, an Australian intelligence body that reports directly to the Prime Minister of Australia, often using intelligence gathered by agencies such as ASIO, ASIS and the Australian Signals Directorate (ASD).

PNG	*persona non grata*, a person who is unwelcome. Under the Vienna Convention on Diplomatic Relations Article 9, a receiving state may 'at any time and without having to explain its decision' declare any member of a diplomatic staff *persona non grata*. A person so declared is considered unacceptable and is usually recalled to his or her home nation.

RAMC	Royal Army Medical Corps.

SIS	UK Secret Intelligence Service (sometimes known as MI6), responsible for supplying the British government with foreign intelligence, undertaking counter-intelligence activities and cooperation with other intelligence agencies overseas.

SOE	Special Operations Executive, a secret British World War II organisation, ordered by Winston Churchill to 'set Europe ablaze'. Its main tasks were to conduct reconnaissance, espionage and sabotage in occupied Europe against the Axis powers, and to assist local resistance movements.

SVR	*Sluzhba Vneshnei Razvedki*, the Foreign Intelligence Service of the Russian Federation (post-Soviet era).

USASIS	United States Army Signal Intelligence Service, the U.S. Army's code-breaking division, based in Arlington, Virginia.

USSR	Union of Soviet Socialist Republics.

Author's Note

For simplicity's sake, I have described the Soviet Union's most famous spy service and secret police as the KGB throughout this book. It has, of course, been known by other names during its existence from 1917 to 1991. It started its life as the Cheka, a Russian acronym for 'All-Russian Emergency Committee to Combat Counter-Revolution and Sabotage'. It was later re-named at various times the GPU, OGPU, NKVD, MGB and, finally, KGB.

Acknowledgements

I wish to acknowledge here my grateful indebtedness to my editor John Ballantyne, who, with unstinting and elaborate skill, helped in the editing and verification of this work and is responsible for the location and addition of the considerable references supporting relevant paragraphs of my text.

I also wish to acknowledge the valuable insights of 'Chris', my good friend and colleague from my days at ASIO's former national headquarters in Melbourne. He witnessed much of what I have attempted to describe in this book, and it is my sincere hope that he will write his own memoirs one day.

I am most grateful to the managing director of Connor Court Publishing, Dr Anthony Cappello, for being willing to publish this controversial book. Connor Court's distinguished layout editor, Michael Gilchrist, deserves a special mention for his sterling work in preparing this book for printing, and for achieving such a high-quality finished product within a very tight production schedule.

Finally, I wish to thank my dear husband Albert, for his unfailing encouragement and support for me throughout this entire project. He devoted many hours typing on the computer and struggling through all the hundreds of hand-written pages that I generated in the production of this book.

Introduction

For almost 40 years it has been my intention to write about my life. In retirement one has time to evaluate the past. Peace of mind and serenity are achieved by acceptance of life and destiny. The story of my life involves much happiness and definite successes, but also many disappointments, sad events, failures and heartbreaks.

Because of my work for the secret services in three countries — the United Kingdom, the Netherlands and Australia — much of my life has remained a closed book. Now that sufficient time has elapsed and I am legally able to divulge certain things, I feel the need to disclose facts in order to set straight the historical record.

My experiences in the Australian Security Intelligence Organisation, both in Canberra and later in ASIO's then national headquarters in Melbourne, drove me to the necessity to extend the scope of my book to review and discuss the reality at that time, notably in three distinct areas:

1. the presence in Australia, during the Cold War, of confirmed spies for the Soviet Union, who were allowed to operate unimpeded in the country for many years;

2. setting the record straight on the false and malicious reporting by the Australian media – especially by the Australian Broadcasting Corporation in 2010 – of the long and distinguished career of ASIO's second Director-General, Brigadier Sir Charles Spry, after his death; and

3. to push the case for the public release of a report by a former Soviet KGB officer Vasili Mitrokhin, who defected to the West in 1992, bringing with him evidence

of Soviet penetration of ASIO. As will be described in Chapter 15 of this book, his testimony to the Australian Federal Police launching a secret probe into ASIO, which resulted in a number of the organisation's senior personnel being forcibly retired for betraying their country.

Others have written books about ASIO, covering its history, administration and structure.[1] My story is different. I am writing about my personal experiences as a loyal employee, in a true rendition of the situation as I lived it at that time: that of a woman in a man's world.

During my life, many of the circumstances, changes in direction and evolving situations I experienced were beyond my control. I travelled to many lands, was involved in a world war and was brought to Australia – all while pursuing my career in intelligence over 40 years. During that time I monitored National Socialism and communism — and now we face global terrorism!

In early 1983, on the day of my retirement, I cleared my office and vacated my desk, the last day of my employment with ASIO, which was marked by a pleasant lunch with 15 friends with whom I had shared plenty, including a few from different departments.

In preparation for that day I had a suitcase packed, with an air ticket to Frankfurt, destination Wiesbaden in southwest Germany. This was a new beginning where my hobby could now come into its own.

My destination was the head office of the *Fédération Internationale Féline (*FIFe), a worldwide federation of cat registries, situated in a large villa in leafy Wiesbaden. As vice-president of the FIFe, I joined the president and, together, we cleared a vast amount of correspondence worldwide, covering thirty-nine member-countries.

A large itinerary of judging assignments, covering six months, with an international show each weekend throughout Europe, awaited me.

I travelled by railway and air, covering thousands of miles across Europe and the Middle East, training many judges, giving talks and dealing with problems in different countries, including the United States of America, Canada, Malaysia, Singapore and New Zealand.

I ran training programmes for all cat breeds and supervised examinations. Meanwhile, my husband was touring Australia's Northern Territory and sailing in the Bay of Islands in New Zealand, and our Siamese were with good friends still enjoying the Australian way of life, climbing gum trees and meeting up with some wildlife including a frill-necked lizard in the friends' rockery.

After my time in ASIO, I proceeded to undertake another type of service in Australia, when I accepted and carried out the assignment of Consul-General of the Republic of San Marino. My association with this republic dates back to 1946.

Truth is stranger than fiction in the sometimes unbelievable journey that I have taken in my life.

In hard times, my belief in God and in what I was doing, my good friends, my life-long love of animals and beautiful music have always been a consolation and provided me with a source of inner peace. Also, my grandmother's wise words have been very important to me: 'Life is but a whisper', 'Make the most of each day within your capacities and remember', 'I shall pass this way but once; any good thing therefore that I can do, or any kindness that I can show, let me not defer it or neglect it, for I shall not pass this way again.'

As it has been said, 'In the beginning was the word'. These are my words, through which I have endeavoured to convey to you my experiences, my personal journey.

1

GROWING UP BETWEEN THE WARS

It was a sunny, crisp winter morning on the day I was born, and it was a Sunday! Children born on the Sabbath Day are supposed to be very fortunate according to an old English poem:[1]

> Monday's child is fair of face,
> Tuesday's child is full of grace,
> Wednesday's child is full of woe.
> Thursday's child has far to go,
> Friday's child is loving and giving,
> Saturday's child works hard for a living,
> But the child that is born on the Sabbath Day
> Is bonnie and blithe and good and gay.

(In the nineteenth century, when this poem was written, 'gay' was described in the Oxford Dictionary, as 'disposed to joy and mirth, light-hearted, exuberantly cheerful, sportive, merry'.)

There was much happiness and great relief after I had been delivered by caesarean section, healthy and well. My mother had previously lost two babies, and her dearest wish to become a mother was now realised. However, I was destined to be, and remain, an only child – a mixed blessing with definite rewards and some drawbacks.

I had a wonderful start in life with an outstanding, talented and devoted mother who was a brilliant professional pianist. She had also studied violin as her second subject at the Royal Academy. Her talents included painting in both oils and watercolour. She gained high praise wherever her works were exhibited. We still treasure some of her paintings in our home today.

She had spent three years in France, before and during World War I. During that time, she worked for the War Office in both England and France, making use of her knowledge of French. I have no knowledge of the nature of her work as it was secret and was never discussed in the family.

She met my father at a London choral society. They both loved classical music and, as a soprano and baritone, they soon sang duets. My father was tall, dark, handsome and musical. After his academic studies and his marriage to my mother in 1919, he accepted the offer of a position that involved much travel to and from the continent of Europe. He developed a thriving business of his own involving trade in gentlemen's hats.

We occupied a three-storey house in a quiet residential area of Putney, southwest of London and the Thames. The basement was full of unused items such as boxes, suitcases and a sleeping place for one or more stray cats that often sought refuge from the rain and cold via a trap door. It also served as a maternity ward for the odd litter of kittens.

The ground floor had a dining room, drawing room, father's study, music room and a large kitchen, which housed a big AGA stove. What a great invention that was! It was fed by wood and coal and included six heating rings on top and a large oven. It supplied constant heat for cooking and provided hot water throughout the house via a system of pipes. Our bathroom had a huge bath with four curved legs and a separate large gas geyser that provided the hot water just for the bath. This was adjacent to my parents' bedroom, which had a balcony. Next door was my bedroom, and on the opposite side was a guest room.

The housekeeper, Bernadine, worked for my family from 1924 till 1939. She occupied the top floor of our house, which contained a bedroom, a small bathroom and sitting room. She had a busy but comfortable life. She did the washing, all the cooking and sometimes some shopping. Most of our groceries were delivered. The greengrocer came twice a week with fresh produce. He drove a horse and cart, and his friendly horse named Nellie came close up to the garden gate in anticipation of titbits. I enjoyed giving her a crust of bread or some carrot and always some water.

Bernadine was German, a solidly built individual with a pleasant, kind personality, who had, thankfully, acquainted herself in the art of British cuisine. Nevertheless, her potato salad appeared a little too often. Sausages were her favourite, but were banned from our table, as mother never trusted their content. Bernadine travelled to Rosenheim, Bavaria, each summer to see her aged mother and sister and always brought me back a small souvenir. She spoke very understandable English but when annoyed would break into muttered German.

The author when young

The housemaid, Mary, came and went each day. She did the light daily cleaning and ironing. 'Mrs Mop' came once a week to do the rough work, thoroughly cleaning the floors inside and the pavement and tiles outside. It was a really happy home as I recall. When my father was there, everything was on time and in place. Things were much more relaxed when he was away on business.

Mother coached students preparing for exams at the Royal Academy and practised the piano and violin for three to four hours each day during the week. She still spent much of her time with me, and I often 'sat in' if and when she deemed it beneficial towards my musical development. There was always music in our house. Mother often invited colleagues and friends for afternoon tea on Sundays. These occasions were always enriched by three or more musicians performing. I was surrounded by talent.

When I was an infant, mother would place me beside her in my high chair to listen to her playing. She told me years later that I was clearly enjoying the music and moving with a distinct sense of rhythm before I could speak. By the time I turned three, she was teaching me to play nursery rhymes on the piano. From about this time my own personal memories come to life and I can recollect the wonderful things we did together.

From this early age, I was taught to behold and enjoy the lovely, simple, yet so complex beauty of nature. I have loving memories of walking through our garden holding mother's hand while she told me stories about the flower fairies who always came out to play when we were not there. We fed the many birds that came each day for breakfast in our garden and admired the colourful flowers, bees, frogs and all that lived there. She would pick several special blooms, carry them inside and sit down with me while she sketched each flower and painted them. I had my own sheet of paper and paint box and coloured my version under her instruction. What beautiful times those were. My childish curiosities and interests were never ignored or left unanswered.

At the age of four I developed measles and the doctor ordered me to stay in bed, which I was loath to do. Several weeks before, mother had taken me to the 1927 Cat Show at the Crystal Palace in London when pedigree cats were a rarity. This show was a momentous occasion for cat-lovers. I fell in love with the Siamese cats on show, and mother had difficulty dragging me away from them.

With this recent visit in mind, my darling mother decided, with her kind and loving heart, to purchase a Siamese kitten on the understanding I would be a good patient and obey doctor's orders. Mother thus returned home with a square wicker-basket, which she placed on my bed and told me to open. I had no idea what was inside, so the surprise was very real. I lifted the lid, squealed with joy and removed 'the most beautiful kitten on earth' out of the box. This memory has so often returned to me and is from where my life-long love for Siamese cats was born. Mother later told me I was obedient for many weeks afterwards.

We named the kitten Ming and all in our household loved him. Naughtiness, such as climbing curtains, scratching chairs and carpets, was largely overcome by directing Ming to a cocos mat by the kitchen door, which had become the perfect 'scratch'. He soon learned some rules and became an adorable, loving pet. He sat for hours at mother's side on the piano stool, spellbound. He loved classical music, particularly Chopin.

The arrival of Ming was a great event in those childhood years. What a character he was and an expert at inventing games. He had a great life roaming our garden and living like the oriental prince he was. He provided joy to us all and gave us his unconditional love and affection throughout his life, which ended at 12 years.

The single misdemeanour we can recall was a visit he paid our neighbour one Sunday lunchtime, from which he returned with a roast chicken! Bernadine was very confused as we too had roast chicken on the menu that Sunday. It was only several weeks later that mother spoke with our neighbour who told her the black and white cat from 'down the road' had stolen his lunch that day. I am not sure whether mother left it at that or told him the truth!

My father was always busy and somewhat remote in my life. He was a good man, a devout Catholic and generous to the poor and needy. He was awarded the papal order, the *Pro Ecclesia et Pontefice* (also known as the 'Cross of Honour'), for his distinguished service to the

Church. His religion was precious to him. He gave me the best start in life and a happy, healthy childhood. My education was carefully considered and I went to one of the best schools known at the time.

My maternal grandmother came to England from Ireland to marry my grandfather, who worked at the Colonial Office in London. Sadly, she was widowed in 1935 when I was twelve years old. She later devoted much of her time visiting and caring for maimed and crippled soldiers who had survived the Great War. She had previously opened up her house to a Belgian refugee family – a clergyman with his wife and daughter. She was always ready to relieve suffering around her.

My grandmother was a strong lady whom I loved dearly. She played a large part in making my childhood years so memorable. Being her only grandchild, she lavished much affection on me. Very much like my mother, she was an artist who painted and played the harp for which she had a special room. Sensitive, compassionate, caring and loving, she encouraged me in every interest I displayed.

We all loved animals and cared for stray cats and dogs, when and where necessary. I have always seen animals as a great gift of nature to humanity. They are, inevitably, part of our lives and dependent on our care and consideration. Whether they are pets or working animals, each is an individual being and deserves understanding, patience and compassion. This also goes for wildlife. With all our knowledge, scientific advancements and theories, we are still discovering remarkable facts about animal life around us. From my grandmother and mother, I learned to respect and admire animals and to appreciate the wonder of their real companionship.

Granny occupied a large house in Gloucester Gardens, Paddington, where we spent many days doing exciting things together. Granny would collect me and take me shopping, often to Harrods, where we would have afternoon tea or lunch together.

On one of these outings we visited my favourite place, the pet section, where they sold birds, fish, puppies, kittens, rabbits and, to my delight, also monkeys. These energetic little chaps were ready and waiting to play with any passer-by or onlooker. In one section there were two cages, one above the other, each containing a monkey. While I was bending down to take a closer look, Gran knelt down on one knee beside me. This protective gesture cost her dearly. The monkey in the cage above was attracted to her large hat covered with ribbon and tulle, which was fashionable at that time. We did not notice the eager paw reaching for her hat through the bars, which were meant to keep the monkey inside.

Within a second, he was pulling and tugging yards of ribbon into his cage. My startled grandmother removed her hat, which by now was denuded of all its colourful decorations. The monkey, shrieking with delight, was greatly enjoying draping himself with this finery, while my grandmother, mortified and embarrassed, took me by the hand, making a speedy get-away. She was carrying the remnants of her once attractive chapeau, much to the amusement of the many onlookers who had gathered around us. A rather shocked shop assistant offered to collect the remains. This offer was politely refused as we made a hasty exit for home. This incident was difficult for Gran, as she never went shopping without a hat.

The annual Christmas parties were unforgettable. As we had quite a small family, close friends were always included, some with children, so there was company for me among the grown-ups. The large Christmas tree in the entrance hall was the highlight of the season for me at that age, even though all Christmas parcels were kept out of sight till Christmas Eve. We all attended Midnight Mass and, on returning home, found plenty of parcels under the tree. These memories remain a precious part of my childhood.

Mother always played special music after Christmas dinner, followed by my grandmother who played the harp. Often, one or more guests joined in and we had a chamber orchestra! After my grandfather's death in 1935, Christmas was never quite the same.

We missed him greatly. His jovial, jolly personality was a great asset and he always brought crackers and other exciting parcels for us and organised games.

My paternal grandparents had both passed away in the late 1920s, so our family became even smaller. My paternal grandmother was a tall, elegant woman. I recall her perfume, shoes, jewellery and large hats. She fascinated me, but we were never close, which on reflection I attribute to the fact that she did not like children. I have good memories of my grandfather who wore a monocle, drove a car and was always ready to give me a piggyback. But best of all he gave me Rupert, my teddy bear, who accompanied me through life! I still treasure his presence. He is now 88 years old. For years he sat on an armchair in my bedroom when he was not taken out. He still sports his original check waistcoat and trousers, muffler, brown jacket and leather boots. This precious chap shared the joys and tears of my childhood with patient understanding and always offered comfort and solace in exchange for a hug.

I was never attracted to dolls. Kind friends gave me dolls over the years. They all ended up in a chest of drawers, waiting for my friends to play with them. My three-storey dolls' house was in great demand with my friends, and we spent a great many hours taking out and replacing furniture to and from different rooms.

As a growing child, I was encouraged and taught to make presents for friends at Christmas — articles such as calendars, cards and small paintings. Mother taught me pen-painting on silk, which was used to make pin-cushions, handkerchief sachets and other small gifts that were popular in those days. I learned fretwork, how to use plywood, make dolls' house furniture, blue and red velvet chairs, and tables and lampshades depicting Walt Disney characters. My work brought me unexpected rewards in the shape of prizes for winning children's handicraft competitions, such as a Reeves Paint Box and several books.

During my early years, I was blessed with a nanny named Ann. She arrived daily at breakfast time. Ann had long, black hair that was held up with a black ribbon, which I often used to pull. She was rarely angry. She managed to teach me the alphabet, reading and writing well before school. We always included Rupert in our outings and games. Ann left when I was seven to join another family in the United States of America.

I had a number of friends who were my parents' friends' children. They were usually on their best behaviour when they entered the house, until they saw me sliding down the banister and promptly joined in, only to be reprimanded by Bernadine who had a loud, penetrating voice – enough to terrify a child!

As I was growing up, I started to value money. I received a shilling a week when I was six, which would be increased each birthday, if deserved. This was never enough, but mother and Gran often bought me small things when we went shopping. At age seven, I am told, I developed an entrepreneurial streak and went 'into business'. Now Ann had gone, I enjoyed more freedom and filled up my small, red wheelbarrow with sand from my sandpit and went from house to house selling sand for cat trays. Not all families had cats, so this was never going to be a lucrative venture. Furthermore, a kind neighbour informed my mother jokingly of my efforts, which were swiftly ended that very week.

I badly wanted and needed a scooter to get around. My pocket money had increased to two shillings a week, which carefully went into my moneybox. I was also saving up for a tennis racquet and a gift for mother's birthday. I visited the shop where I had seen the scooter I wanted, one with bright red handlebars. I felt confident the shopkeeper would remember me as I had been there previously with my mother. I entered and asked to speak with the owner to discuss buying on credit. The owner appeared with a friendly smile but my enquiry did not go down very well. I explained that I did not have enough money in my moneybox to pay cash down, but assured him I was honest and badly in need of transport, so what could he suggest? This kind man picked up my chosen scooter and told me to bring in my pocket money each week until the debt was paid off. I thanked him with all my heart and sped off down the street, victorious.

My joy was to be short lived. Bernadine was the first person to see me arriving home on the brand new scooter. 'Where did you get that?' she bellowed. I started to explain that I was paying for it each week, when mother appeared. She was shocked and forbade me to take it out alone. Then came the questions and answers. Finally her advice was to ask Father Christmas to help out later that year, but for now, the scooter had to be returned to the shop with due apology to the kind shopkeeper. Mother was quite adamant about this and no amount of pleading could change her point of view. Happily and luckily father was not at home as he would have been very angry indeed. So mother and I, with a heavy heart, returned the scooter and walked home. This defeat was hard to bear, so a letter was written to Father Christmas, counter-signed by my mother. What do you think I found on Christmas morning?

This episode was described to me in detail many years later with much laughter, when I called into the shop before it closed down. This little scooter gave me much pleasure and enabled me to make new friends. Several years later I gave it to a young boy who had no toys.

Although, on reflection, I had a wonderful life with every opportunity and my parents' great love and attention, I often wished that I had brothers and sisters like most other children. Mother frequently invited friends over who had children my age. She was acutely aware of the situation. When I felt 'lonely', my darling Ming would talk to me in his very own language, as Siamese cats characteristically do, and Rupert, my bear, would always listen to me. Friends visited frequently and Bernadine always managed to find a treat to offer them. We also played many games. One game which turned into a most unfortunate incident took place when I was pretending to be a 'hairdresser'.

A friend named Jane had beautiful, long, natural, red hair. Before she went to school each day, her mother made one, long, waist-length plait. This hairstyle caused her much embarrassment. First, she was the only redhead in class and, secondly, this plait was often pulled, causing her pain. Jane happily joined in our game and unsuspectingly took her place in the 'hairdresser's chair'. Using large kitchen scissors I cut off her plait! She screamed and ran home with her plait in hand. Soon after, her mother arrived to enquire about what happened. My dear mother dealt with the crisis, but I could not replace the lost hair. I clearly recollect Jane's very kind mother, who was not angry with me, telling me not to worry, as it 'would grow again in time'. I was devastated but grateful for her gracious attitude and acceptance of this very thoughtless act I had inflicted on her hapless daughter.

Some months after this incident, I joined two boys, the sons of our local GP, who were good at breaking windows in empty houses in the district. This sounded like fun to me at the time, so we set off one afternoon and apparently did much damage, breaking a number of large windows with bricks from an adjacent building site. Two days later, the police came to the house while my father was home. They informed him of my misdemeanour and prepared him for the payment of one third of a large bill that would be presented to the parents of the three offending rascals. Thus it was not really surprising when, several months later, my father announced his decision to send me to boarding school. It was almost time for the start of my secondary education, so I had a few months to prepare myself for the inevitable.

We had made many trips abroad during my first twelve years of life. I recall holidays in France, Switzerland, Germany, Austria, Hungary, Belgium and Holland. Some special memories include sitting in the golden coach at Schloss Wernigerode, a castle located in Germany's Harz Mountains, and climbing the Brocken Mountain (the highest peak in the Harz range) to see the *Hexentanzplatz* (the Witches' Dance Floor), where the witches danced all night. I have a very clear memory of sitting by the window of the hotel looking out for witches on broomsticks who never came. I also visited the travelling 'Lilliput Town' in Holland, where dwarfs lived together in their caravan community; the Puppet Show in Salzburg; and the Liszt Academy in Budapest. There was the two-month-long winter holiday at Hotel Eden in Interlaken, where I was supposed to learn to ski but preferred the bobsleigh. We had holidays in Nice with Aunt Ethel, a distant relative, who lived at the Pola Negri Hotel each winter to escape the English weather. I also recall our stays at Hotel International au Lac in Lugano, which still exists and is now run by the grandson of the manager we knew, Mr Schmidt-Dressler. We spent a holiday there in 2014. It was lovely to be back at this hotel, where we were made very welcome by the 88-year-old son of Mr Schmidt-Dressler, who was a little boy in the 1930s.

In the meantime, my education was a regular topic of conversation between my parents and grandmother. Everybody felt they knew best. France was high on the list as all were agreed I should learn languages properly. Much deliberation and many enquiries led to Montreux, but my father was disappointed with the school and curriculum, so this proved a dismal failure. A business contact informed my father of an excellent school where he had recently sent his daughter, Anna. My father flew to the Netherlands to make further enquiries and see for himself. He returned well satisfied. Anna was very happy there. Anna and I were pen pals and she had spent a holiday with us. So, all things considered, plans were in the making and I was consulted.

This International Ladies' College was located six miles from The Hague and rated as one of the best available at the time. Students from many countries were educated there. It sounded exciting to me, as we had been to The Hague previously. I was happy and ready to take the plunge, but I still had a few months to wait. Life in England in the thirties was very difficult for many people. The Great Depression caused unemployment, poverty, hunger and often hopelessness. I recall hearing King George V's first Christmas Day broadcast in 1932. We were all at my grandparents' home enjoying Christmas Day. Later that day, my mother and a group of friends combined to arrange a Christmas gathering for poor, local families. Christmas presents had been collected from neighbours and friends, wrapped and labelled for this occasion. Our local priest acted as Father Christmas, and I was allowed to be his helper, dressed as an angel with large, clumsy white wings positioned on my back. These wings weighed heavily on my shoulders in more ways than one.

After Christmas, I was to start at my new school. I remember all the preparations prior to my formal arrival. Summer uniform was white; in winter it was navy blue. There were black shoes with straps, and black patent for dress wear with a long, white gown. Night attire was as we wished. We had our own bedroom, small and practical, with a wash-basin with hot and cold water. A schedule of two baths per week was mandatory.

The day of my arrival was drawing ever closer. Cases and possessions were packed, Rupert included among them. After a tearful goodbye to Ming, I left with my parents and we headed to the port of Harwich. From there we sailed to the Hook of Holland and onwards by taxi beyond The Hague.

We were received graciously by Mother Superior, who charmed my parents but was distinctly 'wary' of me. She gave me some piercing looks over her teacup, which did not help me feel at ease. Tea was served by an English nun named Elizabeth, who made me feel much better. She later proved to be a good friend to me throughout my five years at the school. She came from Bournemouth and many years later I visited her niece there.

The school had been a country estate located in woodlands since 1880. It had been modified and custom-built with four extensions to house a convent and school run by Dutch, English, French and German-speaking Dominican nuns, who all held degrees in their countries of origin. The school placed a strong emphasis on languages, artistic accomplishments, etiquette, good behaviour and character-forming activities, such as sports. It was known for its educational achievements and provided entry to university. I loved those school years, my friends and particularly the sports: tennis, riding, cycling and hockey.

Our refectory was simple and practical. Meals were wholesome, the food plentiful and well prepared. Much, if not all, of the produce was grown at the adjoining farm, which was both dairy and agricultural. As far as I could see and remember, the school was self-supporting. The convent housed many nuns from many European countries as support staff. They were accommodated on a separate site on the estate. The chapel was relatively large. The boarders occupied the front seats, while the nuns filled the many seats at the back, which contained two long rows on either side. The choir was upstairs at the side of the organ.

The first few days were strange, meeting all the tutors, staff and fellow students. Anna welcomed me with open arms and we remained close friends for many years until her death in 1992. Gradually, I became accustomed to my tutors. Sister Hyacinth was my music teacher who often grew tearful when I sang with her. She called me her angel. My German and Dutch teacher, Sister Cyrilla, left the Order to get married (almost a scandal in those days). Sister Gabrielle, the French teacher, enjoyed speaking French with my mother when she visited the school.

There were three male tutors, including a grumpy, elderly gentleman who was our physics teacher and a Belgian bishop who was assigned as chaplain to the convent and school. He was a pleasant monsignor who tried hard to control his sometimes unruly class of teenage girls.

We teased him mercilessly and now, on looking back regretfully, it is too late to apologise. On one occasion I put a frog in his lector. He got a terrible fright, which amused us all at the time. But such tricks were not worth the inevitable consequences, the main one being the damage to one's reputation within the hierarchy. This was hard to repair.

Best of all the tutors was a very handsome, dark-haired doctor who came to teach us anatomy. He used to blush frequently and we named him 'Bashful' after the character in Walt Disney's *Snow White and the Seven Dwarfs*. We found out he was engaged, and when he got married at the Park Street Church in The Hague he invited us all to his wedding.

Sister Francisco, the Mother Superior, looked every inch the part. She was a tall, stately presence with a look of steel. One glance was enough to make us feel guilty, even if we were innocent of whatever it was she accused us. Frankly, we were all terrified of her and when we were summoned to her office there were always plenty of reasons to feel scared.

During the first year, I was close to disaster after setting off the fire alarm during Sunday Mass by pulling down a lever on the wall. It caused total chaos in the chapel; nuns were running everywhere. I shall never forget that Sunday. Only my closest friends would speak to me. I was in disgrace!

An official appointment was made for me to see Mother Superior at 10 o'clock on the Monday morning. Worst of all, my father had been advised by phone and such calls were known to precede 'expulsion'. Numbed with fear and anxiety, I found my way to this dreaded appointment. This was to be the end.

Timidly I knocked on the door, which was instantly pulled open by Mother Superior herself. She seemed to tower over me and addressed me in a loud, firm voice. I remember my knees were shaking and I was much relieved when she told me to 'sit down and listen', which I obeyed. Why, she asked, did I set off the fire alarm, as I must have known it would disrupt Sunday Mass and upset everyone? This was not only very disrespectful, but caused chaos which ruined everybody's Sunday. She told me that she had spoken to my father to explain that such behaviour could not be tolerated at this school.

He was very upset with me, but she emphasised how much my parents loved me, that they were happy to pay for many extras available at the school and that I should be grateful for this and be of good behaviour. She continued by saying that she had discussed expulsion with the school committee (which consisted of six senior sisters and the bishop) and they were prepared to forgive me if I was truly sorry and would promise never to commit such a disruption again.

I listened to this long, long sermon after which I must have oozed repentance. I was ready to promise anything, so I solemnly declared not to disrupt anything ever again. This was a huge promise but the alternative was unthinkable, as I loved my school and most of my tutors. Thus a new leaf was turned over and I abandoned 'naughtiness' in all its variations. We parted with a handshake and a repeat of my promise.

My remaining years at high school were happy and successful and I look back with much gratitude and appreciation for all the care, patience and trouble that were taken each day to help and guide me towards becoming a responsible adult. I am certain that, together with my upbringing, this schooling enabled me to muster the moral courage to see me through the arduous times that lay ahead, which nobody could have foreseen. I was able to attend two school reunions in 1956 and 1958, when everything seemed unchanged. But the Order left and the school closed down soon after, as did many other convent schools at the time – probably because of a shortage of funds and nuns, or to streamline and amalgamate elsewhere.

On my turning seventeen, after my five years in boarding school, my future career had now been decided. I was to be a singer of classical music. From the age of fourteen I had developed a high soprano voice (coloratura) and had a wide octave range with 'perfect pitch'. I frequently sang solo in chapel and on all festive occasions at school. They dubbed me 'Deanna Durbin', after the well-known young film star of the time. Vocal training therefore took first place in my course, with pianoforte as my second subject.

Though there were air raids, blackouts and rationing, these did not interfere with my wish to start a singing career. Opera pieces, German *Lieder* and French *bergerettes* were studied daily, with scales and breathing exercises undertaken at the Academy of Music in London. I was dispatched to churches, dinners, parties and home concerts by my professor, Albert Howe. Most Sundays I would sing at the services at the Church of St Anselm and St Cecilia in Kingsway. I was a dedicated student.

The seriousness of the war struck me sharply as the Battle of Britain and regular raids developed over the skies of London during the summer and autumn of 1940. News bulletins over the radio and the sounds and havoc of planes overhead drove us to run for safety under the massive oak staircase, which offered the best shelter in the house, as well as three storeys above us for additional protection. At night we took to our cellar with beds and some emergency supplies, comforted by the chimes of Big Ben reaching us on the radio.

The worst attacks took place during the month of September 1940, starting on a sunny Saturday afternoon on September 7. Some 375 German bomber fighters attacked London, concentrating on our docks, the City, Kensington and Westminster. This was followed by 250 night-raiders with high explosives and incendiary bombs, leaving thousands of houses destroyed and three main-line railway terminals out of action. At least 430 men, women and children lost their lives and over 1,600 were seriously wounded.

The following night there were 412 killed and 747 wounded; and on the third night 200 bombers scored 370 dead and 1,400 injured. London was attacked by bombers every night during this month of September, during which a total of 5,730 people died, with 10,000 seriously injured. A total of 12,696 civilians were killed in London, and 20,000 were seriously injured. We can only imagine, and give grateful thanks, as to where we would have ended, without the superiority achieved by the Royal Air Force in the Battle of Britain and their success in forcing the stoppage of this carnage.[2]

With my experience of many visits to continental Europe, particularly Germany, with my parents before the outbreak of World War II, I was conversant with reality. I was haunted by my recollection of a visit in 1934 to the Free City of Danzig, where we watched the Brownshirts of the National Socialist German Workers' Party (NSDAP) singing as they marched through the town with their swastika armbands. I even remember the name of the street in Danzig, the Karthauserstrasze, I was singularly dismayed after watching this parade and others that we witnessed in Cologne and Mannheim.

I had now become a lover of German *Lieder* and specialised in church music, selected opera arias and the many beautiful songs composed by Schubert, Schumann and Strauss. My role models were Elisabeth Schwarzkopf and the Peruvian singer, Yma Sumac. Though I loved music with a passion, I was now drawn by a strong sense of duty and patriotism in quite a different direction. I decided that my musical career could be put on hold until after the war, and I was determined to join the Royal Air Force. I was not yet old enough to enlist, so I continued my music studies until I was finally able to join the RAF.

Sadly, as will be described in this book, I never did return to my music studies, but my love and passion for music never waivered. In fact, music has often sustained me during hard times in later life, and is still a source of great comfort and much enjoyment.

2

WAR SERVICE IN THE RAF

After plenty of thought and preparation, and even though my parents were anxious, I walked happily and confidently into the RAF recruiting office in Kingsway, London, to offer my services as a driver. The sergeant on duty asked for my papers and studied my CV and told me to take a seat and wait, as somebody else would need to see me.

Soon afterwards, an officer arrived, greeted me with a broad smile and a handshake, and invited me to follow him into a small adjoining room. We sat down and he spoke with me in fluent German, the last thing I expected.

Three weeks later a letter arrived 'On His Majesty's Service'. The letter informed me to report for duty on the date given, at the Kingsway office with an overnight bag to await further instructions. I must confess I had some last-minute feelings of concern and some apprehension as to what was to come.

On arrival at Kingsway I was placed in charge of a draft of 30 women recruits from all walks of life. I was handed an envelope containing relevant documents and a railway warrant to take us all to our destination. A three-tonne truck was waiting outside to take us to Kings Cross station. We all climbed in as best as we could. There were benches fixed along the sides but some of us sat on the floor. We were on our way to six weeks of serious training. None of us could have imagined what was to come.

All went well until we needed to change trains at Crewe, where a two-hour delay was announced. I managed to herd the group into the station canteen while counting the 29 bodies. There was a strange mood of excitement and uncertainty amongst the group who had all met only today for the first time. Our train finally arrived at the platform and the girls started boarding. I counted 27. Two were missing, so the search was on. The stationmaster assisted me in searching the platform and beyond, while the train was held up. The two missing girls were located at the very end of the platform with two young men they had met during our prolonged wait at the station. They were surprised when we appeared, suggesting that we catch the next train to our destination, Wilmslow, Cheshire, a town 11 miles south of Manchester. We pointed out the urgency of their cooperation and, luckily, they agreed to board the train that was waiting for us. What a start that was!

We finally arrived late in the afternoon in the pouring rain. Another three-tonne truck was waiting to take us to the RAF School of Recruit Training station, our home for the next six weeks. We scrambled out of the truck into the many puddles while the driver hastened to tell us, 'It always rains here'. And so we arrived at reception. I handed over the envelope I had been given in Kingsway and each recruit was identified.

We were given an enamel mug and 'irons' (knife, fork and spoon) and taken to the canteen for tea. The canteen was a large space with benches and trestle tables where hundreds of airmen and airwomen

RAF Wilmslow, Cheshire (photo taken by Corp. D.I. Frank Arnall)

were already having their tea (evening meal). In addition, there was a large queue waiting to be served at the long, busy counter. Five cooks were serving the 'passers-by' with bacon and baked beans on toast, bread and butter, cheese, jam and tea. We were all hungry and glad to find food and a seat in this very noisy, crowded place.

Thereafter we walked to the billet assigned to us. It was a Nissen hut with twelve beds on either side, a stove in the centre, and two cubicles for the two NCOs (non-commissioned officers) in charge. The bed was covered with a three-piece mattress filled with straw, colloquially referred to as 'biscuits', three horse blankets, two sheets, a hard bolster and pillow slip. The washrooms and toilets were situated at the end of the hut. Finally, we were all taken to the medical section to have an FFI (free from infection) check-up. Three of our group were retained for 'treatment' and the rest of us were returned to our billet.

The next question was how to sleep on this bed with such a pillow – a most uncomfortable prospect, yet there was no other option and no room for complaints. The Tannoy (loudspeaker) woke us at 6 am daily. We were responsible for our own bed space and each morning we had to strip the bed and fold each blanket and sheet, neatly stacking them in a straight line with the beds on either side. The floor had to be swept and polished daily and kept squeaky clean. Inspections took place each morning before parade. A shower preceded breakfast. We soon learned to march to breakfast in our civilian clothes and shoes. During this first week, drill, which included a few long-route marches, caused most of us to develop blisters as the shoes we were wearing were mostly unsuitable for this purpose.

After the first week we were issued with our uniforms and full kit. However there was a problem. Some sizes were out of stock, so a choice had to be made, particularly for shoes and hats, whether to go for too small or too big. The first produced blisters and our route marches turned into agonising ordeals. The hats swallowed up faces.

This was not all. We learned to march, to obey, to take orders and insults, to not answer back, to enjoy discipline the hard way, to make friends, to assist others always, and to swear! This experience was the precursor to further rigorous training in other areas. This training was a great culture shock, which brought us down to earth and into the reality of living with bare necessities. These six weeks seemed like a long time but they did eventually come to an end. For five members of our intake, it all proved too much and they were discharged as not suited to service life and returned to civilian life. The remainder of the intake was now ready to go forward to further their respective training courses in different units and locations.

Sergeants and corporals seemed to wield great power in the eyes of the humble recruit. There was, of course, an explanation for everything in those early days and, on reflection, I thoroughly enjoyed the entire process. I believe such training was truly beneficial. We all learned to work together, assist one another and care about each other. There was a good, healthy competitive spirit that prevailed and I experienced only helpfulness and cooperation throughout my training. There was a bond of comradeship and loyalty, which permeated throughout my service career. I never felt inferior as a woman. All members of each course took their studies seriously, and there was a sense of mutual pride, shared in being members of our chosen service. We were always made to feel that our work and commitment played an important part and contribution to the Royal Air Force.

Life after initial training took me through many specialist courses, focusing on languages, intelligence matters and graduation. I was the youngest and the most junior on the advanced intelligence course of 23 senior officers, as well as the only female! It was tough, as I had made up my mind to study hard and do the best that I could. Most evenings I studied, while the others enjoyed a drink or two in the 'mess' hall and local pub at Uxbridge. This course lasted six weeks. The final exam had most of us panicking. My work was rewarded as

I came 'second' – but the squadron leader who came first cheated his way there. He had lots of pieces of paper up his sleeve and was not caught.

My first posting was to the Special Investigation Branch (SIB) headquarters in Kensington, London. This was a huge block of flats in Exhibition Road, which had been requisitioned by the RAF for the duration of the war. It housed all our offices and provided our accommodation, which was very convenient. My work started with further German and Dutch studies in preparation before taking a specialist civil service commissioners' examination in both languages part-time, while reading thousands of German letters that were subjected to censorship.

Any letters of security interest would be translated and forwarded with comment. Many other German and Dutch documents came my way, followed by duties that took me away from my office to other areas in the UK to interview German prisoners-of-war (POWs) and civilians of security interest. No outstanding event or people can be recalled, but there were cases of dubious characters whose data was passed on to other authorities such as immigration, police or the Security Service, MI5.

After an interval of time, I was invited to apply for a posting to the Air Intelligence Unit at Monck Street. This required attendance at a special selection board. This board sat at 0930 at Adastral House, London. It was always customary to appear: (a) on time and (b) in best blue, and (c) immaculate. With this in mind I left the mess well prepared, on time and ready to face the board's many questions.

My bus, however, was late and packed with people, so I jumped off at the Strand and started walking towards Adastral House. Very soon I caught my shoe on the pavement and fell full length amidst the passing crowd. I scrambled to my feet only to see a huge bleeding hole in my stocking and knee. I had to find help from somewhere before appearing before the board. Miraculously, I spied a small drapery store in Kingsway run by an old lady who took pity on me and supplied me with a large plaster for my knee and a pair of *very* old-fashioned thick grey cotton stockings. I was able to at least hide the injury and cover up the plaster. It was in this fashion that I presented myself to the board, still on time, joined by smartly-dressed candidates for the post.

By this time, feeling quite dishevelled after my fall, I never thought I stood a chance. I was called in to face six serious-looking officers. After the conventional salute I was invited to sit down and feel 'at ease' while many questions were fired at me for which I struggled to provide reasonable answers. I discerned that some eyes were focusing on my knee, so I apologised for my appearance and explained in some detail what had happened. This provoked laughter from all the officers and the rigid atmosphere vanished with many smiles and friendly comments. However, I left the gathering with even less hope of success but was requested to wait for the results. All the other interviewees had left. Then the president of the board called for me to reappear, and to my utter amazement congratulated me on having acquired unanimous pass verdicts and the appointment of my posting to air intelligence.

In Monck Street was another large, old building, which housed a war room where Prime Minister Winston Churchill was known to pop in unannounced to see how things were going. During this period I was accommodated at the officers' mess in St John's Wood, a pleasant house in Avenue Road that accommodated ten women officers. Later, the facility closed down and we had to seek our own accommodation. Luckily, I found a pleasant flat (with a piano) in Buckingham Court, St James.

3

IN THE RUINS OF HITLER'S REICH

In November 1944 I was attached to a detachment unit of the Allied Military Government for Occupied Territories, headed by a lieutenant colonel and including a captain (a happy-faced, red-cheeked somewhat overweight gentleman), a lieutenant (a refined, aristocratic gentleman who was always ready to help), myself, as well as fourteen other ranks. We travelled in a convoy of eight vehicles carrying all our supplies. I was the one and only German interpreter for the detachment. Our final destination in Germany was Verden, a town in Lower Saxony, north-western Germany, on the river Aller. We preferred to travel by night as all roads were dangerous in daylight; but some days we took a chance and covered some mileage, particularly where roads had been bombed and we desperately needed to see where we were going.

Our route was planned on a daily basis and we travelled through northeast Belgium into Germany via Holland. It was a hazardous, dangerous time even though we all knew that Germany had lost the war and there could be no turning back. Our task was to bring law and order, closely following our troops and the retreating German army. The Irish Guards and Royal Artillery were fighting ahead of us. After the initial bombing, they went in and occupied villages and towns. Needless to say, we were confronted with the true horror of war, death, destruction and misery.

Hitler was determined to fight on to the bitter end, prolonging his inevitable defeat and, in doing so, killing millions during these last months of certain failure. Albert Speer, the German Armaments Minister, managed to continue a huge volume of armament production despite the Allied invasion and regular bombing. Millions of Germans were fleeing west from the killing fields of the east, and women were escaping rape from the Soviet Red Army. They came together with thousands of displaced persons and prisoners who had escaped from various displaced persons' camps and prisons. Those who fell by the wayside were callously shot by marauding SS soldiers. We encountered teenage boys dressed in uniform, quite dazed and bewildered without orders. Individuals trying to protect their towns and villages from bombing by negotiating surrender were shot in cold blood by local Nazi leaders while the British Liberation Army was approaching.

Terrified, lost and orphaned children were severely traumatised at being exposed to terrible scenes of badly injured, dying parents and relatives. There was total chaos amidst the bombing, with devastation, death, hunger and misery. The population seemed stunned with disbelief at our arrival wherever we went. Our tasks were many and varied. Suspected war criminals were interrogated, local prisons emptied and political prisoners interviewed and removed. War criminals were interviewed, apprehended and later tried at the criminal courts in Hamburg and Nuremburg. Captured German soldiers of intelligence value were held and interrogated.

Between Borken and Bocholt we were under fire from both Allied Spitfires and German Stukas (dive-bombers). We were always aware of snipers and pockets of resistance emerging in the countryside during the closing months of the war.

We were housed in requisitioned buildings in towns and villages for the days when we had an immense amount of work. One of our Royal Army Medical Corps field dressing stations was located at Groenlo on the Dutch/German border. We encountered two schools filled with many corpses and the remaining seriously wounded

German soldiers left behind, many dying of gangrene. My task was to interview each one of these desperate and abandoned men. The local authorities removed the corpses by horse and cart.

I cannot describe the agony and pain I witnessed while gaining much intelligence from these helpless, disillusioned, dying men. Their pathetic pleas for help could not be ignored and our wonderful medical team from the RAMC field dressing station at Groenlo was able to treat a small number of POWs with amputations.

But the majority died without help. I shall always remember these sad, young men and some of their last words, pleading for God's mercy. There was no chaplain available. Many wanted to pray with me and needed reassurance in prayer and tears, as well as help and sympathy, in order not to die alone. These were enemy soldiers reaching out in their last hour of life. It was a sobering experience.

The intelligence we sought was the location of SS troops (the most feared in the conflict). On most days progress was made and, wherever our detachment went, we were empowered to arrest any citizen, confiscate vehicles and requisition buildings for accommodation. In fact, the Allied Military Government was in command and responsible for all occupied territory as we moved forward throughout the captured region. As I was the only interpreter/translator for this detachment, I helped my colleagues conduct countless interviews, house searches and investigations.

At this stage we were still at war and on duty twenty-four hours a day. We were following the spearhead, which consisted of dispatch riders of the Irish Guards and troops of the Royal Artillery. These units were often closely engaged in heavy fighting with SS troops, capturing towns and villages ahead of us. Thus we were often under fire from both sides! Some areas in this conflict changed hands several times, and it must have been very hard for our bombers and fighters to be aware of what was already occupied, and what was about to be occupied. The ever-changing details of these fluid but intense situations must have been confusing.

There were misunderstandings within the German Military High Command. Some senior officers refused orders and false rumours abounded. Chaos ruled supreme in some quarters, when the truth was simple: the game was up for the Nazis and the day of reckoning was nigh. The 'war criminals' were to be held responsible for their dastardly deeds; there would be no escape for the guilty, the cowardly and the treacherous. Many arrests were made, requiring hours of interrogation. War criminals were uncovered and material for countless court cases was to be organised.

Out of the town of Bocholt, our convoy stopped and our commanding officer requisitioned a 'strategically situated' flower shop where we were all to spend the night. It was of moderate size with, naturally, many flower pots, buckets and plants everywhere. I found a cosy spot in the shop window where some torn curtains provided some privacy. We all settled for the night except for the two guards who were detailed to protect us. Our short-lived peace was disturbed when we were bombed several hours later! Thankfully, we survived under rubble, but many people in the small township were killed and there were many wounded civilians whom we rallied to assist with first aid and stretchers.

Before and after we arrived in Verden, a pleasant, small town on the river Aller, we were bombed several times. The court house in Hamburg was declared a War Crimes Tribunal for local offenders we had encountered travelling through. A suitable house was requisitioned in Verden. It was large enough to accommodate our offices and staff and became our residence for the remainder of our stay.

Once established, we were able to function in the region as intended. We spent three days a week dealing with war crimes; all the interpreting and translation of documents kept me more than occupied. We had particularly tiring days at the Hamburg court due to the many urgent cases awaiting trial.

On one particularly late departure, dusk was setting in and I had to return to Verden on a 250cc motorcycle, which was the only transport available to me on that day. I would have preferred to travel in daylight as the main road from Hamburg to Verden had been frequently bombed, creating many large potholes which demanded careful driving and slow progress. Also, the road was particularly dangerous. We knew that pockets of SS troops were hiding in the woods along that road from where we had quite recently lost our staff sergeant dispatch rider.

There was no time to waste as I was expected back at the mess and it was almost dark. The first part of the journey, some 20 miles, was uneventful. Then suddenly, the motorbike engine stopped. All my efforts to restart it failed. This was serious. I was stranded on a dangerous road with no known means of assistance. I decided to push the bike along the road in preference to staying put. There was no traffic to rely on and there was a strict curfew for civilians.

Suddenly, out of the dark, two enormous lights were advancing and a huge American army truck came rattling along. I dumped the bike and frantically waived my arms hoping it would stop for me. The huge wheels were brought to a stop by screeching brakes and all I could discern in the dim light was a row of sparkling white teeth. An American voice then came from above: 'Do you need help?' I gratefully replied that my bike had broken down and I was stranded. A six-foot-tall black American army sergeant jumped to the ground, lifted the bike onto the truck and invited me to join him in the front seat with his black co-driver, promising to drive me back to the mess in Verden.

After a few minutes of friendly, helpful conversation, I felt at ease, confident and grateful. These men were polite and gentlemanly. I was most impressed by their conduct and genuine assistance, which I reported to my CO on arrival in Verden. I had been through a scary experience, and my thanks and gratitude were expressed in a letter from my CO to their commandant. I do hope this genuine 'thank you' was appreciated.

Victory in Europe Day finally arrived on May 8, 1945, and was a day of cautious rejoicing in Verden. There was an immense feeling of relief amongst us all, even though we were on constant alert for hidden SS troops holding out in the woods around the town. We could not go out at times. While in Verden, our detachment lost a three-tonne utility truck and later our wonderful staff sergeant, previously mentioned, who was also a dispatch rider, a teacher in civilian life and a married man with two small children. He never returned from a journey to Hamburg, and his body was found floating in the river three days after he went missing. He had been decapitated. We were all devastated. Thin wires were stretched across roads to decapitate motorcyclists. How grateful I was that my motorbike broke down where it did. Fanatics were operating, and thus constant vigilance was required for many weeks after Germany's official capitulation. All those serving at that time were warned to observe care and be accompanied when out and about, particularly after dark.

The British government was well prepared to deal with its zone of occupation of Germany. The military government detachments brought law and order after capitulation, followed much later by the Civil Control Commission, which ensured correct handling of finance, trade and commerce. Furthermore, the part of Germany occupied by the Western powers, the U.S., Britain and France, was well aided by Washington's Marshall Plan. On looking back, it could be argued that Germany, in fact, 'won the war' by emerging as the most economically sound country in the European Union. *Das Wirtschaftswunder* (the 'economic miracle') became a reality.

Germany's Bergen-Belsen concentration camp: a crematorium oven where corpses were incinerated

About one month after the cessation of hostilities, the Americans took four of us to Bergen-Belsen to witness the aftermath of the intense horror of these concentration camps. Seventy thousand Jews perished there. Thankfully, those who survived had been removed and were now in care, endeavouring to recover from their shocking ordeal. The scene was quite indescribable, a deserted place of death and suffering with a pungent smell of rotting, burnt flesh. We were shown the remains of cubicles, quarters and huts. We were all quite overcome when we realised we were visiting death chambers. It sent cold shivers down my spine. It made me think of the many Jewish friends I had known and I wondered where they had been during the war. Were they still alive? We returned to the mess that night, deeply affected, sad and sickened, but so very grateful that this war was now over.

Soon after, I returned to London.

Early in 1946, I was posted to Germany to the city of Bückeburg in Lower Saxony, where our Special Investigation Branch headquarters were in Germany, in an old, attractive castle situated in beautiful grounds. All personnel were well aware of the hidden dangers caused by a certain feeling of 'revenge' harboured and expressed by some defeated fanatics. Bückeburg was, and still is, extremely proud of its historic castle, owned for 700 years by the princes of Schaumberg Lippe. It was luxuriously furnished and, at that time, due to its convenient proximity to the airfield, in use by the Royal Air Force.

During my stay in Bückeburg, my work involved translating many official documents connected with war crimes, preparing arrest warrants, and interviewing arrested suspects. We worked closely with the established German police force. They were always polite, cooperative and concerned. Our task was part of the British Occupation Zone, which shared responsibilities with the British Military Government detachments around the regions, later to be taken over by the Civil Control Commission.

One important feature of the castle complex is the Princely Riding School. The stables are more than 400 years old and, even today, accommodate noble stallions of baroque breeds. In the historic riding-school hall, visitors can watch top-notch riding displays in the styles of various periods.

At the time I was stationed in Bückeburg, the then Baron von Lippe owned two beautiful horses who were allowed to remain stabled and cared for in their own quarters, situated separately some distance away in the castle grounds. It did not take long for me to find them, and 'fraternising' with horses was not prohibited. Via one of the grooms, I obtained permission from the baron to ride a beautiful chestnut named Max. In fact, two British army officers were already riding the other horse, a black mare. For three months I enjoyed this privilege of riding through the verdant grounds twice a week, including weekends. Max was a spirited, happy horse who, unlike so many others in Germany during the war, had enjoyed good care. Thanks to him, I had become fully acquainted with the local scene and environs, or so I thought.

One evening, I attended a big party in the mess, where I was always expected to play the piano. This occasion was no exception. Drinks were flowing freely. I cannot drink alcohol as I am allergic to it and have always avoided it. I had asked for lemonade and my glass was well filled. But unbeknown to me, it was laced with Steinhäger! This was a wartime brew, consisting of gin flavoured with juniper berries. It was quite potent and almost lethal to a non-drinker. Whilst playing the piano, I began to sense a strange, floating feeling that I was playing out of control, with a strange cramp in my arms and legs. I realised it was high time for me to leave quietly.

Unseen, I managed to exit through a door behind the bar leading me into the castle grounds. The fresh air was a great relief and I started walking in what I thought was the right direction towards my quarters. The further I went the more unlikely this seemed, and eventually I had to admit to myself that I was lost. I knew that the RAF police patrolled the grounds with dogs, so I tried not to panic, desperately hoping that I would meet one of them soon.

It seemed I had been walking for hours, so I decided to aim for the dim lights flickering ahead. My somewhat dulled and befuddled brain led me to believe this would be my rescue. On the way, I came to a small creek. The water had a steady current and though I could hardly see, I could hear flowing water. I had to overcome this obstacle, so I took a blind leap into the dark and, mercifully, landed on the other side, covered in mud. Then came a wooden fence, which I managed to clamber over and, for the first time, was walking on a paved road. Warnings of not going out alone in the dark in this possibly still hostile environment returned to my mind with a vengeance.

I walked along this road towards some houses until I heard

jackboots behind me, which seemed to be getting closer. I started running, then turned a corner, and then another, when I spotted a trap door partly covering the pavement. I wrenched one side upwards and jumped inside, locking myself inside and out of sight. Anything was better than being caught by a German fanatic. I landed on a solid floor, covered with straw. After a few moments the jackboots walked overhead and I felt relieved and grateful that I was at least out of sight.

The important question now was where I was. I sensed a pungent smell of hay and sewerage and wondered how I would get out again. I tried to move and started feeling my way in total darkness. Something was moving, and I heard a heavy snort. There was a large pig sharing my space. I started to feel very uncomfortable and needed all my strength to hoist myself up along the iron bar attached to the trap door. After an enormous effort I reached open air. All was quiet and I hurried down the street. Exhausted, I sat on a windowsill.

Soon a vehicle came around the corner with two military policemen on patrol. What a relief! They asked where I was going, but thankfully not where I had been. I told them my story, which they must have believed as I was exuding a most unpleasant odour from my encounter with Mr Pig. Laughs all round followed. It appeared I had walked for two hours, round the park and out of Bückeburg. I was grateful for their help, understanding and good humour. They returned me to the mess. Thankfully, after a hot bath there was still some time left for a rest before 0800 parade.

4

A different sort of engagement

I returned to London for an interview at the Air Ministry, Kingsway, in June 1947, followed by due leave. The outcome had a big impact on my life. Following that interview, as I was about to leave the ministry using the revolving door, a very handsome RAF officer was trying to enter by the same door. We exchanged glances while going round, and round, and round, while he kept pushing the door! Both of us finally ended up outside the building. With a broad smile he invited me for a drink across the road. I hesitated and tried to walk away. He followed me and repeated his offer, several times. I was finally persuaded and we went to a small pub off Kingsway.

He was quite charming and kind and told me his life history over our first drink. I was impressed and was secretly hoping I would see him again. When it was time to leave he insisted on taking me for dinner and suggested the dining room at Paddington Station, as he was planning to catch a late train for Newport, Monmouthshire, that night. I accepted the offer and we went to Paddington by taxi. He chose a corner table away from the window and noise and we settled down for the evening. He made a phone call to advise his family he would catch the last, midnight train so we could spend more time together. I had to admit to myself that I was enjoying every moment of his presence. This was not like me. This was different, very different.

We had a wonderful chatty evening as perfect strangers, yet I felt I had known him for years. The restaurant was almost empty and, at 10:30 pm, the time had come to say goodnight. We exchanged phone numbers and I saw him off on the night train to Cardiff. At that moment I knew I would see him again. I took a taxi to my flat feeling happily confused and trying to come to terms with what I had done. I tried to shake it off thinking, 'Time will tell.' After years of avoiding romantic attachments, trying to concentrate on my service life and career, was I now falling in love?

The next morning he phoned, inviting me to visit Newport, South Wales, to meet his family. I tried to appear too busy, but he insisted and was coming to London by car to collect me. On the one hand, I was thrilled; on the other, I was concerned. What was happening here? He arrived, as planned, and we had an enjoyable drive to Newport, arriving at his family home in time for afternoon tea. His two charming sisters were there to greet us, as well as their two faithful members of staff, Ethel the housemaid and Mary the cook, who had worked for the family since his parents were married. They provided us with a luxurious afternoon tea with delicious scones, cakes and more. I felt very comfortable and at home with his sisters Kathleen and Vivienne. I was shown family photographs of their father and mother, both much loved and respected by the family, but sadly deceased.

I heard many stories about their family. His father had been a much admired councillor, and for many years his mother had been responsible for running the big hospital fête, which took place annually in Newport. In fact, they seemed like a good, happy family. Then came the invitation for dinner with Kit, the eldest sister. We left together by car and drove to their beautiful home, Glasllwch House, a stately house on its own beautiful grounds. We met Kit's husband Percy, who was the Mayor of Newport, and their children, Heather and Ron, two delightful teenagers, who had other plans for the evening. It was a most enjoyable night and I heard Robert, my new friend, agreeing with his sisters that I was the image of their mother when she was younger. I was given a beautifully furnished bedroom for the night and Robert went back to stay at 'Bromley' where we had tea. On Sunday we all met after a service at The Tabernacle, the

My first husband Robert in his RAF uniform

church where the family always worshipped and where their father had been a leading figure. On Sunday afternoon we visited an old castle close by and had tea on the lawn.

I was soon to leave on a train for London, as I was on duty the next morning. Robert took me to the station, held my hand and gave me our first kiss. He told me he would never let me go now that he had found me. I boarded the train that came thundering in and my head was spinning. The train was moving and he was waving outside, throwing me kisses. I waved till I could see him no more and then slumped into my seat, unsure of what was happening to me. My life was about to change. I was falling in love, and, even though I was telling myself not to do so, I could not help myself. I was in love, undeniably.

I was due in Florence, in five days' time, to be the bridesmaid at the wedding of my school-friend, Anna. I told Robert, who promptly said he would meet me in Lugano after the ceremony. I could not believe he would be there! I returned to work and pretended to myself that everything was back to normal. On Tuesday I was scheduled to take the train from London to the North Sea port of Harwich, in Essex, then take the night ferry to the Hook of Holland, and from there travel by express train to Milan and onwards.

I arrived at London's Liverpool Street Station, platform nine, and thought I was seeing things. There was Robert, smiling, to wish me *bon voyage* with a box of chocolates. I must say I was dumbfounded. After this surprise, he could very well meet me in Lugano. As the train was about to leave, I felt I was standing on a precipice and about to lose my grip. Robert gave me an embrace that only a lover could and kissed me with loving fervour. The train took off and I was left with my mind and thoughts in turmoil.

I finally arrived in Milan on a busy, bustling station and had to find the train to Florence. It was a steam train which emitted sounds that could have come from an angry dinosaur. Hundreds of people with huge amounts of luggage were boarding the train and I managed to squeeze into a seat, feeling lucky I had made it in good time, as trains in Italy were overcrowded and notoriously late. I managed to sleep much of the way to Florence. On arrival, there were no taxis, so I took a carriage with an unhappy-looking horse, who cheered up after I gave him a lump of sugar that I had in my pocket from the train.

My friend Anna was the only daughter of a wealthy Italian businessman, so she was to have a magnificent wedding. She looked stunning in a white lace dress with a long veil, which I had charge of. My dress was a pale rose-coloured pink, embroidered with white roses, which matched the bride's bouquet.

A six-horse-drawn carriage took us to the famous Cathedral

Santa Maria del Fiore where the magnificent organ was being played. Everything went like clockwork as we left the carriage and walked straight up the beautiful aisle, Anna being escorted by her loving father. It felt like miles but we finally reached the high altar, which was a sea of flowers. A heavenly choir sang the 'Alleluja', and the wedding ceremony was under way. Anna's handsome husband was Swiss and they made a beautiful picture together. After the wedding ceremony we were all invited to their palatial home, in the Via dei Renai, for a sumptuous spread of Italian delicacies, including an assortment of special wines. The party lingered on till we were escorted to the hotel where her father had booked us all into for three days to see Florence. It was a fabulous trip with an excellent guide, and one I shall never forget. The group consisted mainly of the groom's family and a few close friends from Barnet in north London, where Anna and her parents had lived pre-war. We all had great fun together exploring this beautiful city of the arts. However, I had to admit to myself that I was really looking forward to getting to Lugano. After three days of sightseeing and entertainment, I said my thanks and farewells and boarded the train for Milan, as booked, and caught the connection for Lugano. I could not afford to miss that train.

At last the train pulled up at Lugano Station, and I spotted Robert running along the moving train looking for me. I soon alighted and he embraced me, squeezing all the air out of me. After I caught my breath, I was still wondering how I found myself in this situation. I still wanted a career, so how would all this end? I could certainly not deny that I was enjoying being courted by Robert. He had turned into Prince Charming and I had started to feel lonely without his attentions when we were apart.

Robert had arrived in Lugano earlier that day and had booked accommodation for two nights at the Hotel Majestic, with two rooms on different floors, overlooking Lake Lugano. In those days, when a gentleman respected a lady, it would have been unthinkable for

With Robert on the Isle of Wight

him to have booked a double room. This place held many childhood memories for me and I loved being there. We decided to drop our bags at the hotel and look around Lugano. It was late afternoon and Robert suggested taking a small boat to the other side of the lake to a well-known restaurant. The restaurant was indeed special, with soft music and dimmed coloured lights at the waters edge. All that was needed now to complete the picture was for the moon to appear. We dined, held hands, danced cheek to cheek, and life felt wonderful.

The next day we took another boat trip, this time to Morcote, a beauty spot on the lake with a fifteenth-century church on a hill overlooking Lake Maggiore, close to Monte San Salvatore. It was here, standing under the clock tower of this old church that Robert embraced me, took both my hands to his heart and asked me to become his wife. In my heart of hearts I knew we had fallen in love at first sight and there would be no escape, no matter where I went. Here I was confronting my destiny. Happily and almost relieved, I said, 'Yes', and we embraced heart to heart, sealing our fate. We had covered much ground in the little time we had known each other and we felt we had a lot in common – service life, dancing, music and beautiful things – but, above all, we really wanted to be together. Despite the rigours of service life, he promised I could stay in the Royal Air Force if I wished.

Then the question of an engagement followed and the prospect of meeting my parents for 'approval' loomed ahead. This was a great worry for me, as my father would have very different ideas for my marriage. Robert was divorced, had two sons at boarding school aged ten and twelve, and was sixteen years my senior. My father would never agree. I was fearful and worried. A meeting with my parents was arranged. They did not know the full story, so we were well received, initially. I was heartened to hear my father cracking jokes with Robert. Then, I left the room and spoke with my mother who was always more understanding. I told her my worries while Robert filled father in with the facts of the matter. He was horrified at the idea of his only daughter wanting to marry a divorcee with young sons, who was so much older and of a different religion. This was all too much. When Robert approached him with our plan of marriage within three months, he bluntly stated he would not agree under any circumstances. He tried to reason man-to-man, suggesting that Robert could apply for an overseas posting to give me a chance to meet someone else. No church wedding was possible as he was divorced. I decided to see the bishop in my diocese. Not a hope. There was no way out.

We were on our own and had to make a decision. We thus had a quiet wedding at Caxton Hall, Westminster, with service friends. It was sad for my parents and sad for me. This action caused a rift with my father for a number of years and I lost my monthly allowance, which had always been a great help in paying my mess bill each month. My mother was much more understanding; she knew me like no one else, and we had many long phone calls together which gave me hope for the future.

My service life continued as a married officer. Then, unexpectedly, Robert was posted to Singapore early in November 1947. I saw him off when he left by ship from Liverpool for Tengah, Singapore, on a two-year assignment, after which I returned to Bückeburg in Germany.

One cold evening in late November 1947, a fortnight after my arrival in Bückeburg, I was enjoying the cosy warmth of the mess when an excited airman came running up to me with the message that Air Commodore Owen W. de Putron, from the Air Ministry in London, wished to speak to me, and that it was urgent. I hurried to the phone and heard the well-known voice of the commanding officer of our Special Branch, where I had served previously. It was a pleasant call with the order to 'pack an overnight bag and report to me by 11:00 am tomorrow morning'. Message understood. There was no further explanation.

Before leaving, I had to cancel arrangements for the following day, as it would need to be an early flight to keep my appointment in London. No sooner had I gathered my thoughts when the operations officer rang to say that our aircraft would take off at 0630 hours, weather-permitting. It did, on time.

5

On assignment for British secret intelligence

We arrived at Hendon Airport where a car was waiting to drive me to Kensington. By 1100 hours I was led into the air commodore's office. Fortunately, I had worked for him before and knew him to be far less fierce than he looked! However, he was not alone. Two very well-dressed gentlemen rose to their feet and were introduced to me as senior officers from the Home and Foreign Offices respectively. I learned later they belonged to two of Britain's secret services, MI5 and MI6.

We all sat down and, judging by their grave expressions, I knew something very much out of the ordinary was afoot. First, I was asked many personal questions, which is not unusual when one is about to undertake a special operation. Secondly, total and complete secrecy was impressed on me in no uncertain terms. In fact, if I was to take on the task at hand, I was to disappear for an unspecified time and would not be able to tell anyone where I was or what I was doing. I would not be able to see relatives or friends for the duration. Thirdly, I had been selected for this Top Secret assignment because of my previously proven loyalty and dedication, as well as my proficiency in the German language.

By this time I was more than curious and formally agreed to undertake whatever was required of me. The two gentlemen then told me I would be officially loaned to them from the Royal Air Force for the duration of this commitment and that service life would cease from today. I would become a civilian with another name and identity. I was handed a German passport with a new name and ration cards. I was then told I would be assisting the world's most top secret refugee, Russia's – and, at that time, the world's – top rocket scientist. It was now clear I was not returning to Bückeburg and I was on the job immediately. This man, his wife and nine-year-old daughter were to be smuggled out of the Soviet Occupation Zone of Berlin and brought to London. It then was explained to me how both MI5 and MI6 would be involved.

The author in her RAF uniform, 1947

British experts would be in a high state of excitement over the scientific and technical marvels that would soon become available to them.[1] Grigori Aleksandrovich Tokaev, born on October 13, 1909, in Stavtordt, Ossetia, a small state in the North Caucasus region of the Russian empire, was a colonel in the Soviet Air Force and was formerly head of the Zhukovsky Air Force Engineering Academy in Moscow. Stalin personally appointed him to be in charge of all Russian troops in the Soviet-occupied zone in Germany in 1946. He moved from Moscow to Berlin with his wife Aza and daughter Bella to take up this appointment. Tokaev did not agree with Russian communism and Stalin's wartime deportation of whole ethnic groups, from the Caucasus region and elsewhere, to Siberian slave labour camps.[2] He was a German scholar and a Russian patriot who had become disillusioned with the Stalin regime. Britain's Secret Intelligence Service, MI6, became aware of the situation, as did the Soviet spy agency, the KGB. Tokaev was in grave danger of being arrested, and there was no time to lose.

As a matter of extreme urgency, prompt steps were taken in late 1947 to assist his immediate defection to the West. In a highly secret and dangerous operation he, his wife and daughter were removed from their flat and flown out of Berlin, under the very noses of the Soviets, to RAF West Drayton, a Royal Air Force station west of London. They fled without belongings, except for a bag of special documents. The tension and fear were most noticeable in his wife, Aza, who was not prepared for this traumatic journey and change in their circumstances. She feared for her aged parents and the possible repercussions that could affect them. After a few nights at RAF West Drayton, we moved to a safe house, well situated in Chelsea under the watchful eye of MI5 and other agencies. My all-absorbing task was as an escort, confidante, guard, guide and translator in the German language, spoken and understood by this family during their first eighteen months of debriefings, acclimatisation and adaptation to the British way of life.

Grigori Tokaev (Tokaty), the famous Soviet aeronautics scientist and critic of Stalin, who defected to Britain in late 1947

The intense security that surrounded us was essential. The Soviet KGB, the GRU (Soviet military intelligence), not to mention other Soviet personnel from Intourist and the TASS news agency, were on high alert, searching for Tokaev dead or alive. I was always armed to meet a possible emergency. We seldom ventured out of the house and, on the rare occasions when we did, it was in MI5 armoured transport with our assigned driver, Martin.

Tokaev received many visitors, including scientists, British Foreign Office officials and allied diplomats, for briefings, debriefings and scientific discussions. All meetings were arranged and approved by MI5. The sole Air Force contact for me throughout this period was with Wing Commander Christopher Hartley, assigned by the Air Ministry to assist in the logistics under the pseudonym of Mr Osborne. He was a kind and compassionate man, always thoughtful and well aware of the constant danger we lived under. He would occasionally drop in, usually on an evening when we were all tired from the many visits of the day and were relaxing together. Frequently, he would bring Tokaev's daughter, Bella, a small toy, a puzzle or a book. Wife Aza would receive flowers, and Grigori an interesting paper, magazine or a bottle of wine. As for me, I would be given a pat on the back, which was very much valued. It was a strange situation for all of us, but his visits provided a welcome distraction, all communications being translated into and from German.

Christopher (now 'Mr Osborne') was henceforth my only contact with the outside world. All my correspondence was through an address that went to him at the Air Ministry. My parents were not aware of the nature of this new assignment, nor was my husband in Singapore, with whom I kept in touch by correspondence. It was Christopher who brought and took my mail on a regular basis and always enquired on Grigori's state of mind. He was a remarkably sensitive man, and so well suited to this case. Many years later, he was promoted to the rank of air marshal of the RAF and awarded a CBE, then a knighthood, all well deserved.

It was an extraordinary, busy life – unquestionably a full day-and-night occupation to meet every need of this very stressed and anxious family, coping with threats of kidnapping, murder and abduction, as well as satisfying the requests of friendly government intelligence agencies clamouring for information and interviews. These only occurred after being granted official approval, and increasingly more and more visitors were allowed access. The media were kept strictly away. The permitted visits always took place in the safe house, to maximise the safety of the entire family.

We were very cautious in the early stages, as Tokaev had been handpicked by Stalin to command Russian troops in the Soviet-occupied zone of Germany. He was also a personal friend of Stalin's son, Vasili. My early briefings made this point very clear, and it took many months to confirm Tokaev's genuine feelings towards Britain.

Tokaev suffered great frustration during the early months of his defection. He distrusted those who came to interview him and would voice anxiety to me, seeking assurance relating to their background and loyalty. After all, his life and future, as well as his wife's and daughter's, were at stake. He was in a foreign country and depended entirely on our perception of his status. Could he have been 'double agent' material? This was a necessary question for our internal security services. All the early evidence of his dealings with MI6 and their important decisions to facilitate his defection to the UK would seem to contradict this concern. Yet we could not blindly assume the truth of his intentions. Time was needed to prove his loyalty to Britain. He certainly achieved this. He became a well-trusted British subject in 1952, brought his great knowledge to service in the Northampton College of Advanced Technology and became a trusted adviser to Britain's Department of Defence.

About six months after Grigori's defection to the UK, another Russian official, Lieutenant Colonel Yuri Davidovich Tasoev, an intelligence officer in charge of the Soviet Reparations Mission in Bremen, arrived alone in England claiming to be a 'Russian refugee' fleeing communism. He, too, was provided with a 'safe house' and was treated with respect and consideration as appropriate, including interviews with the object of establishing his bona fides. His initial statements and family history sounded plausible and he was given a

On my 250cc BSA motorcycle

level of credence, which enabled him to be accepted as a 'refugee' and granted the protection he requested.

After a number of weeks, Grigori Tokaev was consulted and asked for his cooperation in identifying Yuri Tasoev. Initially he did not recognise the name and it was decided to bring the two men together to see their reactions to the other, first to establish that Soviet Tokaev was indeed the Tokaev who was in the UK; secondly, for us to assess Tokaev's bona fides as a refugee we could trust; and, thirdly, to verify Tasoev's story. I had to question the wisdom of this confrontation as I felt that there was a real danger for Tokaev's security, the Russians having always found the means to annihilate an adversary.

Tokaev was approached and arrangements were made for a meeting with Tasoev in a safe place accompanied by a ministry official and myself. Tasoev was waiting at the rendezvous when the three of us entered. Immediately Tokaev shouted at him in Russian, 'You are an impostor, a traitor!' Tasoev in turn accused Tokaev of being a traitor. There was no polite handshake, just anger and abusive language on both sides, not understood by the bystanders. The ministry official took Tokaev by the arm and led him back to the door through which we had just entered and we left hastily. Tasoev remained behind muttering to another official who had been interviewing him. The question still remained: was Tasoev his real name? Tokaev was furious and alerted our official that there was something very sinister about Tasoev's presence in the UK. He identified him as a prominent Party official, but did not know him personally. Tokaev was agitated, worried and clearly disturbed by the meeting.

The next day, Tasoev left his safe house and accosted a policeman on street patrol, requesting that he be escorted to the Russian embassy in Kensington. The policeman promptly escorted him to his local police station where he was detained and the Foreign Office advised of his presence. He was interviewed by the FO and insisted on being taken to the Russian embassy. Instead of that, on May 20, he was flown to Berlin and taken to the Russian Commandantur. A few days later, the Soviets issued a press release, angrily denouncing the 'British secret services' of kidnapping one of their personnel.[3] Tasoev himself was then put on a flight to Moscow, 'mission completed' – probably the positive identification of Tokaev. After this episode, security was further increased and our very few permitted outings were curtailed for the time being.

My heart went out to Aza and her small daughter. Aza was often deeply depressed and would weep for hours. She felt homesick, and clearly this life was having an adverse effect on her health. The little girl was not allowed to leave the house and was being tutored by her mother, while I taught her English. She too felt the lack of being at school and making friends. Bella and I played games together when there was time. I gave her a teddy bear, which was her constant companion for the whole time I was with them, and we bonded well. She was often comforted by me when her mother was unable to do so. Psychologically, all three refugees/defectors were affected by their abnormal but now necessary way of life. I often had long talks with Grigori, and I would relay his thoughts and wishes at my weekly de-briefings. I suggested we go to the Battersea Dogs' Home with Grigori so that he could select a little friend. I was delighted that this was approved. Two days afterwards we acquired a cute little wire-haired terrier we named Bonny that I was allowed to walk round the block. What a difference that little dog made to Grigori! He became the centre of that household for quite some time and was well looked after for the rest of his doggy life.

One day we were allowed to go on a trip on the Thames. It was a beautiful, sunny day and the riverboat was crowded with people. We were enjoying this day out and Grigori was in awe of all the beautiful buildings we passed. Suddenly, we spotted a little tail wagging above the water and our little dog swimming for his life trying to keep up with our boat – we never found out how he fell overboard! All the passengers were concerned, but the captain did not want to hear their pleas to turn the boat around. The situation was desperate, as we were moving away, not closer. The family were so upset that something had to be done. I slipped off the jacket I was wearing and jumped into the water – it was quite a scene! I swam towards Bonny, our doggie, who knew he was about to be rescued. The captain then took action as he may have thought we might both have drowned. He turned the boat around. By this time I had reached Bonny, and the boat came alongside. A deckhand was standing with a long hook, and I was able to slide the hook through the ring on Bonny's collar and he was lifted out of the water. Cheers from all the passengers followed, while I was left wondering how I was going to re-join the vessel. A rope ladder suddenly appeared and all our problems for the day were solved. As the Thames then was not as clean as it is today, I had a good bath after returning home and life was back to normal.

In 1948, Ernest ('Ernie') Bevin, Britain's then Foreign Secretary, visited Tokaev at his 'safe house' for afternoon tea, accompanied by another gentleman from his department we had not met previously. Bevin had long been a prominent figure in British public life – a former secretary of the powerful Transport & General Workers' Union (TGWU) between the wars, an energetic Minister of Labour and National Service in Churchill's wartime coalition government and, after the war, Foreign Secretary in Clement Attlee's Labour government. Despite his leftist background, Bevin would be instrumental in the formation of the North Atlantic Treaty Organisation (NATO) in 1949.

Bevin's visit was mainly to personally meet and thank Tokaev for his valuable information and assistance given to the Ministry of Defence and various branches of Britain's armed services. It became an enjoyable, friendly hour, while Aza and I served tea, scones and a specially-prepared home-made Russian cake which Aza presented with pride.

Tokaev did his best to speak in English and it amazed me how much he had learnt from our mornings' language sessions. My interventions to translate here and there were thus minimal. Tokaev always refused tea, so he was served black coffee, explaining that he would always prefer vodka or even whisky! A few months later he became a tea drinker.

Bevin's conversation with him covered Stalin's Soviet Union, Tokaev's career and, naturally, his courageous decision to defect to the free world, Tokaev expressed profound gratitude to be in England. Bevin stretched out his two hands and said: 'We extend our warmest welcome to you in Britain and repeat our thanks to you for so much valuable information passed to our government.'

This was quite a moving moment for all of us to witness. It was at this point that Bevin turned to me and thanked me for the important support I was giving to Tokaev's family and my country. He thanked me for my German translations when they had been necessary. Then he graciously thanked Aza for her superb cake … of which he had two servings.

Some further comments and questions on Russia and England were exchanged, causing some laughter, while the hour passed away all too quickly and the official driver arrived to collect our important visitor and his escort.

It was such a joy to see Grigori and Aza so relaxed and happy. This visit gave him a much-needed psychological boost and confirmation of his status in our community. After so many months of incarceration and intensive work, while still feeling a foreigner, not yet fully trusted or understood, and understandably fearful of reprisals against his family from the Soviet Union's powerful spy agencies, he was now reassured that he was accepted for who he was and what he stood for.

Ernest Bevin himself was a kindly man, and this quality came well to the fore during his short visit. By expressing the government's gratitude in this way, he was doing something very special for this, in many ways, lonely and fearful scientist.

Each week I reported on Tokaev's health, mood, attitude and needs. I can now say that the most pertinent and valuable occurrences during my period with this family were (i) Mr Bevin's visit and (ii) the arrival of 'Bonny', the little wire-haired terrier, who gave Tokaev's family hours of pleasure and great companionship, followed by his rescue from the Thames.

We had been in our safe house for nearly nine months and were beginning to feel more secure. Late one evening, after Grigori had had a tiring day, he said goodnight before taking a bath. Aza and I were listening to some music, when we heard a scream coming from upstairs. Grigori was in big trouble. I ran upstairs, gun in hand, to find him on the bathroom floor, hiding from the window behind the bath. The window was situated all along the wall, and Grigori said that a man wearing a black hat and holding a pistol was looking straight at him into the bathroom window. Naturally Grigori took fright and tried to hide. By the time I got up there and looked out the window, the man with the pistol confronted me. I aimed my gun to shoot him, and he immediately started running away along the flat roof, which led by way of the fire escape into the entry of a Woolworths supermarket. He was soon out of sight. Grigori was shaking all over. I told him to leave the bathroom immediately and get dressed. I promptly phoned my emergency contact number, then ran downstairs to alert Aza and Bella. We had twenty minutes to leave the house, as the 'official car' was on its way with our helpful driver, Martin.

The necessary precautions were in place and we were ready to undertake a long journey to an unknown destination in the UK. It was a dark night and we set off through the streets of Chelsea and Knightsbridge, taking a circuitous route, just in case we were spotted or followed.

Both Aza and Bella were frightened and Grigori was sitting on the car floor trying to remain out of sight and out of shot. It was not until we were well on the way, after about two hours of suspense and discomfort, that we were able to relax. I had a message that we were heading for a house in Devon for three weeks for safety. We were all much relieved and were able to relax until finally, at three in the morning, we arrived at a beautiful farm in Kingsbridge, where the charming lady who owned it came to meet us.

We remained there for three weeks. A lovely, quite unexpected holiday followed at this delightful farm where we could all enjoy the freedom of the countryside, the animals and, in addition, an Austin 7 car that I could use to explore the surroundings of Kingsbridge with the family. Our kind hostess prepared beautiful meals for the duration of our holiday, and we all benefited greatly from this change of scene. Of course, this would not last and we awaited further news about our next residence in London.

We were specifically informed that the KGB was still searching for us and that this would go on for many years. However, we gradually were allowed more freedom as the first year passed with six moves around London. Tokaev was there to stay. He wrote three books in English: *Stalin Means War*, published in 1951; *The Betrayal of an Ideal*, in 1954; and *Comrade X*, in 1956.[4] During the 1980s he tried to publish a book about his escape to life in the UK. The U.S. film producer, Arthur Rank also intended to make a film based on this, but I was told that neither would be allowed, as both MI5 and MI6 feared they would reveal too many secrets of their *modus operandi*.

Tokaev — who now preferred to use the Ossetian version of his surname, Tokaty — was instrumental in setting up the Department of Aeronautics and Space Technology at the Northampton College of Advanced Technology in London, where he served as a professor from 1967 until 1994. He received many overseas invitations and appointments, including the opportunity to witness American rocket-launchings in Cape Canaveral in the state of Florida. He wrote a number of scientific books in that time. He became a distinguished and loyal British citizen and died in London in 2003. He was survived by his daughter Bella, who still resides in London.

My assignment with Tokaev's family gave me the wonderful opportunity of meeting some very interesting people in London town at that time: politicians, ministers, ambassadors, scientists, service chiefs and senior police officers. Apart from Bevin, another eminent visitor was Sir Alexander Cadogan, a senior official of Britain's Foreign Office and friend of Winston Churchill's. Most of those who visited and spoke with Colonel Tokaev needed a translator, and I was happy to oblige. Tokaev himself was always willing to cooperate with the never-ending stream of visitors, even though he was frequently very tired.

It was often clear to me that the feeling of uncertainty about their future and the ever-present fear with which they lived was affecting each member of the family in different ways. Because of the shared stress we felt, we all needed one another to work through our days in the best possible way. There were regular meal times; specific appointments were made for the many visitors; and hours were set aside for Bella so she could listen to English and learn to read. Our breakfast time was always important as Grigori needed to be advised of the daily news in English. Newspapers were delivered early and we dealt with all important news at that time. This was also a good way for him to learn English. We also often dealt with English grammar at breakfast. Grigori made considerable progress and kept his good sense of Russian humour, often different from English wit. I gradually succeeded in teaching all the family English. Grigori was the first to start speaking, albeit with a heavy accent; but after one year he was writing fluently and conversing well. He still needed me, however, for official translations, technical terms, difficult words and English idioms and sayings.

Aza was very slowly settling into this new, very strange life that had been thrust upon her. Her depressed mental state improved with quiet understanding and, after the first year, we were laughing and joking together about everyday things. Her depressive moods never completely left her, but she learned to manage better. We all got along very well and I began to feel like a family member. Grigori used to say, 'You are like a sister to me', and I continued to have their confidence and affection long after they became British citizens.

I left the Tokaev family in 1949 and attended the first permanent officers' course for women in the RAF, which was held in Folkestone. On completing it, I went on to the Air Ministry at Parliament Square House in Whitehall to work in the Directorate of Foreign Liaison

(DFL). I was assigned to the desk covering Belgium, the Netherlands, Thailand, Burma and Indonesia. We worked closely with the foreign air attachés posted in London and formed links with our RAF units concerned with the training of foreign students. In that post-war period, allied air forces, which were re-grouping and building up their post-war defences, flying and other training courses, including the RAF Staff College at the RAF Andover station in Hampshire, were much in demand. Hundreds of trainees passed through our office and left our training facilities fully qualified. Overseas visitors were escorted to training establishments.

At RAF Hawkinge, near Folkestone, Kent, in 1949

It was my pleasure to escort very senior foreign air force representatives to the Society of British Aircraft Constructors' annual shows and to aircraft manufacturers in the UK. Many important social and professional exchanges were established, some of intelligence value to them and us. Important delegations were received and top-level planning undertaken towards the purchase of aircraft and the training of pilots. I worked with high-ranking officers of the Thai, Indonesian, Belgian and Netherlands air forces, many of whom later became ministers and airline executives in their own countries.

Shortly before leaving the Air Ministry in 1952, on the recommendation of the Thai Ambassador in London, I was to be awarded by the Thai government the prestigious 'Order of the White Elephant' in recognition for the special service I had rendered to the

Visiting senior air force representatives from several countries attending a luncheon, hosted by the Air Ministry, at the Savoy Hotel, London (the author is seated at the head of the table)

air force of the kingdom of Thailand. Sadly, British service protocol determined that I was not allowed to accept it, and the Air Council did not permit it. This was a great disappointment to a life-long elephant-lover.

6

BRITAIN ROCKED BY TREACHERY OF THE CAMBRIDGE SPIES

Meanwhile, since 1945, the tensions of the Cold War had been steadily escalating.

On March 5, 1946, Britain's former wartime PM Winston Churchill delivered his now famous 'iron curtain' speech in Fulton, Missouri, in which he described how half of Europe was now living under communist servitude. He said:

> From Stettin in the Baltic to Trieste in the Adriatic an iron curtain has descended across the Continent. Behind that line lie all the capitals of the ancient states of Central and Eastern Europe. Warsaw, Berlin, Prague, Vienna, Budapest, Belgrade, Bucharest and Sofia, all these famous cities and the populations around them lie in what I must call the Soviet sphere, and all are subject in one form or another, not only to Soviet influence but to a very high and, in some cases, increasing measure of control from Moscow....
>
> The Communist parties, which were very small in all these Eastern States of Europe, have been raised to pre-eminence and power far beyond their numbers and are seeking everywhere to obtain totalitarian control. Police governments are prevailing in nearly every case....

A year later, American President Harry Truman declared that the U.S. was prepared to support Greece and Turkey with economic and military aid to prevent their falling under Soviet control.

A major early episode of the Cold War was the Berlin Blockade. For a brief period after the war, the city of Berlin had enjoyed a special status under the joint control of the four victorious powers: it became an island of relative freedom in the midst of communist-controlled East Germany. In June 1948, the Soviet Union imposed a blockade on the city, cutting off Western powers' road and rail access to Berlin. It was Moscow's attempt to starve the city into submission in order to bring it under communist control. In response, the Western powers organised the Berlin Airlift to carry essential supplies to the besieged population of West Berlin. The blockade lasted almost a year.

More evidence of the Soviet Union's hostility towards the West emerged with the dramatic testimony of former spies, Whittaker Chambers and Elizabeth Bentley, in the U.S., and a former Soviet military intelligence officer of the GRU, Igor Gouzenko, who defected to Canada in 1945.

In April 1949, the North Atlantic Treaty Organisation (NATO), an intergovernmental military alliance was established to create a Western counterweight to the Soviet armies stationed in the Iron Curtain countries of postwar central and eastern Europe.

Thereafter followed a particularly alarming sequence of world-shaking events:

- On August 29, 1949, the USSR exploded its first atomic bomb.

- On October 1, Chinese Communist leader Mao Zedong declared the creation of the People's Republic of China (PRC).

- Early in 1950, a German-born British nuclear physicist Klaus Fuchs was arrested, tried and sentenced to 14 years' jail for passing British and American atomic secrets to Soviet military intelligence.

- On June 25, 1950, communist North Korea, with Russian and Chinese backing, invaded South Korea with 135,000 men, instigating the Korean War.

The now full-blown Cold War necessitated unceasing undercover vigilance and action, as the Soviet embassies in Western countries were highly active. Secret intelligence officers of the Soviet Union's two principal spy agencies — the KGB (the Committee for State Security) and the GRU (Soviet Military Intelligence) — were present in large numbers around Europe at this time.

In May 1951 we were alerted after the sudden disappearance of two diplomats, Donald Maclean and Guy Burgess, from the British Foreign Office. They fled Britain via Southampton, where they took a cross-Channel ferry, the SS *Falaise*, to the French port of St Malo. From there they vanished from view without trace, causing considerable alarm in both Whitehall and Washington. All of us working for British intelligence at the time were interviewed at least twice regarding their mysterious departure and any helpful information we might have.

We had many diplomatic contacts with resulting invitations to international gatherings and interesting functions, from Buckingham Palace garden parties to dinner and cocktail parties as well as plenty of free tickets to selected musicals, variety shows and plays. Needless to say, we often encountered the Soviets, usually GRU officers, who were more than keen to be wherever they could meet secret service personnel. It was a known fact that that there was an inordinate number of embassy personnel at the Soviet embassy in Kensington, far in excess of requirement.

It wasn't until five years after the disappearance of Maclean and Burgess that their new whereabouts was finally confirmed. The Soviet leader Nikita Khrushchev revealed that they now lived in Moscow.

The defection of Maclean and Burgess rocked the Western intelligence world. It was discovered that the pair had been recruited in the 1930s by Soviet intelligence shortly after they had graduated from Cambridge. But their subsequent espionage activities were only the tip of the iceberg. From the 1960s until the end of the Cold War, the public slowly learned that Maclean and Burgess were only two of a much larger number of communists, most of them from Trinity College, Cambridge, who had been recruited in the mid-1930s at, or shortly after leaving, Cambridge. Intelligence historian Christopher Andrew, who himself teaches at Cambridge, has described the Cambridge spies as 'the ablest group of British agents ever recruited by a foreign power'.[1]

Popularly known in the media as the Cambridge Five or the Magnificent Five, in fact the spies numbered more than that. Moreover, new evidence continues to come to light revealing the damage they did not only to the United Kingdom but to many other countries, not only during World War II, but for many years afterwards.

Most notorious of the Cambridge spies was Kim Philby, who succeeded in penetrating and being promoted to one of the most senior positions in the UK's Secret Intelligence Service (sometimes called MI6). After he defected to Moscow in 1963, twelve years after Maclean and Burgess, the British press christened him the 'Third Man'.

The identities of some of the other Cambridge spies gradually trickled out the next two decades.

Dr Arnold Deutsch

The successor of the Soviet KGB's foreign intelligence arm in today's Russia is called the SVR. It has neither disowned nor repudiated its communist past. On the contrary, it cherishes the history of the clandestine operations its predecessor organisation ran against the Western democracies. The SVR's Moscow headquarters contains a small history museum, known as the Memory Room. On its walls hang portraits of some of the Soviet Union's most successful spies and spy-handlers of the 1920s and 1930s. One portrait in particular stands out – that of Austrian-born Dr Arnold Deutsch. The SVR, in its official citation, describes how his portrait immediately 'attracts the visitor's attention' to 'its intelligence, penetrating eyes, and strong-willed countenance'.²

Deutsch's claim to fame is that he was the principal recruiter of the Cambridge spies. He was altogether an extraordinary figure, whose impact on 20th-century history, although little known, was immense. He was highly trained in every aspect of espionage. He used false identities to operate undercover, and successfully evaded police surveillance. He set up clandestine radio communications, forged documents and established secret border crossings between countries in northern Europe.³

Dr Arnold Deutsch, the charismatic recruiter of the Cambridge spies

He was posted to England at various times in the 1930s, sometimes using aliases such as Stefan Long or 'Otto'. His aim was to recruit from Britain's most prestigious universities academic high-fliers with communist sympathies who were destined for key positions at the highest levels of government, where they could then operate as long-term penetration agents (or 'moles').

During his time in England, Deutsch is credited by the KGB with having recruited some twenty agents,⁴ the most successful (from the Soviet point of view) being ones most of whom were enrolled at, or had recently graduated from, Trinity College, Cambridge. (The only known exception was Donald Maclean, who graduated from a neighbouring college, Trinity Hall).

Academically brilliant though most of his recruits were, Deutsch if anything surpassed them in academic attainments. In 1923 he enrolled at the University of Vienna, studying philosophy, psychology, physics and chemistry. In 1928, less than five years later, and aged only 24, he was awarded a doctorate of philosophy, with distinction.[5] During the 1920s, he forsook his religious Jewish upbringing and embraced the ideas of Marx and Freud. Widely read and highly cultured, he possessed great charisma and an uncanny understanding of human psychology. He became a spy-recruiter beyond compare.

When he chose, he could employ great charm: Philby, his first recruit succumbed to it, recalling in later years:[6]

> He was a marvellous man. Simply marvellous. I felt that immediately. And [the feeling] never left me. … The first thing you noticed about him were his eyes. He looked at you as if nothing more important in life than you and talking to you existed at that moment. … And he had a marvellous sense of humour.

To others, though, he could be abrupt and dismissive. A leading figure in the Communist Party of Great Britain in the 1930s, who had had regular dealings with Deutsch, found him to be most unappealing. An MI5 penetration agent, Olga Gray, who has infiltrated the CPGB, described him as 'a small man and rather bumptious in manner'.[7]

Above all, however, Deutsch was effective. The communist 'moles' he recruited from Cambridge in the mid-1930s achieved successes beyond Moscow's highest expectations. They managed at various times to penetrate the British Foreign Office, the War Office, and Britain's four principal intelligence bodies: the Security Service (MI5); the Secret Intelligence Service (MI6); the Government Code and Cypher School (GC&CS) at Bletchley Park, which collected and decoded signals intelligence; and the wartime Special Operations Executive (SOE) – Churchill's 'secret army', whose members were under orders to 'set Europe ablaze'.

Here are eight of the Cambridge spies:

1) Harold Adrian Russell 'Kim' Philby (codenames *Söhnchen*, or 'Sonny', and *Stanley*)

The first Cambridge spy recruited by Arnold Deutsch, Harold Adrian Russell 'Kim' Philby became one of the most successful in the history of espionage, and probably the worst traitor in Britain's history. Recruited in 1934, he served the Soviet Union as an undercover penetration agent for thirty years. During World War II he succeeded in joining Britain's Secret Intelligence Service, MI6, rising to become head of its counter-intelligence section. After World War II he was posted to Washington as MI6's liaison officer with America's intelligence agencies, the CIA and FBI. Many hundreds of good people died as a direct result of his treachery.

Philby adopted his communist beliefs while an undergraduate, when he was an active member of the Cambridge University Socialist Society (CUSS).[8] On graduating from Trinity College in 1933, he expressed his conviction that 'my life must be devoted to communism'. He travelled to Austria, which was then in a state of civil war, and undertook dangerous courier work in Vienna for the underground Austrian Communist Party.[9] While there, he fell in love with a young, recently divorced communist, Alice 'Litzi' Friedmann (née Kohlmann), whom he married in February 1934. She returned with him to London.[10] One evening she informed Philby that she had arranged for him to meet a 'man of decisive importance'. In June 1934 Philby had his first meeting, on a bench in London's Regent's Park, with a short, stocky man, with vivid blue eyes and fair curly hair, who introduced himself as 'Otto'. This was none other than the chief recruiter for the Soviet KGB in Britain, Dr Arnold Deutsch.[11]

Philby was won over by Deutsch's captivating charm and 'considerable cultural background'.[12] Deutsch, with his deep understanding of human psychology, appraised his prospective recruit with clinical detachment. He immediately noticed the insecurity and resentment that lay at the heart of Philby's personality, owing to Philby's upbringing by an overbearing father. As a result, Philby had a stammer and was 'a very timid and irresolute person'. Deutsch nevertheless informed Moscow that Philby was 'ready, without questioning, to do anything for us and has shown all his seriousness and diligence working for us'.[13]

Philby later looked back with some degree of personal pride at Deutsch's invitation for him to work as an undercover penetration agent for the communist cause: 'One does not look twice at an offer of enrolment in an elite force.'[14]

Deutsch asked Philby who else at Cambridge might be suitable for recruitment. Philby recommended two of his contemporaries, Donald Maclean and Guy Burgess.[15]

Deutsch instructed Philby and his wife to break off 'as quickly as possible' all personal contact with their communist friends,[16] and told Philby to re-invent himself politically and pose as a right-wing pro-German sympathiser.[17]

A short time afterwards, Philby became a correspondent for *The Times* and travelled to Spain to report on the Spanish Civil War. In 1940 he joined Britain's Special Operations Executive (SOE) as an instructor. In September 1941 he succeeded in joining the Secret Intelligence Service, MI6, with a reputation as a counter-intelligence expert.[18]

In early 1944 Philby was instrumental in setting up in MI6 a new body, Section IX, for the 'professional handling of any cases coming to our notice involving Communists or people concerned in Soviet espionage'. He then organised a ruthless palace coup to ensure that he, rather then his rival, the strongly anti-communist Felix Cowgill, headed the new section. Philby's contemporary, Robert Cecil, wrote later:[19]

> Philby at one stroke had got rid of a staunch anti-communist and ensured that the whole post-war effort to counter communist espionage would become known in the Kremlin.

The history of espionage records few, if any, comparable masterstrokes.'

Philby's most recent biographer Ben Macintyre has characterised Philby's success in this way: 'The fox was not merely guarding the hen house, but building it, running it, assessing its strengths and frailties, and planning its future construction.'[20]

During all this time, Philby cut a reassuringly respectable figure with his pipe, flannels and old tweed jacket.[21] His colleagues never suspected a thing. Macintyre describes how Philby 'was adored by his colleagues, who recalled his "small loyalties", his generosity of spirit, and his distaste for petty office politics'.[22] The novelist Graham Greene, who served as one of Philby's deputies, later recalled:[23]

> He had something about him – an aura of lovable authority like some romantic platoon commander – which made people want to appear at their best in front of him. Even his senior officers recognised his abilities and deferred to him.
>
> No one could have been a better chief than Kim Philby. He worked harder than anyone else and never gave the impression of labour. He was always relaxed, completely unflappable.

'You didn't just like him, admire him, agree with him; you worshipped him,' said one his contemporaries.[24]

At end of World War II, the Kremlin secretly awarded Philby the Soviet Order of the Red Banner, in recognition of 'conscientious work for over ten years'.[25] In 1947 Philby was posted to Istanbul as SIS head of station; but the culmination of his career was in 1949 when he was posted as SIS liaison to Washington.[26] A senior American FBI officer, who frequently met Philby during his two-year posting to the U.S., wrote: 'In 1950 and 1951, as far as the KGB was concerned, Philby was the perfectly placed spy with access to MI5, MI6, the CIA and the FBI.'[27]

Philby during 1947-1951 was also directly responsible for the deaths of many hundreds of émigré anti-communist Estonians, Lithuanians, Ukrainians, Armenians, Georgians and Albanians, who had been offered clandestine assistance from Britain's Secret Intelligence Service and America's newly-created Central Intelligence Agency to infiltrate their native countries and establish contact with anti-communist activists.[28]

Yuri Modin, Philby's principal KGB handler during this time, has described how he (Philby) betrayed hundreds of Albanian insurgents who were seeking to overthrow the hardline Stalinist regime of Enver Hoxha. Philby reportedly supplied Moscow with 'vital information about the number of men involved, the day and the time of the landing, the weapons they were bringing and their precise programme of action'. Modin adds: 'The Soviet authorities duly passed on Philby's information to the Albanians, who set up ambushes on their coast. The commando force was surrounded.'[29] Philby additionally betrayed to Moscow the identities not only of these insurgents, but also of their contacts and relatives living in these countries.[30] Ben Macintyre estimates that for every Albanian guerrilla Philby betrayed, as many as forty of his contacts and relatives were shot or jailed.[31]

An even more shocking betrayal occurred during World War II. Just as the Soviet Red Army was poised to enter Germany, Philby provided the KGB with a top-secret list of thousands of leading members of the German Catholic resistance to Hitler, who, the Western Allies hoped, might help them establish a democratic and non-communist government in Germany after the war. The Soviets, on entering Germany, tracked down these individuals and liquidated them all.[32]

After the 1951 defections to Russia of Donald Maclean and Guy Burgess, suspicion fell on Philby. He managed to brazen his way out of the affair. In 1963, when Philby was in Beirut working as a journalist, his former MI6 colleague and long-time friend, Nicholas

Elliott, confronted him with new evidence confirming his treachery. Philby confessed he had been a KGB spy for three decades. The next day he vanished, and was spirited away by a Soviet trawler to commence a new life in Moscow.

2) Donald Maclean (codenames *Waise,* or 'Orphan', and *Homer*)

Donald Maclean was the third of five children of a British lawyer and Liberal politician, Sir Donald Maclean. While still at school, he repudiated the strict Christian values on which he had been raised and eagerly embraced communism.[33] At Cambridge he became widely known for his militant left-wing views.[34]

Maclean was a tall and striking-looking individual. Robert Cecil, a contemporary of his, both at Cambridge and in the British Foreign Office, met him for the first time towards the end of 1932, when Maclean was in his second year at Cambridge. Cecil vividly recalled his 'handsome face, the hair swept back in Rupert Brooke style from a high forehead', adding:[35]

> In those days he was slimly built and this exaggerated his height, which was nearly six foot four inches; height apart, he had the air of looking down on the company and, though softly spoken, he could give his voice an edge if he chose.

In June 1934, Maclean graduated from Cambridge with first-class honours in modern languages.[36] In August he was approached by Philby to work for Soviet intelligence. In December he met Deutsch, who recruited him as a Soviet spy and instructed him to sever his links with the Communist Party.[37]

The next year Maclean sat for the entrance exam for joining the Foreign Office.[38] Only six or seven high-flying Oxbridge graduate were admitted each year. Maclean succeeded on his first attempt.[39] Thus, in October 1935, the first of the Cambridge spies succeeded in penetrating the corridors of power.[40]

In September 1938 he was appointed Third Secretary to the British embassy in Paris, a 'Grade A' posting, where he started drinking heavily. Although he was shy and awkward in the presence of women, he had an affair with an American woman, Melinda Marling. In June 1940, during the tumultuous weeks when France was succumbing to Hitler's military onslaught, they married, before swiftly returning to England. Their marriage, which lasted twenty-five years, was a deeply unhappy one for both of them.[41]

In May 1944, the couple were posted to the British embassy in Washington, where Maclean was appointed first secretary to the Ambassador, Lord Halifax, and given responsibility for handling information surrounding the secret Anglo-American collaboration on the development of the atomic bomb. This turn of events was an incredible stroke of good fortune for Moscow, and a personal triumph for Maclean, who had concealed his anti-American feelings to gain this promotion.[42]

Maclean regularly commuted from Washington to New York, more than 200 miles away, to deliver highly classified intelligence to his Soviet controller. In February 1947 he was appointed joint secretary of the Combined Policy Committee responsible for coordinating Anglo-America-Canadian nuclear policy.[43]

Sometimes, while in America, when he was away from the British embassy, he would indiscreetly express pro-Soviet and anti-American views; but few of his colleagues attached any significance to them.

Like the diligent spy that he was, he made himself indispensable to his employers and colleagues in countless ways. One of his superiors at the Washington embassy, Sir Roderick Campbell, spoke highly of Maclean's 'skill at drafting and his ability to unravel complex issues'.[44] Maclean's friend, Robert Cecil, observed:[45]

> No task was too hard for him; no hours were too long. He gained the reputation of one who would always take over

Clockwise from top-left: Kim Philby, Donald Maclean, Guy Burgess and James Klugmann

a tangled skein from a colleague who was sick, or going on leave, or simply less zealous. In this way he was able to manoeuvre himself into the hidden places that were of most interest to the NKVD.

In October 1948, aged only 35, Maclean was appointed to a senior post at the British embassy in Cairo. By then, the strain of his double life was taking a severe toll on him. He often went on alcoholic binges and verbally abused his wife.

In May 1950, an old friend of his, Philip Toynbee, came to stay with him. (Toynbee, during the 1930s, had been the first communist president of the Oxford Union).[46] Maclean and his friend embarked on a drunken and particularly destructive rampage. The pair broke into the flat of two young female staff of the U.S. embassy, ripping up the contents of their wardrobes and vandalising their bathroom. Years later Toynbee later gleefully recalled how Maclean raised the large bathroom mirror above his head and smashed it down onto the bath, which, to Toynbee's 'amazement and delight', broke in two while the mirror remained intact.[47]

After this particular outburst Maclean was sent back to England, where he was treated by a psychiatrist for overwork, marital problems, alcoholism and repressed homosexuality.[48] Surprisingly, in view of his fragile mental state, the Foreign Office deemed him well enough by autumn 1950 to head its American desk in Whitehall.[49] Only a short time previously, in June, communist North Korea, backed by the Soviet Union and communist China, invaded South Korea. Maclean's old friend, now his deputy at the American desk, Robert Cecil, later acknowledged that Moscow would have found the intelligence provided by Maclean during this period to have been 'of inestimable value' in forewarning the communist Chinese and North Koreans, via Moscow, 'on strategy and negotiating positions'.[50]

3) Guy Burgess (codename *Mädchen*, or 'Maiden')

A contemporary of Maclean's at Cambridge, Guy Burgess was recruited by Deutsch to work for Soviet intelligence at the same time as Maclean.[51] He was a most unusual choice. Although he was intellectually brilliant, self-assured and a charming and witty conversationalist, he was also an habitual drunkard and a flamboyant homosexual at a time when homosexual acts were illegal in Britain and punishable by prison terms.

Cambridge academic Christopher Andrew and former KGB officer Oleg Gordievsky have remarked: 'A more doctrinaire and less imaginative NKVD controller than Deutsch might well have concluded that the outrageous Burgess would be a liability than an asset.'[52] However, for Burgess, the best cover for him was no cover. Nobody could believe that a man who liked to shock polite company with open displays of his promiscuous lifestyle could have anything left to hide.

Like Philby and Maclean, Burgess ostensibly broke with Marxism. At the end of 1935 he became employed as an assistant to a young, right-wing, homosexual Conservative MP, Captain 'Jack' McNamara, a prominent member of a pro-German organisation, the Anglo-German Fellowship.[53] The following year he did a stint of work at *The Times*. Later that year he commenced employment at the BBC as a talks producer.

At one stage, Burgess's Soviet controllers told him to court and attempt to marry Winston Churchill's niece, Clarissa, in order to create a respectable-seeming operational cover for his espionage. This did not eventuate. Instead, she married Sir Anthony Eden, Churchill's Foreign Minister and successor as Conservative Prime Minister, and became Lady Avon.[54]

At the outbreak of World War II Burgess joined the Foreign Office's News Department.[55] By then he had established a network of valuable contacts, both in Britain and overseas, from which he was able to gather both secret intelligence and political gossip for his Soviet masters.

In 1944, Burgess joined the Foreign Office, first on a temporary basis, then, in 1947, on a more permanent basis.[56] A cipher clerk who worked in the KGB's London residency from 1945 to 1948 recalled how Burgess would hand over 'briefcases full of Foreign Office documents which were then photographed in the Soviet embassy and returned to him'.[57]

In November 1948 he was transferred to the Far Eastern Department of the Foreign Office. By then, like Donald Maclean, he was finding his double life an increasing strain. His behaviour, always peculiar, became even more bizarre. During a trip he made to Gibraltar and Tangier in 1949, Burgess embarked upon what a friend from his Cambridge days, Goronwy Rees, described as a 'wild odyssey of indiscretions', including leaving a trail of unpaid bills and debts, publicly identifying British secret intelligence officers, and going from pub to pub drunkenly singing, 'Little boys are cheap today, cheaper than yesterday', to the tune of 'La donna è mobile', from Verdi's opera *Rigoletto*.[58]

Appearances notwithstanding, Burgess possessed a purposeful and disciplined inner-core and was frequently able to function highly effectively. He was one of Moscow's most productive spies and was unfailingly punctual with appointments.[59]

From his post in Whitehall, in the Foreign Office's Far Eastern Department, he was able to supply Moscow with details of Britain's policy towards China's new communist rulers and towards Korea in the months preceding communist North Korea's military attack on South Korea in June 1950.[60]

In August 1950 he was appointed second secretary at the British embassy in Washington, working alongside, and for a time living as a house-guest of, Kim Philby.[61]

In the spring of 1951, Kim Philby and his wife, Aileen, threw a dinner party to which a dozen or so guests from the intelligence and diplomatic communities were invited, along with their spouses. Among those present were senior CIA identities Bill Harvey and James Angleton and their wives. The evening was an unqualified disaster. Bill

Harvey's wife, Libby, struck up a conversation with Philby's house-guest, Burgess, and discovered to her delight that he could sketch portraits. She invited him to sketch her. Thereupon, according to a senior FBI officer who attended the party:[62]

> Burgess executed a caricature so lewd and savage that Libby demanded to be taken home immediately. Bill Harvey had to be restrained from physically attacking Burgess, and was walked around the block by Angleton until he calmed down. After that, the party broke up.

In April 1951, not long after this episode and other indiscretions, Burgess was sent home to England in disgrace.[63] In May, Burgess and Maclean fled England and defected to Russia.

4) John Norman 'James' Klugmann (codename *Mer*)

One of the most significant Trinity College spies – although one whose career seldom receives the scrutiny from historians that it deserves – was John Norman 'James' Klugmann. Before coming to Cambridge, he had been a fellow student and close friend of Donald Maclean's at Gresham's School in Holt, Norfolk. While there, Klugmann embraced communism and was a decisive influence in persuading Maclean to embrace it too.[64] At Cambridge he introduced Maclean to Burgess, who may have had a romantic dalliance with the bisexual Maclean.[65] Klugmann was recruited by Deutsch to work for Soviet intelligence in 1936, shortly after Maclean and Burgess.[66]

American historian David Martin maintains that Klugmann, who graduated with a double first in modern languages, was 'by far the most brilliant of the Communist group at Cambridge'.[67] His treachery during World War II contributed greatly to consigning a whole country, Yugoslavia, to communist police-state tyranny. Only in 1975, two years year before he died, did his role in this affair first become publicly known.

During the war, he served in the Special Operations Executive (SOE). In February 1942, he joined its Yugoslav Section, which was based in Cairo, and immediately impressed his superiors. His first boss, Major Kenneth Greenlees, recalled, upon first meeting Klugmann:[68]

> I soon realised his sterling qualities – conscientious, a glutton for work, much travelled; speaking several languages, a double first in modern languages at Cambridge; of an intellect way ahead of myself and many of those around me.

It was from his pivotal post in Cairo that Klugmann was able to influence decisively the course of events in wartime Yugoslavia. At the behest of Moscow, he conducted a clandestine influence operation designed to discredit, in the eyes of the Churchill government, the royalist Serbian leader in Yugoslavia, General Draza Mihailovich, whose army of Chetniks was doing the bulk of the fighting against the German occupiers. The aim was to eliminate from Yugoslavia any non-communist political movements and to install a Soviet-backed one-party communist dictatorship. American historian David Martin writes: 'Klugmann was a mole whose great accomplishment was to falsify information in a manner that resulted in handing over a nation of 15 million people to Communist control.'[69]

Influenced by the highly misleading maps and reports emanating from the SOE's Yugoslav office in Cairo,[70] the Churchill government and British Foreign Office came to the view that Mihailovich was the wrong horse to back in the Balkans conflict. In December 1943, they switched their support from the Chetniks to the communist Partisans.[71] This led to the strange paradox whereby the Churchill government was simultaneously backing royalists in Greece and 'reds' in Yugoslavia.[72]

The communist Partisans subsequently used the weapons supplied to them by the British not to fight their German and Italian occupiers but to annihilate their political rivals, especially the Chetniks.[73] Josip

Broz Tito's communists refused to cooperate or share power with any other political groupings in the country. In the territories they seized they set up Soviet-style police-state rule and conducted a reign of terror, summarily executing prominent people.[74]

In contrast, Mihailovich's Chetniks, despite being greatly weakened by being abandoned by the British, nevertheless continued to resist the Axis occupiers throughout 1943 and 1944. In 1944, they rescued several hundred American airmen, risking deadly reprisals from the Germans by doing so.[75]

Exactly a year after his government had abandoned Mihailovich's Chetniks in favour of the communist Partisans, Churchill expressed deep misgivings about this policy. In December 1944 he admitted to his Foreign Secretary, Anthony Eden, 'I have come to the conclusion that in Tito we have nursed a viper… he has started biting us.'[76]

Towards the end of May 1945, a few weeks after Victory-in-Europe Day, Tito's Partisans massacred thousands of anti-communist civilians from two of Yugoslavia's other major ethnic groups, the Croats and Slovenes, who were trying to escape the red terror and flee into neighbouring Austria.[77] At about this time, the Partisans also tried to annexe Trieste. This confirmed Churchill in his growing conviction that he had been seriously misled about Tito.[78] In December 1945, Churchill, a few months after he had fallen from power, recalled: 'During the war I thought I could trust Tito … but now I am well aware that I committed one of the biggest mistakes in the war.'[79]

In July 1946, the victorious communists proceeded to hold a show trial of General Mihailovich, after which he was executed by firing squad.[80] This enraged the many hundreds of American airmen who had been rescued by, and owed their lives to, the Serbian Chetniks. In 1948, on the recommendation of General Eisenhower, President Harry Truman awarded Mihailovich posthumously the Legion of Merit in the Degree of Commander-in-Chief for rescuing American airmen and contributing to the Allied victory.[81]

Towards the end of his life, Churchill's wartime Foreign Secretary, Anthony Eden, was asked what weighed most heavily on his conscience in the twilight of his political career. He replied: 'Our betrayal of Mihailovich.'[82]

The Soviet mole Klugmann who contributed so much to this outcome, unlike Philby, Maclean and Burgess, never bothered to camouflage his communist convictions. Hugh Seton-Watson, who shared an office with Klugmann in Cairo during 1942-43, reminisced decades later:[83]

> Of Klugmann's absolute devotion to the Communist cause there was no doubt.... If ... the Party had instructed him to order my execution, or to execute me in person, I don't suppose that he would have hesitated. Nevertheless ... I cherish his memory as a brilliant man who was once my friend, and as a person of selfless, almost saintlike, character.

In March 1948, the Soviet Union broke with Tito, denouncing the Yugoslav Communist Party as ideologically heretical and filled with British spies.[84] So obedient was Klugmann to Stalin that he immediately followed Moscow's new policy and excoriated the man he had previously championed, denouncing the Yugoslav dictator in a pamphlet, *From Trotsky to Tito*.[85]

5) Anthony Blunt (codenames *Tony* and *Johnson*)

A few years older than Philby, Maclean, Burgess and Klugmann, Anthony Blunt arrived at Cambridge in 1926 with a scholarship in mathematics, although the following year he changed to studying modern languages and became a French linguist and art historian. In October 1932 he was elected a fellow of Trinity College.[86] By the autumn of 1928 he had clearly adopted communist beliefs, even though in later years he would dishonestly claim that he only came to communism in the mid-1930s, when Marxism was gaining a large

Clockwise from top-left: Anthony Blunt, Paddy Costello, John Cairncross and Leo Long

following among Cambridge undergraduates.[87] Like Burgess, Blunt was a lifelong homosexual.

In August 1935 Anthony and his brother Wilfred sailed from

London to Leningrad aboard a Soviet vessel, the MV *Sibier*, to visit Stalin's Soviet Union. They returned a few weeks later.[88]

In early 1937 Burgess introduced Blunt to Deutsch. From that time until World War II, Blunt was given the task of talent-spotter for the KGB.[89]

In June 1940, after almost two years of effort, Blunt succeeded in joining Britain's Security Service, MI5.[90] A few months later he was sharing lodgings in London's Oxford Street with fellow Cambridge spy Guy Burgess.[91] Tall, distinguished-looking and self-possessed, he made a favourable impression on everyone. A future Director-General of MI5, Dick White, later recalled Blunt's ability to befriend his superiors:[92]

> He made a general assault on key people to see that they liked him. I was interested in art and he always used to sit next to me in the canteen and chat. And he betrayed us all. He was a very nice and civilised man and I enjoyed talking to him. You cannot imagine how it feels to be betrayed by someone you have worked side by side with unless you have been through it yourself.

Blunt became one of the KGB's most productive agents, photographing and passing on to his Soviet controllers a prodigious hoard of intelligence, including copies of secret files and the names and 'all possible details' of serving MI5 officers and their agents.[93] He impressed one of his KGB handlers, Yuri Modin, as 'a man who matched his deeds to his words'. Modin recalled: 'In all the time we worked together he never once broke a promise or forgot a detail.'[94]

One of Blunt's major wartime responsibilities was to conduct clandestine surveillance of neutral countries' diplomatic missions in London, which were obvious targets for exploitation by German and Italian spy agencies. Robert Cecil said of Blunt's work: 'Surveillance extended to couriers and their diplomatic bags, and Blunt proved adept at the delicate manoeuvres necessary to deprive couriers of their bags for just long enough to permit scrutiny of their contents.'[95] Blunt was able to pass on this information to his Soviet controllers,[96] and additionally to advise them of any MI5 surveillance of the activities of Soviet spies and agents in Britain.[97] Each month, from March 1943 until the end of the war, Blunt was responsible for producing summary reports of MI5's work, which were sent directly to Churchill. He doubtless ensured they went to Moscow as well.[98]

At the end of the war, Blunt requested the KGB to allow him to retire from espionage. He was surprised that he was allowed to do so. Two historians of the Cold War have speculated: 'It was possible, if not likely, that the KGB already had a well-placed mole inside MI5, and did not need Blunt any more.'[99] We will revisit this question in a later chapter.

6) Desmond Patrick 'Paddy' Costello (codename *Long*)

New Zealand-born Desmond Patrick 'Paddy' Costello joined the Communist Party while studying at Cambridge and married a fellow communist in 1935. He came to the attention of Anthony Blunt, and in 1937 was believed to have been recruited by Deutsch to the KGB.[100]

During World War II Costello became general staff officer responsible for intelligence for the New Zealand Division of the Middle East Forces GHQ. In July 1944, he was discharged in order to take up a diplomatic appointment at the New Zealand legation in Moscow, where he became first secretary in 1947 and *chargé d'affaires* in July 1949. New Zealand's then Secretary for External Affairs, Alister McIntosh, had nothing but praise for Costello, whom he described as 'our most brilliant linguist and diplomatic officer'. In October 1950 he was appointed to the New Zealand legation in Paris.[101]

According to a KGB file of 1953, Soviet intelligence regarded Costello (known by his codename *Long*) as a 'valuable agent' of its Paris residency.[102] In May 1954 Costello issued New Zealand passports, with fake identities, to two veteran American communist spies Morris and Lona Cohen, who had fled from the United States after the arrest in 1950 of the famous nuclear spy, Julius Rosenberg, and his wife Ethel.[103] The Cohens would doubtless not have thought lightly of the prospect of being convicted for espionage and sharing the fate of the Rosenbergs, who had been sentenced to the electric chair.

Thanks to Costello's provision of New Zealand passports with false identities for the couple, the Cohens' espionage career, instead of being suspended, was given a new lease of life. Using the aliases Peter and Helen Kroger, they moved to England, settling in northwest London and adopting a low-profile cover as antiquarian book-dealers. During this time, however, they were working closely with a Soviet intelligence officer, Konon Molody (himself using a false alias, Gordon Lonsdale). In January 1961 British authorities arrested the Cohens for their role in servicing a major Soviet espionage network known as the Portland Spy Ring that had succeeded in penetrating the Royal Navy. They were sentenced to twenty years' jail, but served only eight.[104]

As for Paddy Costello, he left Paris, and in October 1955 was appointed to the chair of Russian studies at the University of Manchester. He came under suspicion of espionage in 1961 and died of a heart attack in 1964.

7) John Cairncross (codenames *Molière* and *Liszt*)

One of the later spies recruited by the KGB, and whose career of espionage for Moscow first became known to the British public in 1981, was John Cairncross. He was a Scotsman with a prickly personality but with a great gift for languages. Unlike most of the other

Cambridge spies, he came from a working-class family. Nicknamed the 'Fiery Cross', he did not disguise his left-wing views. Philby and Maclean had already left Cambridge before Cairncross enrolled there as an undergraduate.[105] But, in early 1937, he came to the attention of Blunt and Burgess. Klugmann recruited him in April and arranged for him to meet Deutsch the following month.[106]

With his mastery of foreign languages, Cairncross was successful in his application to join the Foreign Office, coming top in the entrance exams. In 1940, he was appointed private secretary to one of Churchill's ministers, Lord (Maurice) Hankey, the Chancellor of the Duchy of Lancaster. Hankey was a pivotal figure in Whitehall during the first half of the twentieth century. During World War I, under the then wartime Prime Minister David Lloyd George, Hankey had been appointed Secretary of the War Cabinet and was responsible for creating and directing the Cabinet secretariat, the central administrative mechanism of modern government.[107] One of Hankey's many tasks was overseeing Britain's intelligence agencies. As a result, he had ready access to highly sensitive government documents. One of Cairncross's KGB controllers in London, Yuri Modin, later recalled:[108]

> The most important reports on foreign policy, defence, industry and the orientation of scientific research regularly passed across [Hankey's] desk. John Cairncross, as his private secretary, suddenly became a major asset to us. Any time the name of his boss was omitted from the list of recipients of top-secret papers, he would write personally to complain to the Foreign Office. Result: the documents arrived by the next courier, who delivered them straight into the hands of the agent.

According to Modin, Cairncross became the first agent to inform the KGB that the Americans and British had been collaborating since late 1940 on jointly developing the atomic bomb.[109] In March 1942 he ceased working for Lord Hankey and succeeded in gaining employment at the top-secret code-breaking facility, the Government Code and Cypher School (GC&CS)[110] at its wartime location at Bletchley Park in Buckinghamshire. So secret was its existence that its vital contribution to the Allied war effort was not publicly acknowledged until 1974. Churchill described the decoders of German secret intelligence traffic as 'the geese that laid the golden eggs but never cackled'.[111]

Cairncross was apparently unaware until 1951 of the existence of other key KGB spies in Whitehall; he thought he was a solitary agent.[112]

8) Leonard Henry 'Leo' Long (codename *Ralph*[113])

In May 1937, Blunt succeeded in recruiting another promising undergraduate from Trinity College to spy for the KGB – Leonard Henry 'Leo' Long. According to Cambridge academic Christopher Andrew and former KGB officer Oleg Gordievsky, Long was 'Blunt's most important recruit'. During World War II, he managed to join MI-14, the Directorate of Military Intelligence at the War Office. During this time, Blunt took personal responsibility for running him as a sub-agent.[114]

Exposure of the Cambridge spies

Following the dramatic defections to Russia in 1951 of Maclean and Burgess, and in 1963 of Philby, many years would elapse before the public would learn the identities of any of the other Cambridge spies. It is noteworthy that on at least three occasions – well before 1951 – Britain's counter-intelligence came tantalisingly close to discovering something of these KGB spies' existence. One occasion was at the beginning of World War II; the other two occasions, shortly after the war's end.

a) The defection of Walter Krivitsky

Walter Krivitsky, a senior officer of the Soviet Red Army's intelligence directorate, the GRU, who ran spy networks in Western Europe between the wars, defected to France in 1937. He and his family fled into hiding to escape Stalin's assassination squads and later migrated to America. In late 1939 he testified before the U.S. House of Representatives' Dies Committee about his career in Soviet espionage.[115] Shortly after the outbreak of World War II, he travelled to London, and in January 1940 was debriefed by MI5's legendary Mrs Jane Archer (née Sissmore), a trained barrister and the Security Service's first female officer.[116]

Krivitsky revealed the names of more than seventy Soviet intelligence operatives and agents operating abroad, most of whom were unknown to MI5 at the time, and mentioned that he had heard of a Soviet spy network operating in Britain. He dropped some clues to the identities of two of the network's agents, but it is only with the benefit of hindsight that they can be seen to have pointed to Philby and Maclean.[117] Krivitsky returned to America, and on February 11, 1941, was found dead in a hotel room in Washington in suspicious circumstances.[118]

b) James Klugmann incriminates himself

Not long after the end of World War II, MI5 had in its possession all the evidence it needed to prosecute at least one of the Cambridge spies with espionage and treason. On August 1945, the Security Service secretly recorded an incriminating conversation between James Klugmann and a senior official of Britain's Communist Party, during which Klugmann admitted working for Moscow since his student days, passing secret documents to Tito's communist Partisans during the war, and doing all he could to discredit the royalist Chetniks.[119]

MI5 failed to act on this intelligence and never interrogated or prosecuted Klugmann for espionage and treason. He went on to become official historian of the Communist Party of Great Britain. It is strange, in light of his contribution to consigning 15 million Serbs, Croats and Slovenes of Yugoslavia to communist tyranny, that he is not accorded more prominence among the Cambridge spies.

c) The Volkov incident

In September 1945, Konstantin Volkov, a KGB lieutenant-colonel stationed in Turkey, visited the British consulate in Istanbul, pleading for political asylum for himself and his wife. In exchange for resettlement, a British passport and payment of £50,000, he was prepared to reveal the names of 314 Soviet agents in Turkey and 250 in Britain. Among the latter were nine particularly highly placed spies in London. Two of them worked in the Foreign Office (probably Maclean and Burgess). Seven of them worked 'inside the British intelligence system', one of whom (almost certainly Philby) was currently 'fulfilling the function of head of a section of British counter-espionage in London'.

Philby was the first person at MI6's headquarters in London to learn of Volkov's impending defection. He hastily conveyed the news to his Soviet controller, who in turn relayed it to Moscow. While Philby played for time by delaying MI6's response to Volkov's offer, Moscow flew two KGB hitmen to Istanbul. A few days later, Volkov and his wife, heavily sedated, bandaged from head to foot and fastened to stretchers, were loaded aboard a Soviet aircraft bound for Moscow. Upon the couple's arrival, the KGB subjected Volkov to a ferocious interrogation until he broke down and confessed everything. He and his wife were put to death.

The failed Volkov defection, as Philby would later recall, had 'proved to be a very narrow squeak indeed'. Had Volkov not been betrayed by Philby, the information he promised to disclose could have exposed and seriously disrupted Soviet espionage operations in the West. With Volkov out of the way, however, Philby, Maclean, Burgess and others were able to continue their treachery.[120]

d) The truth slowly trickles out: 1951–1990

A major breakthrough in identifying the Cambridge spies came as a result of a famous code-breaking operation in the United States, called the 'Venona Project'. During and after World War II, code-breakers at the United States Army Signal Intelligence Service (USASIS) had succeeded in intercepting and decrypting some of Moscow's top-secret radio communications with its intelligence officers around the world.

The first Cambridge spy to be identified by Venona, in the spring of 1951, was Donald Maclean. Kim Philby, from his unique vantage point as MI6's liaison officer in Washington, learned of this discovery and, fearful of being exposed himself, warned his Soviet controller of the urgent need to evacuate Maclean to the Soviet Union. On May 25, Maclean and Burgess fled Britain aboard a night-ferry to France, then travelled via Switzerland to the Soviet Union.[121] Their sudden disappearance caused consternation and alarm in both Whitehall and Washington.

Philby and Anthony Blunt, who were both known to be friends of Maclean and Burgess, were repeatedly questioned by British authorities, but they admitted nothing.

Four years later, however, an American newspaper leaked information that British authorities were investigating the possibility that Philby was the 'Third Man' who had warned Maclean and Burgess about their impending arrest before their defection to Russia. In October 1955, the Foreign Secretary in the Eden government, Harold Macmillan, in a speech to the House of Commons, cleared Philby of any allegations of wrongdoing.[122]

In 1963, new evidence came to light pointing unmistakability to Philby's betrayal of MI6. His former colleague, Nicholas Elliott, travelled to Beirut, where Philby was working as a journalist, and questioned him about the incriminating evidence. Philby confessed to espionage. The next day he vanished, later to reappear in Moscow.[123]

Blunt had left MI5 in 1945 and been appointed Surveyor of the King's Pictures, one of the largest private art collections in the world. (In 1952, after the death of King George VI and the accession of Elizabeth II, his title changed to Surveyor of the Queen's Pictures.) In 1956, the Queen knighted him for his work. In 1963, MI5 learned of his espionage from a wealthy American, Michael Straight, who had attended Trinity College, Cambridge, in the 1930s and whom Blunt had recruited. Under interrogation, Blunt confessed to Soviet espionage and named some of his accomplices. In return for his confession he was granted full immunity from prosecution and allowed to keep his prestigious job and knighthood.[124]

In February 1975, James Klugmann's wartime treachery was publicised for the first time in a speech delivered in the House of Lords by Lord Clifford of Chudleigh, a World War II veteran, who described Klugmann as 'an example of an intelligent, highly educated and dedicated agent of a foreign power; an ideologist and a disciple of hate and subversion'.[125]

This revelation made little impact in Britain at the time. In the United States, however, it was a different matter. Hundreds of U.S. airmen shot down over Yugoslavia during the war had been rescued by, and owed their lives to, the gallantry of General Mihailovich's Chetniks. They had been greatly angered when, after the war, Yugoslavia's communist dictator Tito had put Mihailovich on trial on trumped-up charges of treason and had him executed. Klugmann, as we have seen, contributed greatly to Yugoslavia's falling under communist control. He died in 1977 and did not live to see books which would chronicle his misdeeds for posterity – books such as American historian David Martin's *The Web of Disinformation: Churchill's Yugoslav Blunder* (1990)[126] and British historian Peter Batty's *Hoodwinking Churchill: Tito's Great Confidence Trick* (2011).[127]

In November 1979, Britain Conservative Prime Minster Margaret Thatcher, who had come to power earlier that year, revealed in a speech to the House of Commons Sir Anthony Blunt's former career as a spy for Moscow. The British public were outraged. Blunt was stripped of his knighthood and publicly disgraced.

In 1981, Fleet Street investigative reporter Chapman Pincher publicised another Cambridge spy, John Cairncross, and copiously documented his treachery.[128] Towards the end of that year, Margaret Thatcher exposed Leo Long.[129] Nine years later, with a great fanfare, a former senior KGB officer, Oleg Gordievsky, who had defected to Britain in 1985, confirmed that Cairncross and Long had indeed been spies for the KGB.[130]

Other spies in Britain's MI5 and MI6

a) MI6's George Blake

In this chapter we have so far limited our discussion to the Cambridge spies, mainly because of their notoriety and because there were so many of them. Of course they were by no means the only spies to have infiltrated Britain's secret intelligence agencies, MI5 and MI6, and spied for Moscow.

Another master-spy and traitor, who was exposed in 1961, was MI6 officer George Blake.[131] He was a particularly colourful personality. Born in Rotterdam in 1922, he spent most of his childhood in the Netherlands. His Egyptian-Jewish father, who was also a naturalised British subject, died when Blake was thirteen, and he was sent to Cairo to live with his uncle and aunt. He returned to the Netherlands in 1938. During the war he worked with the anti-Nazi resistance in Holland. He was captured by the Germans but managed to escape. With British help he reached England in 1942.

He was fluent in German and was recruited to Britain's Secret Intelligence Service (MI6) in 1944 to work in its Dutch section. After the war he won a scholarship to Cambridge to study Russian, which he quickly mastered. In 1948 he was posted to the British legation in Seoul, South Korea, where he gathered intelligence on communist North Korea. In 1950, during the Korean War, Blake was captured by the communists and imprisoned. During his captivity he converted to communism and volunteered to spy for the Soviet KGB.

After his release and return to Britain in 1953, he returned to his former job. He was appointed secretary and minute-taker of a joint MI6-CIA committee which had an audacious plan to build a secret tunnel that would run from the American-controlled sector of West Berlin to beneath Soviet-controlled East Berlin. From there the two intelligence services hoped to be able to eavesdrop on communications of the Soviet military command.[132]

MI6 and the CIA were overwhelmed with the vast amount of raw intelligence they were able to gather in this way, to the point that they set up a special centre in London's Earls Court for transcription and analysis. Meanwhile, Blake was betraying their clandestine work to his KGB controller in London, Sergei Kondrashev.[133] For a period, Blake was posted to Berlin, where his brief was to recruit agents for the West. MI6 later estimated that forty of these agents were betrayed by Blake to the KGB and executed.[134]

Blake was caught in the UK in 1961 and sentenced to forty-two years' imprisonment. He served only five years, however. In 1966, with the help of accomplices, he managed to escape Wormwood Scrubs, using a home-made rope-ladder reinforced with knitting needles, and was smuggled out of Britain in a secret compartment with breathing-holes built into a motor vehicle.[135] He was received in Moscow as a hero. Blake is one of the last surviving Soviet spies and, at the time of writing this book, is now 92 years of age.

b) Soviet penetration of MI5

If Britain's Secret Intelligence Service, MI6, was badly compromised by the presence in its ranks of traitors such as Kim Philby and George Blake, so was its Security Service, MI5, by the treachery of Anthony Blunt, as we have seen earlier in this chapter. Did Blunt act alone, however? In chapter 16, we shall examine evidence that points to the presence in MI5 of another super-mole, who, it has been alleged, was run not by the KGB but by the GRU, the intelligence directorate of the Soviet Red Army.

If this individual, who served in MI5 from 1938 to 1965, was indeed a spy for Moscow, it would have had huge ramifications not only for Britain's security, but also for Australia's, because this person was closely involved in setting up, after World War II, the Australian Security Intelligence Organisation.

Serious vetting of employees in MI5 did not take place until the mid-1960s. Until then, both MI5 and MI6 struggled through the years of the Cold War with spies undetected in their ranks.

7

AIR PHOTOGRAPHIC INTELLIGENCE DURING THE COLD WAR

After leaving the Air Ministry in 1952, my next posting was to RAF Nuneham Park, in Oxfordshire, a highly guarded Grade 'A' Station, where a high level of security was in place at all times. This facility was successor to the famous wartime RAF station Medmenham in Buckinghamshire, which had been established in April 1941 to attempt to map everything of strategic value in Nazi-controlled Europe.

RAF Medmenham was responsible for pioneering an entirely new science – the processing and interpretation of aerial photographic intelligence. Like the famous code-breakers at Bletchley Park, who succeeded in listening in on encrypted German wireless communications, the photo interpreters at Medmenham contributed decisively to the Allied victory over Hitler's Germany. As Taylor Downing has shown in his recent book, *Spies in the Sky*, their work shortened the duration of the war and, in doing so, saved countless lives.[1] Only fairly recently has the importance of wartime air photographic intelligence finally begun to receive the attention it deserves.

RAF Medmenham was located at Danesfield House, a spacious mansion in Buckinghamshire overlooking the River Thames. Its staff grew in number to more than 3,000, many of them housed in Nissen huts and other outbuildings on the mansion's grounds.

In an era before satellites and Google Earth, RAF pilots during the war regularly had to risk their lives flying on reconnaissance missions over enemy-controlled territory to gather photographic intelligence. Once they were over a target area, they would activate the aircraft's cameras to take photos 'at regular intervals calculated to allow for an overlap of 60 per cent'. In other words, every object was effectively photographed twice. The results were then passed on to Medmenham personnel, whose task it was to interpret the photos. They employed a special method of stereoscopic viewing, by viewing the overlapping parts of two adjacent photographs through two magnifying glasses in order for the images to appear in 3D.[2] This was not as straightforward as it sounds, but was painstaking and arduous, requiring great skill and dedication.

Objects of particular interest to the air photographic intelligence personnel were enemy-controlled fortifications, airfields, harbours and shipyards, rivers and canals, roads and railways, and weapons factories. Using stereoscopic viewing, they were able to estimate the heights of the objects from the shadows they cast.[3]

The type of intelligence pioneered at Medmenham was critical to the outcome of World War II, as even Britain's American allies were prepared to acknowledge. The Americans, on entering the war in late 1941, lacked experience in air photographic intelligence. Colonel Roy Stanley of the U.S. Air Force described Medmenham as the 'Mecca' of photo interpretation and expressed gratitude for how the British photo interpreters had helped Americans get 'up to speed in record time'.[4] None other than General Dwight Eisenhower, the American Supreme Commander of the Allied Forces in Europe, who directed the successful invasion of France and Germany in 1944–45 from the Western Front, acknowledged after the war the debt the victorious Allies owed to the photo interpreters at Medmenham.[5]

Medmenham could be proud of the role it played not only in winning the war, but also in advancing the status of women. English historian and biographer Christine Halsall writes:[6]

The 800 or so women who had worked with air photographs at RAF Medmenham, and all the other women who had served in similar ways on reconnaissance and interpretation units in Britain and overseas, could be proud of the part they had played in one of the Second World War's great achievements. From a few lumbering aircraft and a handful of civilians in 1939, photographic reconnaissance and interpretation had become the major provider of intelligence used in virtually every wartime operation. Unusually for those times, women had carried out the same work as men, were chosen for a particular job solely on their capabilities and had played a decisive part in winning the war.

One very important occurrence was the discovery in 1943 that Hitler was developing a secret long-range, jet-propelled flying bomb, the V-1 – a forerunner of the Cruise missile.[7] This terrifying weapon, which became known to the Allies as the buzz bomb or doodlebug, was feared by all, as nobody could hear it coming. It would hit its target unheralded by any air-raid warning. The only sound it made just before impact was a short whistling sound. This would be followed by a massive explosion, killing and wounding many innocent and unsuspecting civilians who had been unable to take cover.

The German Propaganda Minister, Dr Joseph Goebbels, named the flying bomb the *Vergeltungswaffe Eins* ('Vengeance Weapon One'), or the V-1.[8] The first V-1 flying bomb hit London in the early hours of June 13, 1944 – exactly a week after the Allies' successful 'D-Day' landings in northern France.[9] Thousands more followed.

The Germans had planned to start firing V-1 flying bombs on London, from mobile launching sites near the coasts of France and the Low Countries, as early as late October 1943.[10] That they were delayed by several months in doing so was thanks to the work of aerial reconnaissance and, in particular, the sharp eyes of one particular RAF officer and photo interpreter, Constance Babington Smith (whom I met after the war). She scrutinised an aerial photograph taken of a German military research facility in Peenemünde, just off Germany's Baltic Coast, and spotted a 'tiny cruciform shape', later confirmed to be a flying bomb in position for launching.[11] She mentioned this sighting in several of her reports, but was initially ignored until Bomber Command re-investigated and the V-1 flying bomb was acknowledged as Hitler's latest new weapon. Colonel Stanley has described Miss Babington Smith's discovery as 'one of the great PI achievements of the war'.[12]

From August to December 1943, Allied air raids flattened V-1 construction sites and set back German work on the project by several months.[13] However, from June 1944 until early 1945, the Germans succeeded in launching many thousands of doodlebugs, which rained down on targets all over southern England. Thankfully, I was never a witness of a hit or I would probably not be here to tell the story.

By end of World War II, then, air photographic intelligence had well and truly come of age and earned itself a permanent place alongside human intelligence (HUMINT) and signals intelligence (SIGINT). After the war, RAF photo intelligence relocated from Medmenham to the somewhat smaller premises of Nuneham Park, in Oxfordshire, which during the war had been the training facility for the Medmenham staff.

As the Cold War between the communist Soviet Union and the free world escalated, so was there an urgent requirement by the British and Americans for continued photo reconnaissance and interpretation. In August 1947, an entirely new organisation was created – the Joint Air Photographic Intelligence Centre (JAPIC). Its task was to monitor Soviet industrial capacity and troop movements in communist Eastern Europe. After the USSR tested its first nuclear bomb on August 29, 1949, an urgent priority for JAPIC was to assess the Soviet Union's growing nuclear capability.[14]

RAF Nuneham Park, Oxfordshire, home of the Joint Air Photographic Intelligence Centre (JAPIC) during the early years of the Cold War

I was appointed to JAPIC in 1952 as head of its intelligence section, staffed by two officers, three NCOs and three airmen. JAPIC was housed and operated in Nuneham Park, a beautiful, old mansion, owned since the 18th century by the Harcourt family, which had been requisitioned by the Department of Defence at the start of World War II. Adjacent to the mansion was a small family chapel and a graveyard with tombstones of departed family and servants.

Specialists from the army, navy and air force were engaged in highly classified work in photographic interpretation, which has still not been made public. We worked very closely with the United States Air Force, the Department of Defence in London and Bomber Command. Working here called for many liaison visits, particularly with the USA. I enjoyed my posting there, in particular meeting and working with the other services. I am still a member of the Medmenham Club, an association of former and serving photographic interpreters and imagery analysts.

My husband Robert, after his two-year assignment in Tengah and Changi in Singapore, had been sent to Malta for a year. During this time he returned to the UK, and in 1951 was posted to RAF Locking in Weston-super-Mare. He was then entitled to married quarters. He lived in a pleasant large house at Banwell, north Somerset, with a beautiful garden. At that time I owned a 250cc BSA motorcycle and enjoyed travelling there at weekends from Nuneham Park, where I was serving. Robert's two sons, John and Christopher, had been at boarding school since 1944. The posting to Weston-super-Mare enabled the boys to stay with their father at every opportunity and it was also to become my home after leaving the RAF in 1954, until our departure for Holland in April of that year.

I experienced an extraordinary event during the first week of my arrival at Nuneham Park. After settling in and being listed as duty officer, the routine demanded a defaulters' parade to inspect certain areas. The duty officer's bedroom was a small room at the end of a long corridor on the ground floor of the mansion. It was customary to relax on the bed if there was time to do so. Two RAF policemen, accompanied by two police dogs, would check all landings, and the stairway leading to the attic, which was normally out of bounds to staff. I found this ruling strange and, on my first night as duty office (D/O), I asked the police to take me there. Soon after midnight they arrived with the dogs and we went down the long passage to the steps leading to the attic. Both dogs started growling; they refused against all commands to go up the steps. They were angry and their hair stood on end. The police could not, and did not, force the terrified dogs. We just gave up; they left the building and I retreated to the D/O room. It was 1:00 am. Duty was done until 6:00 am unless an emergency arose, so I decided to rest on the bed and dozed off.

What happened next was very strange. I woke up with a start and saw a small man wearing a colourful embroidered waistcoat sitting in the old wicker chair in the corner of the room, his short legs dangling from the chair. I shook myself awake and decided I must have been dreaming. Odd though my experience had been, I carried on and handed over to the next D/O. At the risk of being ridiculed I told him of my experience, but he informed me that it was the ghost of an old manservant who was murdered there in the early 1900s. The description I gave was well known. He appeared spasmodically to D/Os, and my colleague told me to report it in my D/O report, which I did. This would require another exorcism consistent with the popular play of the time, *Bell, Book and Candle: A Comedy in Three Acts*, by John Van Druten. The C/O told me that this would be the third time a priest would come from Oxford to exorcise this spirit which haunted the mansion and was well known to all who served there.

I well recall the night of January 31/February 1, 1953, when a terrible disaster struck the lowlands of the province of South Holland and Zeeland, where unusually strong winds and high seas caused the collapse of the dykes of the Oosterschelde (Eastern Scheldt) and Westerschelde (Western Scheldt), flooding all the surrounding land. Hundreds of people drowned. Many well-stocked farms were swept away, along with countless animals and livestock, destroying the livelihoods of many Dutch people who depended upon agriculture. This all happened during that one fateful night without any warning. The country was devastated, and a state of emergency was declared.

The Netherlands government in its hour of need turned to Britain, requesting help, specifically from the Air Ministry, for an expert appraisal of the terrible damage sustained.

For this task JAPIC was the best-equipped facility to provide a complete and detailed assessment of where help was needed to rescue stranded people and animals. The flooded area was vast and our orders were to operate under wartime conditions (that is, eight hours on, eight hours off), to meticulously interpret all aerial photographic overlays and to report our findings on a daily basis.

Our first air reconnaissance of the flooded areas started within hours of the Dutch government's request for help. Then the photographs were developed and our interpreters worked in teams without a break on eight-hours shifts to maximise our output during this emergency. As it was peacetime, the aerial photography could proceed without interruption. The resulting comprehensive coverage and reliable interpretation were of great value to rescue teams and relief and reconstruction workers. I recall that it took about three months to complete this assignment.

The catastrophe and huge loss of life from the North Sea *Watersnoodramp* ('flood disaster') of 1953 prompted the Dutch to design and construct an elaborate flood defence system known as the *Deltawerken* ('Delta Works'). Designed to protect the estuaries of the rivers Rhine, Meuse and Scheldt from storm surges, it is a masterpiece of engineering for which the Dutch, well known for battling with water for centuries, are justly proud.

The work contributed by JAPIC at Nuneham Park would have also been an important element in its planning.

At Nuneham Park we had a wonderful gala night on June 2, 1953, to celebrate Queen Elizabeth II's coronation. It was an unforgettable occasion with lavish fireworks. A grey-haired colonel, from the paratroopers' regiment stationed on the other side of the river from our mansion, took me under his wing for the evening with dinner and 'olde tyme' dancing. As a consequence of the flowing gown with red velvet cloak that I wore that night, I earned the nickname of 'The Duchess' for the next year.

While I was serving in Nuneham Park, I frequently visited the Department of Defence in Northumberland Avenue, London, and often used my 250cc BSA motorcycle. On one particular visit some time in late 1953, I took off for London in reasonably good weather to enjoy the ride via Henley-on-Thames. Soon after departure, a thick fog set in, which steadily increased in density. After about an hour I decided to ride behind the protection of a big lorry on quite a narrow road.

All went well for a distance until suddenly, the lorry braked unexpectedly and I went crashing into it. Thankfully, I was wearing a solid helmet, which was badly dented. While struggling to free myself from the wreck of my bike, a kind man, who had been driving behind me, came to my rescue and pulled me out. I felt OK and very relieved it was not more serious. Other people appeared through the fog, as well as a cow, which surprised me but which I learned later was the cause of the accident. It had walked away from a loaded cattle truck that had left the road and was perched over a ditch on the other side of the road. Many more cows were trapped, injured or roaming around in the fog. My rescuer dragged my ruined bike from under the truck and took me to a local garage where it was left for insurance assessment. It was later declared a write off.

Thereafter this kind Samaritan drove me to the guardroom entrance of Nuneham Park, well out of his way. I phoned the medical officer, who gave me a full examination at the medical centre and was satisfied that I was OK. He sent me on my way with two tablets to take before sleep. Whatever the medication was, it gave me a night dreaming of repeated collisions and I was glad to be back at work the next day without further repercussions. The sad thing was that I had lost my bike. My husband discouraged me from replacing it and gave me his old Austin 7 motor car to compensate for my loss.

In 1954, Robert was offered a branch commission as a wing commander to complete his RAF service of twenty years and to qualify for an RAF pension. He declined and elected to accept an offer he had received from the Fokker aircraft company in the Netherlands working on a NATO project. Soon after he had accepted this offer, I found I was pregnant and realised my service career would soon have to come to an end. There were no provisions for pregnant, married service women, and no options were available to remain in the service and/or return afterwards. I left with a heavy heart. I loved my work, my life and my service friends.

We temporarily settled down in Banwell for several months before our departure for the Netherlands. Robert's son, John, joined the Royal Air Force and became a pilot after training in Calgary, Alberta, Canada. He went on to become one of the first ten Concorde pilots in the UK, serving until his retirement as a senior flight inspector with the Ministry of Civil Aviation. His second son, Chris, decided to follow suit and left for Canada to join the Canadian Air Force and later civil aviation. He married a lovely Canadian girl. They had three children and are now enjoying retirement in Smiths Falls, in Eastern Ontario, Canada.

My RAF service life ended in 1954, and I have always since, and always will, cherish my experience in this noble service.

8

WORKING WITH DUTCH COUNTER-ESPIONAGE

Time had come to leave England for our Dutch posting, and Robert was looking forward to working at Fokker Aircraft Company. Our base was to be in The Hague (Den Haag), from where he would need to travel to Avio-Diepen near Dordrecht, Rotterdam and Amsterdam. For this purpose a car was provided and our temporary residence became the Hotel Central in The Hague. We both wanted to live near the beach and this wish later became a reality after a short period of residence in Scheveningen, one of Holland's most famous seaside resorts. It was extremely difficult to find decent living quarters at that time. Holland had suffered immense damage during the German occupation, and after the war little or no building was done. So we had to be patient, as we might have been required to move closer to Amsterdam where Fokker was established. Although we were reasonably comfortable, we were still on the lookout for a house.

My pregnancy was proceeding well, but returning to London by air or sea was discouraged at the time, so our baby was to be born in Holland. We had arranged a place in a good hospital and, as the date grew closer and I felt more confident in my role of motherhood, we were looking forward to welcoming our baby, boy or girl. The new doctor, a gynaecologist recommended by Fokker, was happy about my fitness and condition and was consulted monthly to monitor proceedings. He was adamant the baby was due in September.

I was feeling very well throughout the entire period of pregnancy. However, as time progressed, we became a little anxious, particularly during the month of August. At this time the specialist was on leave, so we went to see a radiologist who stated the baby was well overdue and, to complicate matters further, was in breach position. Worried and horrified, we spoke to the specialist's locum who stated that my specialist was returning in two days and would decide on appropriate action; and so he did.

Two days later I reported to hospital where I was given castor oil. Labour started at noon and continued. The specialist returned at six o'clock that evening and I told him there was foetal distress as a green substance (foetal faeces) had emerged. At this point an immediate caesarean should have allowed the birth of a healthy baby. He told me that he was off to a birthday party and would call in later. At midnight he rushed me off for an immediate caesarean, which sadly proved too late. The baby was removed with the umbilical cord around his neck, seriously short of oxygen. Life support was applied for thirty minutes and removed thereafter for fear of serious brain damage caused by a prolonged period of lack of oxygen.

After I awoke from the anaesthetic, my husband was sitting by my bed amid a large display of red roses, sobbing. He could not speak and just held my hand. I soon realised the worst had happened. We were both heartbroken; a dark cloud rolled over our lives that day. Thankfully, I was allowed to see and hold our baby. He weighed 12 pounds, the equivalent in weight and size of a month-old baby. He was four weeks overdue with plenty of hair and a healthy body, according to the children's specialist who had tried so hard to resuscitate him during the operation. The specialist was so kind and gentle and said, 'This should never have happened.'

My parents were informed and there was a small reversal in my father's attitude after this tragic loss of our lovely baby. They sent me flowers in hospital, but the relationship remained largely superficial with my father, while it was heart-breaking for my mother who kept in touch by letter and the telephone.

After his three weeks of absence, my specialist attempted to apologise for having delayed surgical procedure. My husband was close to a breakdown and our doctor advised that a long holiday was necessary. An attempt to sue the specialist for negligence was met with a warning from the solicitor that the medical profession would support and protect any wrongdoing in good faith. There was little chance of success and suing would have been quite irrelevant to bringing back our baby.

This was a hard time for us. I left for Portugal to stay with a close friend living in Estoril, a coastal town not far from Lisbon, while Robert took three weeks' leave with his sister in the UK. My friend was married to a Portuguese naval officer and pregnant with her first child. They did so much to help me at that time with support and understanding for which I am still so grateful.

Robert and I returned to The Hague after the break to re-start our lives together. Soon after our return we spoke with an Australian pilot at a Fokker reception, who told us that he and his wife had also recently lost their new-born baby – a sad repeat of our own sad loss with the same gynaecologist.

My dearest wish was to get back to work – but where? And doing what? My experience in the RAF and previous training in intelligence was not, understandably, attractive to employers. I ventured to apply to several international organisations, such as Shell, Elmo and the Peace Palace, as a translator or interpreter, without success.

Out of the blue, I received an unexpected call from Australia House in London, inviting me for an interview with a representative of the Australian Security Intelligence Organisation (ASIO) in London. The happy result was a consular appointment at the Australian embassy migration office in The Hague, the Netherlands. The position was to arrange security screening of intending migrants to Australia. I was delighted to accept this position.

The Hague office was responsible for processing hundreds and thousands of intending migrants from the Benelux countries (Belgium, the Netherlands and Luxembourg) and some other countries. The Dutch Ministry of Justice was responsible for the clearance of individuals with criminal offences and the Dutch Domestic Security Service (BVD) for the security aspects, and each service would issue a report on the possible 'traces' (i.e., adverse records) of the individual applicant. The Australian government issued strict guidelines where certain 'traces' were concerned. ASIO's presence in the Australian embassy migration office was vital to prevent war criminals from entering Australia.

My appointment to the Australian embassy migration office in The Hague took effect, after the necessary clearances, in early 1955. At that time, The Hague office was manned by ASIO's senior liaison officer (SLO) with jurisdiction over all ASIO's European posts. This post was to be transferred to Australia House in London, and the incumbent SLO was due in The Hague to oversee this move. The Hague office would be retained to deal with the much increased migration programme centred in The Hague covering the Benelux countries.

The newly appointed SLO, Max Phillips, invited me to assist him to set up the new office in London involving many changes connected with this transfer. Simultaneously, the Director-General of ASIO, Brigadier (later Sir) Charles Spry, was on a visit to London for talks with MI5. I had the great privilege of being introduced to him soon after my arrival in London. We discussed intelligence matters, espionage in Europe and the revised aims and purposes of ASIO's responsibilities in Europe.

Only recently, in 1954, the dramatic defection of a senior Soviet diplomat, Vladimir Petrov, and his wife, Evdokia, had brought

Australia out of its relative isolation into the world of international espionage and activated renewed attention from the Soviet Union's principal spy agencies, the KGB and GRU.

The defection was also the occasion for some confusion and panic on the part of an Australian-born intelligence officer, Captain Charles 'Dick' Ellis, who had worked for Britain's Secret Intelligence Service, MI6, since 1922. Ellis was a brilliant linguist and, between the wars, had been stationed in Paris, recruiting agents from Russia's émigré community there. His first wife was a White Russian, Elizabeth 'Lilia' Zelensky. During this time he was allegedly 'turned' by a Soviet GRU operative, Vladimir von Petrov (no relation to the 1954 KGB defector with the similar name). On hearing in London about the impending defection of a Russian called Petrov, he panicked and headed to Australia where he took a job as 'consultant to ASIO'. He returned to London to brief Kim Philby on the matter. Meanwhile, in Australia, Petrov, still at the Soviet embassy, realised that someone had tampered with the contents of his safe. He feared that the KGB had somehow learned of his intentions and defected far sooner than he had originally planned.[1]

The Russians at that time were having problems in Britain in trying to collect vital information, which was entrusted to Britain from the United States and the Commonwealth countries, which naturally included Australia. The Russians lost no time in setting up an elaborate programme in Australia. They would now seek the information they sought in Australia. The Americans were already concerned about the political direction of the Australian Labor Party, which, under its then leader Dr H.V. 'Doc' Evatt, they considered to be communist.

In 1955, the Australian embassy assisted me in obtaining a house via the Dutch housing authorities and rented through their agent. It was located at Scheveningen, The Hague's seaside resort, on the dunes overlooking the sea. It was quite an ideal position at the time. We had an important neighbour: the Dutch Queen Mother Wilhelmina, who lived at a place named *De Ruygenhoek* – a pleasant, simple house. She was often seen riding in her donkey buggy to the shops, always dressed in white. It was said she was a spiritualist and somewhat eccentric. As she grew more disabled, she was moved to a place further inland where she later died.

We loved our new house and were told we would need to share it with another family should the need arise. From 1955 to 1958 we occupied this house alone and, with plenty of room, were able to entertain our families during the summer months. In May 1958 a charming gentleman looking for accommodation in The Hague came to the door with the Shell agent responsible for finding accommodation for itinerant staff assigned to their headquarters, also located in The Hague. We met, had a friendly chat and agreed to share the house, which resulted in the arrival of a charming family of six: Albert, his wife Kay, two daughters Rae, 13, and Jacqueline, 10, and two sons David, 6, and Philip, 2. We all fitted in our house and, with the beach on our doorstep, were able to spend much time enjoying that summer by the sea. The children were a delight and we soon became friends and shared the house very happily together. I became 'Auntie Molly'. Our friends and relatives, including Albert's parents, brother and sister-in-law, all mixed in during visits, and we even went on combined sightseeing excursions together. This was such a happy time, which lasted approximately eight months, due to delays in their posting to Indonesia, which finally arrived. We kept in touch over the years and met up intermittently whenever the opportunity presented itself in England, Holland and, later, Australia. We never had a cross word and always enjoyed each other's company, and this was to continue until this day.

Soon after arriving in The Netherlands I saw an advertisement in the newspaper announcing a cat show at the Kurhaus Hotel of Scheveningen, close to where we were residing. This was of interest to me, especially the Siamese cats!

I went along and enjoyed the day seeing Siamese cats and meeting their owners, watching the judging and admiring the winners. It was amazing to see the many different breeds that had arrived from all over Europe for this international show. I went home pondering when I could have a Siamese cat of my own and perhaps take him to a show. While I was in the midst of giving serious thought to this venture, a beautiful Siamese walked into our house one day and stayed. I was delighted, and so he seemed to be until, after three weeks, he disappeared for several months. When he re-appeared, he was wearing a new collar, with his name 'Sam' and a telephone number written on it. I rang the number. A charming voice answered, we met, and Sam became the reason for a long and happy friendship with Rosalie, Sam's owner and a lover of Siamese cats. The next year, after her Siamese 'queen' produced a litter, she presented me with a male kitten we named Samson.

While in Holland we were delighted to host a visit of Colonel Grigori Tokaev and his wife Aza, who were able, finally, in 1959 to take their first holiday out of Britain since their traumatic arrival in 1947. Special arrangements for this visit were made by the British security services for their flight to Rotterdam and onward travel to our home in Scheveningen, where a warm welcome was awaiting them for their week-long stay. The visit was kept very quiet, for obvious reasons, and some restrictions were in place to maximise their safety. We enjoyed a spell of good weather, which enabled our guests to make the most out of the sunshine and the beach.

A list of professionals was scheduled to meet with Grigori, and these visits were conveniently slotted in each day. It was a joy to see the great change in attitude and behaviour that was now apparent: both Grigori and Aza were able to relax, there was plenty of laughter and reminiscences and, occasionally, some tears of relief in safety, at last! They were now British nationals and were able to travel on a British passport; yet our Dutch friends put safety first throughout and made sure to provide a safe return to Rotterdam and London. We all enjoyed a farewell dinner party before their departure, and their short stay was long remembered as a very fruitful visit to those who were able and fortunate to meet Grigori. This visit was to be the first of many future visits to the United States, Canada and other countries, where he delivered many lectures during his lifetime.

In May 1960 my mother phoned me asking whether I could drive her and my father for a holiday in France with her great friend of World War I days, as my father had given up driving. I was delighted and Robert was relieved and generously assisted me to make plans to collect and escort them to the south of France in September 1960. The whole operation went well. My father was friendly and generous, and mother was delighted and happy at the apparent breakthrough in our relationship. We felt this was a great step in the right direction, and our good friends accepted my father very graciously. We all enjoyed each other's company.

Needless to say, we had a very busy office, and working overtime was normal. The Soviet KGB and GRU were well represented in The Hague during my years of service between early 1955 and August 1969. Here, as in the UK, Russian 'diplomatic' staff far exceeded their requirement at the Soviet embassy and the trade consulate.

The first head of the BVD (*Binnenlandse Veiligheidsdienst*), the Dutch postwar Domestic Security Service, was Colonel Louis Einthoven, a close contact of Brigadier Spry, who introduced me to him at the Australian embassy. This kind gentleman gave me a detailed briefing on the current situation in the

Colonel Louis Einthoven, the first head of the BVD, the Dutch postwar Domestic Security Service

Netherlands, stating that his counter-espionage (CE) department was extremely busy and that my professional assistance in certain areas would be much appreciated. Several days later, the head of the CE branch, Pieter Gerbrands, whom I had previously met in London in 1948, returned from leave and came to our office. I would be working with him for over fourteen years.

Our basic necessary liaison was a check of each prospective migrant applying to go to Australia. The BVD's accuracy and level of service were second to none. Twice weekly we received clearances and 'traces' and were thus able to deal with all applications with a minimum of delay. We never had a backlog of 'clear' migrants. Those with a trace needed an interview, which would be arranged with our office, usually within days. Those with serious traces were recommended for rejection. These included criminal cases forwarded by the Dutch Ministry of Justice. Security risks were forwarded by the BVD.

The state of affairs in post-war Europe was tense and unusual.

First, we had Dutch nationals leaving for a better future in sunny Australia. Most would be accepted without or with only minor 'traces'. Many Dutchmen who assisted the Germans during the period of occupation from May 1940 to May 1945 (by joining the Dutch SS or working in some other capacity, such as the civil police force and guards rounding up Dutchmen, Jews or others for transportation to Germany) left the Netherlands for Germany towards the end of the war. They later returned, seeking to leave the Netherlands for Australia, New Zealand, Canada or South Africa. Luckily, there was a register kept of such people, and both the BVD and Justice Department would advise the representatives of the relevant countries. This is how we managed to keep many traitors and unwanted individuals out of Australia. Those that 'got away' fled to Cuba, South America or some other distant lands.

Secondly, there were many foreigners arriving from displaced persons (DP) camps, workers who had originated from different countries and been transported as forced labour to Germany. There was also the influx of refugees from the failed Hungarian anti-communist uprising in 1956. Trainloads of Hungarians would roll into The Hague to seek asylum and safety; most were young unattached men carrying no identification. Clearly this was a profound problem for the Dutch government, which was only too keen to help these refugees. On the other hand, communist Hungary's secret police, the AVH, was very active in sending their agents, disguised as refugees, to carry out assignments in Western Europe. This same dilemma was faced with the many refugees from Yugoslavia. Our office was inundated at times with large numbers of unidentified individuals displaced by war-like operations that Marshal Tito's communist regime directed against civilians in that country. I often felt very uncomfortable when faced with wild-eyed, desperate men demanding to go to Australia when, in fact, they had to face a long wait while certain enquiries into their *bona fides* had to be made. Infiltration by undesirables was something we had to guard against constantly, and the Dutch Domestic Security Service advised us on this accordingly.

I recollect one particular occasion which could have become dangerous. A bearded man with a mop of black hair was shown into my office for a preliminary interview. He spoke little German but enough to conduct a simple conversation. He looked impatient and angry. He sat down and rattled off something in a Slavic language I could not understand. He gradually calmed down as I spoke slowly to him in German. There were a number of questions for special cases such as this, which had to be answered. All went well until I asked if he had ever killed anybody. He jumped off his chair, took up a fighting stance and pulled out a dagger from his trouser leg. His eyes flashed fire as he leaned over my desk, bringing his face up close to mine. 'Killing was my business,' he yelled. 'I am a Partisan!' I immediately touched the emergency button under my desk to summon reinforcement. Our medical officer, Dr John Thompson, whose office was next to mine, came to my aid and dealt with my client and escorted him out of my office. He agreed that my client was behaving strangely and also informed me that he had already terrified a staff member in the migration section. I later learned that he was not accepted for migration.

We certainly had some very strange cases coming through at times and we were certainly vigilant in dealing with unidentifiable individuals, particularly those who offered differing stories at multiple interviews. Many moved to try their luck at other embassies and were often more successful with South American countries.

A great problem during my assignment in The Hague was undoubtedly that of the 'Freedom for the Moluccas Movement', which was often the cause of political demonstrations outside our offices. Angry crowds with banners poised displayed their demands and sought Australia's protection. The police were always present to guard our premises. A man named Dr Johannes Manusama was an important agitator operating from the Netherlands. In 1948 there was a round-table conference in The Hague, and 1949 saw the inclusion of the Moluccan islands and the island of Timor in the newly-created *Republik Negara Indonesia*. Subsequently, on April 25, 1960, the South Moluccas exercised their alleged rights and declared their independence. This caused Indonesian troops to invade the South Moluccas and forcefully re-incorporate it into the Republic of Indonesia, causing the local government, along with 12,000 South Moluccan soldiers and their families, to establish themselves in 1960-61 in the Netherlands and create a government-in-exile.

The exiled community mounted many demonstrations. Certain elements organised and conducted terror attacks. In 1978 a group of Moluccans took 70 Dutch civilian hostages travelling on a train near Assen. The siege lasted 14 days. This put an end to any support the Dutch government was prepared to give to the South Moluccas. Many Dutch settlers and Indonesian residents left Indonesia after 1947 to settle in the Netherlands seeking employment and housing, and this number increased in the '50s, causing an acute shortage of both. The Dutch government provided some camps as temporary residence, to stem the problem. All these displaced people were largely dissatisfied and needed time and patience. These were difficult years for many, in a small, overpopulated country, such as the Netherlands, which had suffered profoundly from five years of German occupation.

Thirdly, there were Turks who had been imported by the Dutch government as 'guest' factory workers by the thousands, initially without their families, but now reunited with families and seeking to migrate to Australia.

* * *

Overall, the Australian embassy migration office in The Hague was a happy environment with good staff. Much depended on the chief migration officers, and the two outstanding personalities were Ted Waterman and Keith Smith. Both these gentlemen raised Australia's profile in the European community in the Dutch capital. Ted became a dear friend of mine, together with his wife, now both sadly deceased. Half a century later, I was delighted to meet their daughter and her husband (who, by an astonishing turn of events, just happened to have worked, in another country, with my present husband at Shell corporation). Such a happy coincidence brought back fond memories of her dear parents and our happy days in The Hague and the many friendly discussions we had relating to problem cases that had cropped up then.

9

DANCING WITH THE ENEMY

The most terrifying and unsettling event hit the world between October 14 and 28, 1962, known variously as the 'October Crisis' or 'Cuba Missile Scare' – a 13-day confrontation between, on the one side, the Soviet Union and communist Cuba, and on the other side, the United States of America. The already existing Cold War between the Superpowers had dangerously escalated to a possible nuclear conflict, and Europe was in a state of shock. I vividly recall the panic experienced by the population and the frequent announcements broadcast on radio and television. Suddenly, Russia did not seem so far away from the Netherlands in terms of nuclear attack repercussions. The Soviet Union had an arsenal of 700 medium-range ballistic missiles, and it was little consolation to know that the United States boasted an even larger nuclear arsenal.

In May 1962 the Soviet Premier, Nikita Khrushchev, wanted to show the United States that he, also, had strategic missiles capable of reaching them, by placing them in the Caribbean on Cuban soil. On the other hand, in Europe, he wanted to wrangle the incorporation of 'West Berlin' into the Soviet orbit and West Berlin became the central battlefield of the Cold War. The Soviet strategy entailed elaborate denials and deception tactics known in the USSR ruling circles as *maskirovska*. All planning and preparations for transporting and deploying the missiles to Cuba were carried out in utmost secrecy under an operation code-named *Anadyr*.

The United States responded by announcing that it would intercept and destroy any missiles being transported to Cuba. The

Soviets responded by warning the U.S. that an attack on Soviet ships would mean a declaration of war and officially denied that missiles had been sent to Cuba. U.S. intelligence knew better, and in August 1962 found and announced eight concealed locations of missiles. The world waited with bated breath in the two weeks after October 14, 1962, for the outcome of this confrontation, which happily ended with President John F. Kennedy's obtaining from Khrushchev the withdrawal of the missiles from Cuba and their return to the USSR.

The 100,000th migrant left the Netherlands for Australia in the early sixties with much fanfare. More and more applications were being received and our office was extremely busy. Even with extra clerical staff it was impossible to keep pace with the workload within normal working hours. Thousands of individuals with large families who had failed to find work in postwar Holland departed for Australia. Most made happy and contented migrants, who did very well in their new country and became fine Australian citizens.

Despite this interesting and demanding job, there were many outside recreational activities. Most of my limited spare time and some holidays were occupied judging at international cat shows, which were very elaborate when royalty was involved. Cups and medals were donated by mayors and other dignitaries, who were invited to award the prizes. International shows were huge affairs all over Europe and the U.S., involving 1,000 to 1,500 valuable feline exhibits. The shows were held in beautiful venues in tastefully decorated halls housing handsome cages, where proud owners watched over their valued exhibits and their many trophies.

My husband, Robert, was an enthusiastic sailor and set up the *Catamaran en Trimaran Club Nederland* with like-minded Dutchmen, and organised events and races. The club grew with time and is still currently thriving. Robert was also a gifted Scottish dancer and performed the sword dance with great skill. He helped set up a Scottish dancing group in Scheveningen, with 250 keen participants attending each week. They accepted invitations to perform in different cities throughout the Netherlands. Robert also worked for a time as president of the Anglo-American Theatre Group, which had existed for some years in The Hague. This group comprised of English-speaking members, mostly employees of embassies and international companies. We performed two shows annually and all proceeds went to Dutch charities. Our plays were usually sold out after three consecutive shows in The Hague, Delft and Rotterdam, and we made substantial donations to different Dutch charities. We both took parts in a number of plays, and I worked as the group's secretary, publicity officer and 'props' assistant. Dr Lloyd Thomson, Australia's Ambassador, was our president for many years during his two postings to The Hague.

Robert was a member of the Commonwealth Club, which thrived with the support of over 150 male members of the English-speaking community. An interesting meeting of minds was established in the 'discussion group' attended by many different nationalities with as many diverse views. It became an outlet for young men and women with strident political views, and a most interesting centre for the BVD, as time would tell. Most of my 'extra-curricular work' was centred in these clubs, attending meetings and, in particular, cultivating the social contacts made.

The counter-espionage (CE) director briefed me each week on certain subjects of interest and I would be ready for a debrief the following week. It was unbelievable how many of the people I watched (our 'subjects') had been approached by members of the Soviet embassy. Most had access to classified or top-secret material. My involvement substantiated these contacts and in many cases I would record meetings in places of interest together with names of previously unconnected Dutch nationals. These persons were often unaware of the seriousness of their contact and did not suspect any ulterior motives. The BVD would always follow up such cases with a confidential interview during which a clearer picture would be obtained and acted upon. Some of the cases necessitated immediate and drastic action.

A few examples may suffice.

My husband and I were attending a Commonwealth Club ball in the Kurhaus in Scheveningen. It was a fabulous night and about 200 guests were enjoying the music and dancing. A handsome male of American appearance came over and asked me to dance. I had not met him before but accepted his request and soon realised that he was not American. There was an accent that I tried to identify when he asked me whether I had served in London. I answered by saying I came from London. Then he asked me where I worked, so I told him 'At home in Scheveningen'. There were many ladies of leisure at that ball, so I felt I would not be considered an exception. He was very charming and suave and tried to invite me to lunch. I asked him where he came from. 'Moscow' he said. 'Do you work at the Russian Embassy?', I asked. A broad smile appeared on his face and he replied, 'Yes, I am the first secretary.' I then realised that I had better be a little friendlier, just in case he was a big fish.

This meeting was certainly the start of some action. He had several more dances with me and, before the ball ended, we exchanged phone numbers. First thing next morning I phoned Pieter Gerbrands, the CE director. He came over and informed me that my dancing partner was the most senior KGB officer in the Netherlands, recently arrived. His name was Nikolai Kosov, a very important target at that time. Pieter was delighted and told me they had been watching Nikolai for some weeks. He had approached several women with access, and two operations had been planned against him. He was interested to learn how Nikolai managed to be at the Commonwealth Club ball. I soon found the answer, quite by accident, in speaking to the personal assistant to our information officer at the Australian embassy. She was describing how much she had enjoyed the night of the ball with her daughter, who had obtained the tickets to include her 'new boyfriend' – and, surprise of surprises, this was Nikolai.

The next day I completed an initial surveillance on the daughter. She was private secretary to the general in charge of the Supreme Headquarters Allied Expeditionary Force (SHAEF), located at the Alexander Barracks in The Hague. She had 'cosmic' clearance to cover her very secret employment. I was later horrified to see Nikolai arrive at her mother's flat at 8:00 pm. He was travelling in his embassy car, CD491, which he parked in a side street, and went inside. He spent the night there. All lights were turned off by 11:00 pm. He emerged at 5:30 am, drove off in his car and returned to the embassy compound where he had a wife and three children. My surveillance paid off. After no sleep and bleary-eyed, I arrived at my office at 8:30 and phoned Pieter, who lost no time in coming. He contacted Colonel Einthoven at home and immediate action followed.

Pieter saw the SHAEF general urgently that morning and the secretary was fired by noon that day. No delays there. The girl was subsequently interviewed and interrogated by the BVD. Her mother was also interviewed and soon after both mother and daughter returned to Adelaide from whence they came. This secretary was a very plain-looking girl who had been wined and dined by Nikolai. She felt flattered and happy, but he never let her know he was married. The BVD took no chances with her, and were delighted she left the country of her own accord with her mother, who had now also become a security risk at the Australian embassy.

Another case that resulted in action involved the 'discussion group', which I always attended. There I met an East German student named Hans. He was having an affair with a Dutch lady working in the Foreign Office. I always spoke in German with him. He was relaxed and appeared very happy about spending weekends away with her on the Veluwe, a beautiful part of central Holland. I reported this to

Pieter Gerbrands, who then interviewed the lady. Hans's visa was not renewed and he left within weeks.

A Dutch engineer studying in Delft, and also a member of our 'discussion group', was seen with Nikolai at the cinema. The next time I spoke with the engineer I referred to the film we had both seen. He told me he liked Nikolai very much having been entertained by him and his wife at the embassy compound. Pieter told me this engineer was working on a classified project for NATO and these meetings would be stopped immediately. He was interviewed by the BVD accordingly.

I witnessed many other similar cases during my fourteen years' close cooperation with Dutch counter-espionage.

I had direct contact from the beginning with ASIO Director-General Brigadier Spry on a special code-machine and kept him abreast of all activities relating to Australians. We had other problems of contact with embassy staff. This was always tricky as some contact was quite legitimate and part of normal duty. However, the Russians also targeted others, and it was these cases with which we struggled. One was an attractive, young Australian officer, employed by the Commonwealth Department of External Affairs. He was handsome and frequently invited to functions as the 'popular bachelor'. It did not take long for me to observe a close liaison between this young officer and the Russian second secretary, Igor. When I reported this to Pieter, he told me they had both been on their watch list for some time and it was known they spent nights together. Being 'gay' was a crime in the USSR at the time, so the BVD was planning how they should approach the Soviet Ambassador to arrange for his possible removal. This was clearly a case for action, also on our part. Several months later, our Australian second secretary left The Hague. Igor remained.

Our migration office receptionist, Natasha, a charming woman, was seen on the Canadian embassy tennis court, playing tennis with

Aleksey, another well-known senior KGB officer. The Canadians were very hospitable in allowing other Commonwealth-friendly embassy staff access to their courts, so I assumed Natasha must have had previous contact with Aleksey to take him to play tennis there. Pieter Gerbrands interviewed Natasha, and it appeared that Natasha's mother was Russian and they had regular contact with Russians in The Hague. She told Pieter that they attended the Russian Orthodox Church on Sundays and were very friendly with the Russian priest, Igor Susemihl. He had come to the Netherlands two years previously and was a known KGB operative. Ever since his arrival he had been in the sights of the BVD. He was left *en poste*, as the BVD were led to other persons of interest through contact with him; but he was a thorn in their sides, nevertheless. It was well known that the Russian Orthodox Church around the world was closely connected with the KGB and many priests were actively engaged in operations. One of their most infamous characters was this Igor Susemihl. He was widely travelled and, after a series of dubious activities in the Federal Republic of Germany, was defrocked and disgraced, and then proceeded to the Netherlands in the sixties.

Many 'White' Russians – that is, Russian refugees from the Red Terror – were members of his flock and would confide in him on matters concerning their relatives in the USSR. He in turn would inform the authorities in the USSR if necessary. According to Pieter, there were many distressed and worried parishioners in The Hague with relatives in the USSR. Susemihl was a rampant womaniser and openly had affairs with members of his church. Natasha and her mother often entertained him to lunch on Sundays at their home in The Hague after the Sunday service they attended. Peter told me they interviewed Natasha who appeared shocked and admitted they entertained other Russian friends. At that time there was a high percentage of KGB and GRU officers working in many guises at their embassies in Western countries. They were targeting Commonwealth embassies, and Australia was certainly on the list.

Nikolai Kosov, mentioned earlier, phoned me several times to take me out to lunch. Pieter Gerbrands encouraged this meeting and wanted me to go along and be 'cultivated'. I declined for personal reasons, as I was first and foremost a member of the embassy and had no intention of being seen in public with Nikolai. The Hague was a busy post but also a small town, and my reputation was important to me. Many people also knew my husband, and for both our sakes I refused further contact in public places.

The BVD were anxious to find a reason to declare this top KGB officer 'PNG' (*persona non grata*); so they devised a plan. My husband, Robert, was invited to lunch by Colonel Einthoven to discuss an operation and request his agreement prior to implicating me. The plan was for me to invite Nikolai for a cosy dinner by candlelight at our home in Scheveningen. Nikolai would make advances as he always did on such occasions, and I would relent and/or refuse, and Nikolai would be thus accused of rape or attempted rape. Robert was supportive of my work and had shared many previous operations when necessary; but this suggestion was extraordinary. He promised to discuss it with me and that we would work something out. We agreed that I would invite Nikolai to a cosy dinner and see what eventuated. If he made advances, I would play along but only so far, and then accuse him of 'attempted rape'. The scene was set and the date fixed. Protective security was supplied in the usual manner, with support teams in place. Robert was close by with Pieter, in a car. The 'distress button' was easily accessible. When that was activated, a 'friend' would ring the front door bell; I would open the door and accuse Nikolai of attempted rape. The friend would be a commissioner of police who would identify himself to Nikolai on the spot. The case would go to the Ambassador with a follow-up demand from Dutch Department of Foreign Affairs to 'PNG' Nikolai.

And so it was and went off without a hitch. It was quite an amusing evening and Nikolai took his time. He became quite vocal and sang me some Russian songs and I sang him some English ditties accompanied on the piano. I kept wondering whether he would mention our Soviet defector, Colonel Grigori Tokaev. Thankfully, he did not; but I suspect he knew all along that I had been involved. When the moment came to press the button, I was taking no chances. He certainly did not see me do it as I put a lounge cushion on his face. He struggled. Then the front door bell rang and he flew up and followed me to the door. The Dutch police commissioner was in plain clothes, but introduced himself and asked, 'What is going on here?' I replied, 'This is a case of Attempted Rape!' Nikolai pushed me aside and scurried out of the door, leaving us to discuss the affair. He was then seen running out of the garden gate towards his car. I never saw him again.

The whole affair was related to Colonel Einthoven, and the BVD in turn dealt with the Dutch Department of Foreign Affairs, which summoned the Soviet Ambassador to complain of Nikolai's conduct. The Ambassador, I was told, spoke highly of Nikolai and stated he had acted naturally. This was clearly a failed operation, but did not serve as a warning to Nikolai, as he was caught soon after, in 1970, following a similar incident with a public servant.

We had a consular officer who occupied a small room at the entrance of the Australian migration office. He would welcome all visitors and direct them to the appropriate officer. I always thought him slightly strange and I often saw children in his office, which was unusual in the circumstances. I mentioned him to Pieter. A few days later I was told he was under scrutiny with The Hague moral police who were dealing with worried parents and their children's 'friendship' with John, our consular officer. Later it was confirmed he was luring young boys with foreign stamps he collected from the mail in our office. He was caught red-handed by the Dutch police and given 48 hours to leave the country, and not to return.

One of our officers arrived *en poste* with his wife June – a strange character, both in behaviour and appearance. On her arrival she stated she would show us all she was a lady. Naturally, we were all bursting with excitement in anticipation of what was to come. She was a rather sickly type with many real or imagined complaints, which caused her stress and possibly pain. None of us could ever find out what the problem was. We all tried to be helpful and accommodating, and this only made things worse. Her husband was driven to find his comfort elsewhere and soon started an affair with one of our secretaries. Somehow, June managed to find the 'Queen's Dressmaker' in The Hague, and would appear in some very costly gowns from then on. It was quite sad, really, as she had become a laughing stock in the English-speaking community and with many members of staff. Then, late one afternoon, the Australian Ambassador called to say that June had been arrested and was waiting in The Hague jail to be bailed out. The Dutch Department of Justice had been advised that special conditions had to apply, as her husband had diplomatic immunity and so did she. It all caused an upheaval. She had, apparently, removed items of very expensive jewellery from two shops in The Hague, which were found, undamaged, on her person when arrested. The ministry made an exception for this case, as June was diagnosed with kleptomania and would most probably offend again. Her husband was recalled several months later after only six months at his post. They left The Hague for Australia quietly.

At Pieter Gerbrands' request, I attended one of the Russian Orthodox Church's 'introductory services' with a brief to stay till the end to see who stayed behind in the church with Igor Susemihl. I agreed to do this and positioned myself out of sight. I got the information I went in for, but realised too late that he and the two subjects had left the church by the front door, locking it behind them. I was locked in for the night, so it seemed. With the aid of the light from the street lantern I could just see enough to walk round the church to examine all the stained glass windows. One small window could be opened, but I had to snoop around to find a chair to stand on to reach an old, rusty lever to push it open. It was impossible to leave without a trace as I could not remove the chair nor close the window once outside. But I did get out, unseen, jumping into the dark garden surrounding the old church.

A covert operation of another kind came my way, very unexpectedly. We were advised of the visit of a high-ranking Australian, now deceased, who was in the Netherlands for formal talks at government level. He was expected that day, and a visit to our office took place accordingly. The next day this gentleman arrived early in my ASIO office, unaccompanied, worried and agitated. He asked for my help in tracing his lost wedding ring. He confided to me that he had been in a shady place the night before, but was not sure where it was! This was indeed a problem, for there were a number of such places in different districts of The Hague; so I agreed to help and our search began. Leaving the office before staff arrived was important, and it was fortunate that I had arrived early that day. We set off in my car, guided by a vague description of unknown surroundings seen at a different time of day, when such areas are alive with activity. As we drove into a maze of streets of similar description, I was slowly getting desperate as time was moving fast and my VIP visitor was scheduled for important appointments to keep that day. He would be missed, and he was in my car with me!

We continued searching for a 'corner house with flowers in the window', and there were plenty of them! Suddenly, my passenger recognised one and exclaimed, 'There. I think so!' I stopped the car, jumped out, proceeded to the front door and rang the bell. All was quiet, with very few people around at that hour, which was lucky. My heart was racing. I was hoping against hope that a face would appear, when a young woman in a dressing-gown opened the door. I asked politely if she had found a wedding ring the night before belonging to the gentleman in the car? She peered into the morning light and, thankfully, recognised him. She went inside and reappeared with the ring. My VIP was overwhelmed and grateful and gave her a handsome tip. He was so relieved, telling me he could not envisage returning home without it. The next most pressing thing was to deliver my passenger to his hotel in time for his next appointment without causing any suspicion amongst the ever-marauding pressmen. A floral piece was delivered to me two days later, beautifully packed and delivered, which I took home without undoing the wrapping. The card, inside, read: 'With my very grateful thanks.' It was unsigned.

10

A special invitation from an eminent Australian

My first encounter with Brigadier (later Sir) Charles Spry, the long-serving Director-General of the Australian Security Intelligence Organisation (ASIO), was in London in 1955. The newly-appointed ASIO senior liaison officer (SLO) in London, Max Phillips, was setting up office in Australia House in London. He had invited me to work with him to assist with the many changes that had to be made in connection with this transfer of the SLO office from The Hague to London. The Hague post, from now onwards, would be dealing exclusively with the Benelux countries (Belgium, the Netherlands and Luxembourg).

Brigadier Spry was on a visit to London at that time for talks with MI5, the British Security Service, and, as mentioned previously, I was introduced to him and had several discussions involving, among other things, the revised aims and purposes of ASIO's responsibilities in Europe. Not long before this, in April 1954, there had occurred the dramatic defection in Australia of a Soviet diplomat, Vladimir Petrov – in reality, a cipher specialist and under-cover officer of the Soviet spy agency, the KGB.

On defecting, Petrov brought with him a huge haul of top-secret documentation of Soviet espionage activities, not only in Australia, but across the world. This defection had brought Australia into the realm of international espionage, and was a regular topic of conversation in Western intelligence circles. The Australian ASIO officer in charge of the Petrov case was Oxford Rhodes Scholar and poet Michael Thwaites.

Brigadier Spry informed me that, since 1943, the United States Army Signal Intelligence Service (USASIS) in Arlington, Virginia, had been intercepting clandestine Soviet radio signals to their intelligence officers around the world. This information established the presence of major Soviet spy rings operating in Australia, Western Europe and the U.S. This confirmed and exposed Soviet covert activity in Canberra of which Petrov had already warned Thwaites. As a result, the then Prime Minister of Australia, Robert Menzies, set up the Royal Commission on Espionage in Australia.[1] Labor opposition leader Dr H.V. Evatt was fiercely against the existence of ASIO and sought to disband it. Brigadier Spry said it was imperative that Australia maintained intelligence exchange with UK and USA, built on mutual trust and rigid security. What hope was there of this, with Soviet intelligence officers 'on the loose' in Canberra!

Brigadier Sir Charles Spry, CBE, DSO, second Director-General of the Australian Intelligence Security Organisation (ASIO), 1950 to 1970

On the next day, Brigadier Spry was to leave London and we had another talk on Benelux migration. Some members of the National Socialist Movement in the Netherlands (NSB), who had fully supported the Nazi cause under Anton Mussert during the war, were trying to escape out of Holland, where damning records of their activities were held. Some of them had returned from Germany and other European areas with false identities. Before the brigadier's departure, I translated a number of important documents for him from and into Dutch and German.

I was included in several discussions on secret intelligence during the brigadier's visit. Our first meeting gave me a sense of deep respect and admiration for a very loyal senior Australian army officer. He, for his part, told me he trusted me as a former RAF intelligence officer. I felt I had his confidence and was greatly looking forward to my further duties in The Hague. On the last day of his visit in London, we lunched at Simpson's in Piccadilly.

Next on Brigadier Spry's itinerary was to call on the head of the Dutch Domestic Security Service (BVD)'s counter-espionage operational division in The Hague. He was accompanied by Ron Richards, ASIO's then Deputy Director-General, who retired soon afterwards. I was invited to attend the luncheon they held during this visit, and operational aspects of both ASIO and the BVD were discussed. The Dutch were already aware of my former service in England, and this experience was well utilised during the full duration of my service in The Hague. We developed a close operational working liaison, and it was very apparent that Brigadier Spry was very highly regarded. There was great respect and appreciation on both sides.

Usually, Brigadier Spry visited Europe once every two years and met the relevant heads of friendly intelligence services, an essential requirement to promoting efficient cooperation and agreement during threatening times of infiltration between communist East and the democratic West in Europe, during the Cold War. 'The Greats of ASIO' I met in London and The Hague (and who are named in David Horner's recent history of ASIO) were Messrs Blair Nienaber, Des O'Leary, Ron Richards, Jack Behm and Colin Brown.[2]

After about six meetings I had with the brigadier, he elaborated on a number of his deep concerns relating to Australia's security. The Communist Party of Australia had long been waging a campaign to discredit ASIO and undermine the justification for its existence. The Australian Labor Party under Dr Evatt's leadership wanted to abolish ASIO, and leftist parliamentarians were known to liaise with Soviet intelligence personnel in Canberra. What weighed particularly heavily on Brigadier Spry's mind was what a high-ranking Soviet defector had warned him about a few years previously, in the early '60s. This defector, a former intelligence officer, had informed him that there was a high-level penetration agent, or 'mole', in ASIO. Australia's counter-espionage operations were indeed regularly failing, and Brigadier Spry concluded that this pointed to the likelihood of some hostile individual, or individuals, clandestinely 'working from within'.

During his long career as ASIO Director-General, from 1950 to 1970, and even afterwards, Spry watched, intervened and was obsessed over threats to the security of Australia, so single-minded was he about protecting Australia's sovereignty. He was a figure of extraordinary influence and, during the first two decades of the Cold War, was at the forefront of Australia's anti-Soviet efforts. In 1956, Prime Minister Menzies gave ASIO legal standing by creating the *ASIO Act*.

Intercepted documents from the Soviet embassy made it clear that Australian communists were spying for the Soviets, and Spry considered it his duty to infiltrate the CPA, a task he took very seriously. Communist parties in the West are now known to have played a major role in espionage. Had this fact been properly appreciated during the early stages of the Cold War, ASIO's so-called 'preoccupation' with the CPA would have been readily understood and supported by any unbiased Australian.

Spry was also deeply concerned and worried about his staff. He described to me how in 1950 he was appointed as ASIO Director-General, taking over from Justice Geoffrey Reed. The staff at that time were so incompetent that he discharged many, including his deputy. He told me he had recruited a number of ex-service members in the UK, but others currently serving had been hired by staff, certainly not by him. It was during this long discussion he said he was well aware of my specialised training in war and peace in RAF intelligence,

The author in 1968

my service in the wartime and postwar Allied military government in Germany, then my attachment to MI5 on special duties, and my qualifications and fluency in languages, which was so valuable in the sort of work I was doing at the Australian embassy' migration office in The Hague. He suddenly turned to me and said, 'I want you in the Canberra office. Would you consider an appointment?'

I was very surprised, as the thought had not entered my mind. I thanked him for his offer and trust in me, adding I would need time to consider the idea and talk with my husband, who was now retired, in order to make this move possible. This subject was not spoken about again until I received a formal invitation from Australia in 1965 with a job offer, which I could not accept immediately. My dear mother was very unwell at the time and I needed to be within reach; Australia was just too far away.

My husband's appointment to the Fokker Aircraft company came under the North Atlantic Treaty Organisation (NATO) project and dealt with 'spare parts provisioning' for the Hawker Hunter aircraft fleet operated by NATO members. This appointment was a five years' engagement, which was to be renewed to his age of retirement at 65. He was looking forward to this commitment. However, sales slumped and redundancies followed, affecting firstly the foreign advisers. By 1962, at the age of 55, he was hit and left Fokker. Through a personal contact he was appointed as manager of an aircraft paint company. This offered further prospects but came to a close a year later when, while Robert was in negotiations, the British company, which was desirous of purchasing the company, failed because Britain was encountering problems with joining the European Common Market (which later evolved into the European Union). Soon afterwards, the Germans bought the company and appointed a German director to run it. This was a great disappointment, but, as it turned out, made it easier for us to come to Australia in 1969.

During Brigadier Spry's next visit, later that year, he firmly repeated his offer with all arrangements for travel, accommodation, and such in hand. He was clearly very happy with my assistance to the Dutch Domestic Security Service, which, he said, had contributed to Australia's standing in Europe and improved liaison with friendly intelligence services. The Australian migration programme had benefited by my linguistic expertise over many years, covering thousands of necessary interviews. Now he wanted me to help identify secret intelligence officers operating out of the Soviet embassy in Canberra.

Each time his offer was very genuine and, finally, in 1967, after my mother's death, and much thought and discussion with my husband, I officially accepted and made the decision to travel.

Brigadier Spry immediately set wheels in motion for my replacement in The Hague and wrote me several welcoming letters, thereafter outlining accommodation details, cost of living allowances and such. We had one more important meeting in The Hague, when he entertained my husband and me at the historic Old Wassenaar Castle (*Kasteel Oud Wassenaar*), where he was staying. He again expressed his worries about the fact that MI5 and the CIA were withholding special classified information from Canberra, as ASIO had lost their trust over the years.

The fear that a Soviet penetration agent, or 'mole', was operating in Canberra was very real. The Soviet threat in Europe was well known to me. Many operations were ongoing, and the European security services were not reluctant to declare a suspicious person

PNG (*persona non grata*), whenever this was deemed necessary. Such action was a rarity in Australia. When I asked why, Brigadier Spry explained that communist ideology had even penetrated the Australian government's Department of External Affairs, which made action to expel spies very difficult. It became apparent that Spry was facing an enormous task, combating both communism and Soviet penetration with a limited number of reliable serving officers and few friends in the government departments of the day. He bravely countered the threats. This man was a committed, loyal and much-decorated soldier with a great love for his country and its values.

I observed how high Brigadier Spry's reputation stood in Europe. He was a much admired, respected and trusted intelligence chief, whose judgements and discussions were highly valued. During his almost twenty years as ASIO's Director-General, he carried a particularly heavy burden. He knew that some Australians were assisting the Soviets. The culprits included a raft of untrustworthy MPs, public servants and, as Spry now was certain, a yet-to-be identified mole, or moles, in ASIO. It was hard to believe. His huge task was to improve and mend relations with MI5 of Britain and CIA of the USA. The stresses and strains he lived with never left him and finally, over time, took their toll on his health. Small wonder he often needed a stiff drink.

In September 1969, he suffered a heart attack, on the very day we arrived by ship in Melbourne. We were scheduled to disembark there, as the brigadier had requested, and report to ASIO's then headquarters in Melbourne, before proceeding by air to Canberra, Australia's national capital. This plan was cancelled and we were told to sail on to Sydney directly.

Brigadier Spry remained in hospital for many weeks. He never really fully recovered and was forced to retire from ASIO for health reasons. I sadly never saw him again. His premature departure from the organisation, owing to ill health, was a disaster for the professional development of ASIO. He had high hopes and great plans, which tragically never came to fruition. His focus was for a professional outfit supported by government. Alas, it was not to be. My admiration and profound respect for this outstanding Australian remains. He was knighted by the Queen, deeply respected by overseas colleagues but maligned at home principally by the Australian Broadcasting Corporation which, on a number of programmes in later years, especially one documentary it broadcast in November 2010, smeared his good name and character.[3] What greatly surprises me is that the government of the day never intervened to refute the unfair attacks on this great man who had put the security of his country uppermost against the many heavy odds he had to face.

The trashing of his reputation as being an alcoholic is quite unjust and ignorant of the times. Most areas of public life involved heavy drinking, not just in ASIO, but also in defence, foreign affairs, the police and more. Spry had just directly emerged from six years of war into the stress and tension of the Commonwealth environment. Those who spent many years in combat in World War II received no counselling or assistance. Post-traumatic stress disorder (PTSD) and war-related stress were as real then as now, and without an antidote. In my experience at the many social functions I attended during my service at the Australian embassy in The Hague in the '50s and '60s, I never witnessed Brigadier Spry over-indulge in alcohol, even though alcoholic drinks were always plentifully available, consumed and thoroughly enjoyed by all present.

In this context, in the course of the weeks following the ABC's November 2010 broadcast of its documentary, 'I, Spry: the rise and fall of a master spy', Melbourne journalist Anthony McAdam and other commentators castigated the national broadcaster for maligning the reputation of Brigadier Spry.[4]

In my view, his respected memory is that of a special, senior officer and also a friend who entrusted me with a task I was, sadly, prevented from completing due to the lack of support, deliberate or otherwise, displayed by my colleagues and others in the organisation at that time. May Brigadier Sir Charles Spry always be remembered as a great Australian. I shall always be grateful to him for bringing me to Australia, as I would not have come of my own volition at 46 years of age; and the proof of this is that, after my retirement, we continued to make our home in Melbourne.

In conclusion, I quote the statement made by Justice Robert Hope in his Royal Commission Report in 1986:[5]

> Until quite recently, ASIO could not be taken seriously as an efficient organisation, still less as an effective security organisation. ASIO may be, or may have been, penetrated by a hostile intelligence service.

Brigadier Spry knew this to have been the case.

11

A COOL RECEPTION IN CANBERRA

We departed The Hague after many farewells from friends and office staff and were bound for Southampton where we boarded the Italian Flotta Lauro Line ship, the *Angelina Lauro*. We had previously been booked on a larger P&O liner, but we had two important passengers to consider, our two Siamese cats! They had been in quarantine in Bedford in the UK for six months to satisfy quarantine laws in those days, and arrived in Southampton to board the *Angelina Lauro*. This all went well; they were housed together in a spacious area on top deck with their comfortable travel box in which they cuddled up together at night.

We were not the only passengers with pets on board. There were a number of dogs. Their caring owners were permitted access twice daily to enable them to be taken for walks on the top deck. We walked our Siamese daily. They travelled well and were taken good care of by an Italian seaman who was in charge of all animal passengers.

We travelled round the Cape of Good Hope as, in those days, the Suez Canal was closed, as a consequence of the on-going Arab-Israeli conflict. A number of ports of call en route made this voyage interesting, especially Messina and Cape Town. In the latter city, my husband visited a wartime friend, a meteorologist, who warned of an incoming cyclone in the Indian Ocean, which we were about to enter. No doubt, our captain was also aware of it, but he did not delay the voyage and set sail as planned.

Two days after departure the full force of the cyclone struck us.

A freak wave engulfed us, and the ship itself suffered severe damage. China and glass were broken; we lost jukeboxes, a piano and other appliances. Passengers were terrified and there were many serious casualties. I saved myself from injury by clinging to the table base while others were being thrown from side to side. Very gradually, we all managed to settle down and reach Perth.

There, we were met by the Australian Security Intelligence Organisation (ASIO) regional director for Western Australia with a large bunch of kangaroo paw flowers. He took us for a scenic drive around Perth. Even though it was dark at the time, it was much appreciated. Our subsequent voyage to the eastern states was far from peaceful, and we were grateful to reach Melbourne and, eventually, Sydney.

We were scheduled to disembark in Melbourne, where we were expected to head to ASIO headquarters there and report to Brigadier Sir Charles Spry, the Director-General. However, on arrival in Melbourne, two ASIO officers boarded the ship to inform me that the Director-General had suffered a serious heart attack and was in hospital. We were to proceed to Sydney. We spent four days at an hotel and took the opportunity to visit Taronga Zoo and much of the city and its surroundings. We were waiting to collect our car, which had been unloaded at the docks; but the waterside workers had been, and still were, on strike.

Thus, without our car, we flew to Canberra. My husband, a former RAF pilot, thought we were making an emergency landing on a flat bush opening as the pilot descended for landing in Australia's national capital. This was amazing! It was midday on a Friday when we eventually touched down and were met by two colleagues who escorted us out of the airport and into a car, which took us to our hotel. This would be our abode until the house that was reserved for us became available, but no time was mentioned. I was collected later that day and taken to the regional office where I met the duty officer in charge, who greeted me with a certain level of suspicion. He was seemingly surprised that a woman had been selected to fill the particular post which had recently been created by Brigadier Spry. After all the introductions had been performed, I was sworn in and shown my office, overlooking a beautiful park, within the sight of the famous war memorial.

My life as a research officer promised to be most interesting and extremely busy with only one snag: I was a woman. The duty officer's 'welcome' alerted me in advance that he would not be the only surprised male to meet me on Monday morning!

Canberra gave us a very strange impression as a 'capital city', particularly as we had just made our acquaintance with Sydney – a lively, busy centre. On Saturday, we were lone curious wanderers exploring the city where the centre piece was a children's roundabout, covered over for the weekend with not a child or adult in sight. Shops were closed and we saw no restaurants. I can still recall the feeling of disbelief and isolation which saw us walk away to a different area in search of other human beings who, we were given to believe, did exist here! We found Telopea Park, with children and parents enjoying weekend freedom and recreation, which made us feel much better. The weather was lovely, warm and sunny – a great plus point to console our confused minds in relation to our actual whereabouts.

As the day progressed, we needed some sustenance and decided to return to the city and once again search for a restaurant to have dinner before returning to our hotel where no meals were served that night. So, out we went. After a fruitless search, my husband asked a policeman to direct us to a nice eating place. He told us to take a taxi up Red Hill where there was a good but expensive Spanish restaurant. We arrived at this attractive building, with numerous tables laid for a large crowd, but nobody was inside and all was quiet. Were we not told Canberra was the 'bush capital'? It lived up to its name for many years. How about the stars on a clear, moonless night, with little background interference and ideal for astronomy, but emphasising the remoteness of the neo-village of Canberra – the half-finished design of Walter Burley Griffin – and the sheer vastness of the surrounding country, and the cold at night?

We walked around, towards the bar. Suddenly, a figure appeared, in the image of Manuel, who could have come straight out of the very popular BBC TV comedy *Fawlty Towers*! It was a Spanish restaurant and here was the one and only waiter, who was, naturally, Spanish. My husband, Robert, exchanged a few words in the waiter's native tongue, invoking great excitement and causing a flood of Spanish in an emotional outburst in which he told us of his arrival in Canberra three months earlier, adding: 'And, if things do not improve, I will end my life!' We did not know whether to flee from the premises or remain and subject ourselves to a Spanish dinner served by 'Manuel'; but we chose the latter.

To this day I do not know what we consumed. We never returned to see whether our waiter survived the stress of Canberra, as we eventually did. We were quite preoccupied with settling ourselves into this strange environment; it certainly was like no other experienced to date, despite much travelling.

I was due to take up my post in ASIO on Monday morning, September 22, 1969. The Office was located on the top floor of a large concrete building occupied largely by the Ministry of Supply, known as Anzac West. Our area was secured by a special door, which appeared on arrival by lift at the top floor. The door opened by pressing a button controlled by a Receptionist who sat opposite the entrance. She directed approved visitors in the right direction with plenty of comings and goings. My arrival had been anticipated for some time, as I later learned they dreaded the 'dragon from The Hague office – a woman – and *British*!'

To say I felt apprehensive would be an understatement. Secretly, I was fearful and worried as Sir Charles Spry might never return. I did not know any of the staff, except for the regional director for Canberra, Colin Brown, who was on four weeks' leave abroad. What I did know was some of Sir Charles' many worries about the Canberra office, which was what had brought me here. There was no escape or turning back now, so I bit the bullet and pressed the button. The door opened and I entered. Little did I realise at that moment what the next years would bring. I was 46 years of age with a mop of greying hair and certainly not a luscious, promiscuous blonde. But I made my entrance into this macho, perhaps misogynistic, kingdom where angels would fear to tread.

The receptionist, a mature lady, received me with a charitable smile. She obviously knew what I did not and may have been secretly sorry for me. She escorted me down the passage to my office where a young male was sitting at a desk. We shook hands while he informed me that he had just arrived in Canberra from Melbourne, where he had been married three weeks previously. He hastened to tell me that he and his family were struggling with residential problems in Canberra.

I was due to see the deputy regional director who was occupying the regional director's office during the latter's absence on leave. Luckily, the regional director, Major Colin Brown, was a good friend of Sir Charles Spry. Both were Duntroon-trained and had served together in army intelligence. The regional director was well known to me; I liked and respected him as a very good friend when he had served in The Hague and London, and we remained in touch until his death in 2008. Meanwhile, I was at the mercy of those I knew not.

The deputy regional director, John Cecil Elliott, invited me to afternoon tea that first day to make my acquaintance. I shall always remember that meeting. As I entered his spacious office, this tall, balding, bespectacled gentleman rose to his feet, kissed my hand, smiled broadly and pulled up a chair. He immediately spoke to me in German, so I replied appropriately and the entire encounter was conducted as such. Though the man was quite charming, there was something quite 'surreal' about this meeting. I recall that I decided not to be too judgmental at this first encounter. However, I couldn't help but think he was a strange, smooth, eccentric gentleman who did not fit into this environment. What was he doing here? I believe there is no record of his ever having been checked!

The late afternoon brought a meeting with the surveillance team. They were a mixed group of young men from varying walks of life, all willing to learn the 'tricks of the trade' and hoping to progress upwards in the organisation, which at that stage was quite disorganised from the top down or the bottom up, whichever way one would want to see it. Without going into details, within days I found valuable intelligence stored away in drawers in my office. It was hard to believe. The information, originally 'hot off the press', was sometimes up to six months old. I'd never seen such a thing in all my years of experience in intelligence work. Important information, as it was received, seemingly tossed straight into a drawer – and insecure to boot.

The Canberra ASIO office's chief target was intelligence officers from the Soviet Union and its communist satellite countries in eastern Europe. Often, valuable information was obtained from four sources on a daily basis:

        a) from our intercept facilities;

        b) from our surveillance teams;

        c) from our static site; and

        d) from our agents.

I was always happy to work with our surveillance team headed by David Schramm, a most competent officer who was far more capable of guiding his team than those 'in charge'. He suffered plenty of frustration and often used his own common sense to produce effective results. He finally left ASIO for greener pastures, joining the

Australian Federal Police, in which he eventually rose to the rank of commander. Sadly most of our intelligent, energetic promising young officers were forced to leave when they realised there was no future working in our unintelligent environment.

It was vital to see and know what was current on a daily basis and to compare and validate all information available. More often than not, combining these sources provided a valuable insight into our targets' movements, meetings and whereabouts. To my horror, this co-ordination and reconciliation of data were not apparently realised or comprehended by anyone and therefore not followed. Something urgent had to be done to change all this.

From that day, I made it my business to study all information available each morning, to whom it referred, and whether it connected with already known (recorded) data. This was compiled daily into a document which was sent by telex, for internal circulation among headquarters and all state offices. It soon became known as the 'Canberra Oracle'. It was vital to ASIO's fundamental functioning, and was particularly appreciated by the mobile surveillance teams and used by analysts at headquarters who had previously not received such assistance. This simple coordination of information became the daily diet for all and proved to be a valuable, but previously untapped, resource. I was told it was greatly appreciated at headquarters, where staff had previously felt starved of timely, relevant information.

Outside the office, we were settling down into our new environment. We had started to make new friends, and some social life was emerging. Then we discovered Bateman's Bay, a 145 km, two-hour drive away on the New South Wales coast, which was a great revelation and delight for us. We spent many weekends lapping up the sun, swimming and sailing. Compared to the North Sea, the beautiful clear water here was a great gift, not to mention the crayfish.

12

HEROES, HAS-BEENS, BUNGLERS, SPIES

Before my arrival in Australia, Brigadier Sir Charles Spry had told me of his great concerns about ASIO's office in Australia's national capital, Canberra,, which, from a counter-espionage point of view, was the most important post for the country at this time. From the time of World War II, the Americans and the British had been reluctant to share intelligence with Australia because their technical operations, as well as Soviet defectors, had revealed conclusively that several 'moles' were operating at the highest levels of Australian government. In the late 1940s, Australian authorities reacted to this knowledge with disbelief, but were eventually forced by the United States and Britain to set up ASIO, which they did in 1949, with considerable opposition from the political Left, both inside and outside Parliament.

The American and British threat to exclude Australia from intelligence-sharing was hard to bear and particularly perilous, given Australia's geographical isolation from its main allies. The two Soviet intelligence services, the Committee for State Security – the much-feared KGB – and Soviet military intelligence – the seldom-reported, but no less proficient GRU – were both well represented and actively operating in Australia under cover of diplomatic, consular and trade positions in the Soviet and eastern European embassies in Canberra and consular premises in Sydney.

Canberra, being located outside the main centres of population, was quite small when we arrived; but, over the course of four decades, it has seen an expansion to the extent that it is clearly identifiable as the national capital. Embassies, many built in the traditional style of the countries they represent, are part of drive-by tours. With its thriving cultural life and fine parks and gardens, the city today, as planned by the noted American, Walter Burley Griffin, and his wife, Marion, is now close to realisation.

'Little Canberra' of the 1970s was a surveillance and counter-surveillance nightmare. During my time, as in all Western capitals, the big question was the identification of all Soviet embassy employees and an accurate assessment of their duties and functions. In a typical Soviet embassy, there were diplomatic, consular and trade personnel. These were limited in number by the Australian government, following the resumption of diplomatic relations in 1959-60. The break had been caused by a major defection of a senior MVD (KGB predecessor organisation) officer, Vladimir Mikhailovich Petrov in 1954.

Major Western intelligence services regarded the Petrov defection as an important coup. But such was the political climate in Australia, obviously influenced by the powerful Communist Party, that ASIO gained neither credit for it nor public recognition for its work in achieving it. A large number of the Labor opposition, the press, academics and trade union officials, all dominated by active communist influence, pursued a sustained high visibility campaign against those who were not of their far-left persuasion – individuals collectively known and referred to as 'cleanskins'. This situation raised the level of necessary monitoring and checking of all newcomers at the Soviet and eastern European satellite embassies in Canberra. Any indication of suspicious intelligence activity demanded further investigation at higher levels, and it could take weeks, even months, to pursue the necessary leads.

Among the Soviet embassy staff abroad were officers from both the KGB and GRU – usually, but not always, under the cover of a diplomatic passport. Although genuine diplomatic and trade officials exceeded their number, they could be and were called upon to act in a variety of support roles, even something as simple as being a decoy, when leaving on legitimate business. Despite a small embassy, the ratio of intelligence officers in Canberra was pretty much the same as that in other capitals and, even though there were travel restrictions (no travel outside 25 miles of Canberra without two days' notice to the Department of Foreign Affairs), the calibre of Soviet intelligence officers posted here was not inferior to that of those posted to Europe, the UK and U.S.

The rival Soviet spy agencies, the KGB and the GRU, each formed its own 'residency' (or *rezidentura*), and the most senior officer of the respective agency was known obviously as the 'resident' (*rezident*). Theoretically, anybody might turn out to be the 'resident'. Wild rumours often floated about lowly embassy staff, such as drivers, being 'the top dog' turned out to be *hocus pocus* or to deliberately mislead. Australian government policy was to deny visas to nominated intelligence officers identified as such to ASIO by friendly liaison services. It was a rare exception, however, for ASIO's advice to be actually followed.

Once I had literally managed to get my feet under the table and start serious work, I had good reason to wonder about the company that surrounded me. My colleagues, with their behaviour and attitudes, were light years away from the British and European people I had previously worked with. I had fallen into a den of misogyny and incompetence. That was beyond dispute; but, worse than that, I often wondered in whose interest these people were working.

In many respects, I had to change my view of what constituted an 'officer' in Australian intelligence. Legend had it that many of those employed in ASIO's early days were heroes of World War II, and it was relatively easy to separate the blowhards from the genuine. The latter were usually rather quiet, private men, and an occasional woman, who kept their own counsel and rarely talked of the war unless they knew that interest was genuine. The loudest often constituted what was known in-house as 'the old and the bold' and surely some were old, others bold, while many managed to be obnoxious with an 'in yer face' attitude quite common in Australia.

My personal dealings with some of these people simply cannot be allowed to slide by without comment, as they reflected the attitudes and mind-set of those who were nominally colleagues, but could be summed up in the words of an old friend: 'Just because you work with them … doesn't mean you have to like them or drink with them.'

All exhibited a similar image and were senior. First, there was 'Maxie', a retired policeman from Sydney who was white-haired, well over 60, flat-footed and self-opinionated. He was a frequent drinker and smoker and a well-known lunch and dinner patron at the Returned and Services League (RSL) Club in Queanbeyan, a short drive over the border into New South Wales. His main obsessions appeared to be beer and gaming machines, often in extended sessions. Quite insensitive to the Soviet secret intelligence presence in Canberra or their identification, he appeared not to care less. Every time I pointed out a threat, the best he could do was laugh and say: 'Go and have a drink', 'Don't rock the boat' or, his favourite, 'A women's place is in the kitchen and in bed.' This last, frequently-made, comment summed up his general attitude to women, and appalled me.

After about three months he relied heavily on my daily reports and would occasionally copy my work verbatim to headquarters, presenting it as his own. Very gradually he apparently became interested in espionage and would ask me many questions, frequently repeated, time after time. I believe he would have been better off and happier directing traffic in Sydney or just enjoying free time!

Another was 'Norm', a retired policeman from Queensland – a swarthy, bull-in-a-china-shop type who resembled a retired weightlifter. He was oversized and overweight, with plenty to say about everything other than work. He too was totally ignorant of the Soviet threat or of what he was supposed to be doing in ASIO. Like 'Maxie', he would laugh off the idea of spies in Australia, stating he wanted a quiet life. 'Just let things be,' he used to counsel. He often accused me of looking for work – surely a cardinal crime! He was basically lazy and not exactly over-burdened with intelligence.

By contrast, and at about the same pay grade, was 'Len'. Relatively short in stature and yellow-skinned, he was an introverted, shifty type. He was rarely seen during office hours, locking himself in his office but readily available for club lunches in the Queanbeyan RSL Club, always returning in late afternoon when he would have a snooze in his office with his feet on the desk until it was time to retire for the day. He always had a smirk on his face and it was hard to know when he was joking or when he had something important to say. He felt ASIO should not employ female officers. He was believed to have been a detective in Sydney, retired and well over 60.

This man had the temerity to put on my last 'annual report', which I was given to read before my departure in 1977 for ASIO's national headquarters in Melbourne: 'This officer's judgments are askew.' Soon after, he received a phone call from headquarters informing him that the results of the two-day special test I had undergone, prior to starting my new appointment, were 'brilliant' and 'well above the normal results achieved'.

'Maxie', 'Norm' and 'Len' were three of a kind and by no means rare at the time. They were part of a continuing problem for upper management because their careers had been allowed to advance in ASIO merely by 'being there'. One colleague suggested that as they were too senior to dismiss, and as their time (if there was such a thing) had come and gone, they could be redeployed sweeping up autumn leaves.

Not least comes Peter Barbour, who in 1970 succeeded Brigadier Sir Charles Spry as ASIO's Director-General. He was a tall male with heavy-lidded eyes behind horn-rimmed glasses, often described as having 'bedroom eyes'. His conduct did not befit his position. He certainly was not the gentleman that his high office demanded. He was a creepy individual whom I instinctively avoided.

This man, previously deputy director, was appointed acting director-general in 1969 when Brigadier Spry was hospitalised, with a huge reservoir of goodwill which he flushed away in record time. He was a very complex character with airs and affairs. He betrayed his office by chronic mismanagement and exploitation of his position for sexual favours. He had a voracious sexual appetite which offended many people's moral and professional perceptions. His palpable dislike of 'foreigners' was made abundantly clear to the British appointees to ASIO. I found it hard to work with him and recall the old verse:

> One day when walking down the stairs
> I saw a man who wasn't there
> I saw him there again today
> I wish so much he'd go away.

In September 1975, Barbour was suddenly sacked as Director-General by Labor Prime Minister Gough Whitlam, apparently with the support of the opposition leader, Malcolm Fraser. One of Barbour's successors, Justice Sir Edward Woodward, wrote in his memoirs thirty years later that Barbour's dismissal had arisen from a lengthy trip overseas, supposedly to review other countries' intelligence organisations. He had taken his 'beautiful Eurasian secretary' with him, wrote Sir Edward, but failed in the end to produce any reports, ideas 'or anything else' of benefit to ASIO.[1]

Barbour was posted as Australian Consul-General to New York for three years, before taking a consular role in Los Angeles. From 1981 to 1984, he served as Australia's Ambassador to Venezuela. He died in 1996.

After several months of battling against these individuals, I managed to maintain my daily intelligence briefing, which had more than proved its value. Initially, my work was derided. After all, I was a woman, and what could I as a woman possibly know or do of value? I felt more than insulted. After a service career in which I had often been in charge of staff and had largely worked with male colleagues, not *one* had ever made a derogatory remark! In fact, quite the reverse had been my experience.

What with some of the staff we had in Canberra, trouble was never far away and occasionally caused a great deal of mirth. On one busy morning, when the usual hustle and bustle was well under way, one of our new recruits, a former RAAF air-crew wing commander, was detailed to deliver a secret tape to another department.

This chap had only recently joined us and it must have seemed like a weird world to him. However, he was full of enthusiasm, vigour and goodwill to make an impression and very determinedly so. He usually ran through the corridors and he stood out in contrast to the less energetic. He entered my office with a big smile ready to do anything 'at once'. He was told to take extra care of the box I gave him, which contained a secret tape, after which he dashed out of the office and was on his way. I was intrigued to see him leave and went to my window overlooking the car park, from six floors up, only to see him running to his car and in doing so, dropping the tape. It fell out of the box onto the road while he entered his car with the empty box.

I immediately phoned the Ministry of Supply doorman and explained what happened. He kindly lost no time and went outside and retrieved the tape. The car and our friend were well out of sight by the time the tape was brought up to me. Later that day, our messenger had not returned as expected. He arrived the next morning looking very sheepish and full of apologies at having lost the tape. For him it was a mysterious disappearance; for me it was an insecure pair of hands. Flying aeroplanes had been his business, distinctly different from this office where very little moved at all.

After this episode, some of his eagerness disappeared and he reverted to reading the newspaper in the office, drinking coffee and doing crosswords before lunch. He kept well out of the way of anybody who was likely to give him a job to do. He had understood it was the safest way to get ahead without upsetting anyone. This was the way to get promoted. One of our 'administrators' tried the same recipe. Then we found out he could not compose a letter. He was almost illiterate and had very childish handwriting. Believe it or not, he was promoted.

Just another example came on the morning that two Russian couriers were due at Canberra airport. Two of our officers were there, as always, to witness their arrival and to see by whom they were welcomed, naturally of interest at that time. All went well until for some reason they were separated and could not locate one another. The airport was busy and one of our two officers realised what was happening and kindly helped direct one of the couriers to find his colleague within the airport!

Russian couriers were always a question mark in our minds, as they have often been discovered to be KGB or GRU case officers, travelling to certain places to brief and debrief agents. We always liked to know where they were staying outside the embassy. Any person who met or was contacted by a courier became of immediate interest to our organisation. It was a strange fact that, on a number of occasions when certain couriers were due, operations were launched with the participation of certain necessary outsiders, carefully planned and prepared, leaving no loopholes. At the last moment, the couriers mysteriously failed to arrive, or else the mechanics broke down and their plans suddenly changed. These incidents happened too often to be accidental. I always suspected that our deputy regional director, John Elliott, who was always 'in the know' on all our operations, must have tipped off the Russians.

A disturbing factor was that I was too often told to not 'rock the boat'. In all honesty, I was often tempted to leave, but always called myself to order that this job had to be done and I was merely a 'cog in the machinery'. After some considerable research I had done on a number of Australian Labor parliamentarians, I felt it was time for some action and support. My findings had produced evidence of a number of our trusted MPs being more than friendly with Soviet intelligence officers, asking them for favours. These favours would also be rewarded. Potentially a dangerous situation from the point of view of national security was developing, and one we should not ignore.

I needed to discuss the matter and went to 'Maxie' with my proposal. It soon became clear that these MPs were politically sacrosanct and strictly off limits, no matter what they were doing. My further investigations were 'sabotaged' and I closed the files; but I took the precaution of keeping the records in my safe and changing the access code regularly. (NB: It is interesting to record that some of these cases were recently exposed in the Australian press – *thirty years later*! Concerned readers would be justified in wondering, 'Where was ASIO all this time?').

I am sorry and ashamed to admit that many obvious threats were left 'un-actioned'. In this context I greatly lament the fact that we were also unable to investigate the possibility that we had 'moles' in our midst — a grave flaw, especially in a security service. It is hard to blame any one person. There was an attitude of complacency, unawareness, inefficiency, lack of discipline and incompetence throughout. My frustration was often, perhaps too often, expressed, and I could never accept the many feeble excuses that were given to me to evade action.

By this time I had collected ample evidence to substantiate my fears and doubts about the likelihood of a 'mole' betraying secret information. I could trust no one to discuss this with, except the regional director for Canberra, Colin Brown. But he felt that such a disclosure would 'open a can of worms' at the time, so we agreed I would continue to gather evidence.

The 1973 Murphy raid

Then in 1973, like a thunderbolt out of the blue, came Labor Attorney-General Lionel Murphy's raid on ASIO. Very early in the morning of March 16, Senator Murphy arrived with a squad of Commonwealth Police at ASIO's then national headquarters in St Kilda Road, Melbourne, demanding entrance to our 'inner sanctum'. An ASIO officer, and later colleague of mine, who was present there that morning has described the dramatic events that unfolded. He wrote:[2]

> When I arrived at headquarters, the building had been secured by a large detachment of Commonwealth Police and we were directed to the auditorium. It was never intended to hold so many people. The hybrid air-conditioner was a closed system, and it was soon hot and rank with a mix of perspiration, fear and loathing. Coppers on every floor had sealed off offices like crime scenes. Some ASIO officers were tipped off by telephone not to come in, but the police had bagged the majority of us.
>
> Shortly after 09:10, the first female fainted, followed by a couple of others. We were captives in our own building....
>
> Most of our very senior ASIO officers stood around paralysed and in a state of shock. One of them, Desmond Vincent O'Leary, then Director of C branch, took the sort of action that was demanded. He went for the senior police officer present and his words, as I recall, were: 'Take these girls out to recover, allow use of the toilets, or, I can assure you, there will be a riot. We will not be held prisoners in our own building.'
>
> Looking at nearly 400 angry people must have prompted a change of heart. Those who had fainted were taken outside to a cooler conference room, and the nauseous and sick followed. There was an inevitable stream of people going to and from the toilets.

A senior officer, showing some backbone, had taken some of the tension out of the situation. However, it was still hot, sweaty and uncomfortable, rather like the old Singapore airport but somewhat more humid and malodorous, with sweat and fear mingled with tobacco smoke.

The same eyewitness to the ASIO raid unforgettably described the entry of the Attorney-General and his entourage, not long after the police had secured the building:

> Around half an hour later, a purple nose appeared through the door, followed by its owner, Senator Lionel Murphy; the [ASIO] Director-General Peter Barbour; a British exchange officer; Murphy's press secretary, George Negus; Commissioner Jack Davis of the Commonwealth Police Force (CPF); and one of his toadies, Kerry Milte....

The police led the way and many offices were invaded and searched and documents seized.

Four-time Walkley Award-winning political commentator and Churchill Fellow, Larry Pickering, was in the nation's capital when he heard about the raid. He later wrote:[3]

> I sat stunned in my *Canberra Times*' office, and reached for a phone to call super sleuth journo Alan Reid, ... surely he would know what the hell was going on. He didn't, well not right then he didn't, no-one did.
>
> It turned out that Murphy was after his own file.
>
> ASIO Chief, Peter Barbour, had let them in and opened the safe that held the file incriminating Murphy with, among other things, a 'close association' with the Soviet spy Ivan Skripov, who had been deported in 1963.

Needless to say, Murphy's ASIO raid, even though very few people at the time knew what had prompted it, caused a furore, with fur and feathers flying everywhere. The Prime Minister at the time, Gough

Whitlam, ordered a royal commission into this unprecedented incident!

The Hon. Robert Marsden Hope, Judge of the Supreme Court of New South Wales, was appointed by Mr Whitlam to head the royal commission. This PM was in office from 1972 to 1975 and would very much have liked to have seen the end of ASIO. He interfered with several of our operations by holding back and not supporting our security service.

Attorney-General Lionel Murphy QC

Some time later it was announced that Justice Hope would be visiting ASIO's Canberra office. I was determined to seek an interview with him and asked the regional director for approval, which I received, and an appointment was made for a generous amount of time. This was an important chance of, hopefully, having some structural changes made in the future; but above all I begged him for a closer, more in-depth look at some members of staff whose anomalous behaviour had filled me with disquiet. He did not appear alarmed, but agreed it deserved attention. I offered him my evidence in writing – six foolscap pages – which he accepted.

In 1977, the report of the Hope Royal Commission finally appeared,[4] which I was allowed to read. A number of points we had touched upon featured with further recommendations. *All* of ASIO's staff, however, remained in place. The years rolled on, but our troubles remained. We had changes of ASIO chiefs, perhaps not always beneficial. Brigadier Sir Charles Spry, with his military discipline and professionalism, was sadly missed over the years and never returned. ASIO was floundering with a public service mentality.

Then, in 1976, Justice Sir Edward Woodward was appointed ASIO Director-General to ensure that new laws and guidelines were upheld, and this raised staff morale. Promotions were given where they had been overlooked, along with an overhaul of our 'conditions of service' urgently craved by many. Correct conditions of employment with suitable contracts were promised, entry requirements were upgraded, and the face of the organisation received an uplift. My deep concern about the likelihood of hostile penetration of ASIO never left me, but was further confirmed as time went by. I had passed pages of vital evidence to Justice Hope, but to no avail.

ASIO Russian interpreter George Sadil

When I arrived in Canberra, I was introduced to our Russian interpreter, George Sadil. The son of a Czarist army officer, who had fled to China in the early 1920s after the communists' victory in the Russian Civil War, he was born circa 1936-37 and baptised in Shanghai as Georgii Sadilnikoff.[5] He migrated to Australia via Hong Kong not long after World War II, when he was still a child.[6]

I was curious to know more of his background. This individual was dealing with our secret intercept material – an important part of our work! My first impression was that he was a young, casual type, with a ready grin who had plenty of 'mates' in our office with whom he enjoyed a drink after work.

During my first months in Canberra, however, I became seriously concerned about the quality and veracity of his work. I observed that the contents and standard of his translations often differed from other intelligence that I was receiving.

During my service in the Royal Air Force, I had been trained as a translator/interpreter, qualifying with the Civil Service Commissioners' specialists' examinations in London. The importance of correct translation was uppermost and it was always emphasised that the exact meaning of the script was paramount. This was not always the case with ASIO's Russian interpreter in Canberra.

Not being a Russian linguist, I needed to refer my concerns to a trustworthy person to confirm that we were not receiving the full value of our facility. This was particularly noticeable after the arrival in Canberra of a new Russian translator from UK, an ex-army captain with a degree in Russian. It was to him that I had gratefully turned for 'special work' and re-translation whenever I doubted the contents I had received.

My fears and doubts were sadly verified. We both had a problem. I decided to visit the Russian Orthodox church in Canberra soon after, and I saw what I had expected: our translator and his sister, Tanya, were laughing and joking outside the church with a group of personnel from the Soviet embassy. I reported these sightings to the regional director. Thereafter there were other more familiar sightings recorded.

Since then it became known that our translator was the godfather of the baby son of the senior KGB officer in Canberra, and had 'many friends' in the Russian church and community. He was close to his sister; they always seemed to be together.

Both translators were maintained in their positions right up until the evening of June 2, 1993, when a squad of twenty Australian Federal Police officers burst into George Sadil's home and found, spread across his living-room floor, confidential files he had taken from ASIO. Sadil was immediately arrested, taken to Woden police station, interrogated and charged with twenty-two offences relating to the unauthorised removal of classified documents from ASIO for a purpose 'intended to be prejudicial to the safety of the Commonwealth, those documents likely to be directly or indirectly useful to a foreign power'.[7]

Next day the newspapers, especially the *Canberra Times*, reported this as front-page news. It was certainly given publicity. The ludicrous story has not yet ended. Bail was not granted at the initial court hearing in Canberra, so the translator spent a short time in detention. The proceedings were held *in camera*, precluding our attendance.

According to *Sydney Morning Herald* reporter David Lague, the court was informed that George Sadil and his wife Jenny (also of Russian parentage) had become godparents to the children of Vyacheslav Vladimirovich Tatarinov, a commercial attaché at the Russian embassy in Canberra,[8] who was believed to be an intelligence officer of the KGB's successor body, the SVR.[9] Furthermore, the Sadil and Tatarinov families had become so close to each other that they often visited each other's homes. Sadil, however, had failed to disclose this relationship to his employer.[10]

A few of Sadil's Canberra mates were selected – to give evidence, I presumed.[11] Then the unimaginable happened: Sadil was *acquitted* – after 'due process'.

I had dealt with the accused on a daily basis. I had collected evidence. I had complained repeatedly to the regional director. I had seen the man in the company of Soviet intelligence officers; but, importantly, I had officially complained to Justice Hope in 1972, 1974 and 1986, identifying the problems we had with this particular translator. Despite all this, I was not interviewed by the prosecution during the trial or called to give evidence as a witness.

After the acquittal, quite a number of colleagues watched a television programme in which one of Sadil's friends lauded him as a loyal friend, a good father, etc, etc. Many other ASIO staff, however, were appalled and dumbfounded. Although the espionage charges against Sadil were withdrawn, he was convicted of the lesser charge of illegally removing documents and given a three-month suspended sentence and two twelve-month 'good behaviour' bonds. He was allowed to retire with reduced pension and retirement benefits. Shortly afterwards, he and his wife moved to Queensland.[12]

We will never know what damage could have occurred during the years between 1968 and 1994. The terrible truth is that nobody seemed to care! Why not?

One of George Sadil's contacts was a Russian migrant who ran an air-conditioning firm in Canberra. He was recommended to install a complete system throughout ASIO's Canberra office during the mid-'70s and was subsequently awarded the contract. As I recall, neither the contractor nor his staff underwent any vetting before commencing work on ASIO's premises. I was not alone in being appalled at the organisation's negligent attitude towards security. What an opportunity for Soviet intelligence! I doubt whether our premises were ever subsequently swept properly for listening devices.

After my retirement I had another opportunity to see Justice Hope and reminded him of the case of our translator. Prime Minister Bob Hawke had called for another royal commission into yet another spy scandal, this time involving an Australian Labor Party lobbyist named David Combe, a former national secretary of the ALP, and his relationship with Valery Ivanov, first secretary at the Soviet embassy. As a concerned member of the public and as a retired ASIO officer, I was allowed to see Justice Hope. The meeting was followed up by a visit from two of his lawyers, who came to my home for further discussions in 1986. I supplied them with written notes and file references.

ASIO Russian interpreter Mrs Tanya Smith (née Sadil)

I vividly recall my impression of George Sadil's sister, Tanya, as a woman who suffered poor health. Like her brother, she was an ASIO Russian interpreter; but she was frequently absent from work and seemed to suffer from a variety of ailments. I often felt constrained from asking how she was in order to avoid long replies outlining real or imagined problems.

Personally, I always suspected she suffered from a high degree of mental stress. There were plenty of signs in her eyes, attitude and behaviour to indicate this. First, she may have known what her brother was involved in. Secondly, she knew I had observed both her and her brother together in the company of Soviet intelligence officers on different occasions. Thirdly, she knew I had up-to-date information of other ASIO ongoing sightings of the pair in the company of Soviet personnel. These three factors could well have explained her distinct 'uneasiness' throughout her period of employment with me.

On my first birthday in Canberra she gave me a very expensive birthday gift, which was certainly over-generous as we had never developed a close friendship. Her mental stress might well have been far greater in reality than she exhibited in the office, but during the nine years I observed her reactions during many encounters. I certainly suspected her of living under great strain. Her work was of better quality and more accurate than that provided by her brother, and Russian documents were correctly translated. During the nine years of my service in Canberra from 1969 to 1978, both brother and sister were accustomed to attending, together, Russian functions and meetings.

A decade after George Sadil's arrest, his sister Tanya admitted to ABC television investigative journalist Andrew Fowler that she had been concerned about her brother's close relationship with Tatarinov. She stated: 'I was against it. Then I was against him having anything to do with the Soviets.' About Sadil's removal of classified files from ASIO, she said: 'I wasn't very pleased with him. I said to him what a stupid thing to do.'[13]

ASIO's deputy regional director in Canberra, John C. Elliott

As mentioned previously, John Cecil Elliott held the position of ASIO's deputy regional director and, frequently, of acting regional director in Canberra. He was privy to all ASIO's operational pursuits in the nation's capital, and read all our overseas communications. Later, he held a senior post in ASIO's national headquarters in Melbourne.

He was multilingual and had served as ASIO liaison officer in both Germany and Hong Kong. During his year's stint in Hong Kong in 1958, he conducted numerous interviews with prospective migrants to Australia and reported any adverse findings. During that year alone, he reviewed visa applications of hundreds of Russians, 997 of whom were allowed to enter Australia, and a further 1,642 who were granted provisional visas. As expected in his position, he was diligent about building good relations with other intelligence services.[14]

To my knowledge, John Elliott was never security-checked by ASIO. He told me his mother was Norwegian and he had served in Germany in the army. I never found out in which army he served.

My suspicions were always aroused when I spoke with him. He was unfailingly kind and pleasant to me, and we frequently enjoyed afternoon tea together in his office, always speaking German and mostly discussing world affairs and Europe. Despite all this, I never felt entirely comfortable in his presence. I was always left with the question, 'Why was he in ASIO?'

I had kept an open mind, but then I observed him at the Swedish Ambassador's residence, engaged in deep conversation with a Soviet GRU officer named Igor Volkov. I left without being seen by him. I asked the regional director, Colin Brown, if Elliott was known to be there – and he was not! Several days later, he was sitting at a Canberra coffee bar with another GRU officer. He was not meant to be there either! What was he doing? Other members of staff often complained to me about their sightings of him with Soviet intelligence officers known to us.

To me, although he was always the gentleman among us, he remained suspect. To my knowledge nothing was done to investigate his reasons for these meetings. We shall now never know the answer. He retired in 1985 and is now deceased. He was a Russian linguist; but why would he want to practise the Russian language with identified Soviet intelligence officers? Such behaviour was quite out of place given his position in ASIO.

After eight years in Canberra, I ventured to apply for an overseas posting. An urgent vacancy in Vienna became available, and ASIO's personnel officer encouraged me to apply for the post. He felt I was the right candidate with my long experience in The Hague and my fluency in German.

There was a huge backlog of applicants waiting for clearance in Austria, who were from the Displaced Persons' camp in Traiskirchen and desirous of coming to Australia. I boldly and happily applied formally. There were plenty of rumours soon after that a mere woman could not do the job. However, the deputy director confirmed that I had been selected and it would be wise for my husband and me to prepare ourselves for an early departure, which we did. Two weeks prior to departure I was informed by the then Director-General that our trip was off as he had selected a male officer. This officer did not speak German but was nonetheless selected. Within three months he returned home, and a local Austrian was appointed to replace him!

Sometime later, I applied for The Hague – an obvious choice. This application also met with negative results. I had been hoping so much for a change of scene away from Canberra! I was told I could not apply for positions advertised in the *Commonwealth Government Gazette*, as these vacancies were for public servants, and we were not public servants! None of this made sense to me at that time. Then, by chance, I met a former RAF officer I had known in Oxford. He told me that the Australian government's Office of National Assessments (ONA) was looking for staff and thought I might be interested. I promptly applied and received a telephone call in reply inviting me to attend an interview. A few hours before the appointment, I received another phone call cancelling the appointment! Later, I was reliably informed that ASIO had intervened.

In 1977 a vacancy came up in ASIO's Melbourne headquarters. I applied and was accepted, subject to a series of tests and exams introduced after ASIO had adopted new rules for appointees within the organisation and for newcomers.

13
ASIO's national headquarters in Melbourne

Implementing Justice Hope's recommendation for the institution of a strict test for entry to ASIO, Justice Sir Edward Woodward introduced this two-day test together with the appointment of a psychologist. I was required to take all the tests on my nomination to work at ASIO's headquarters in Melbourne in October 1977. I passed with flying colours and high marks, much to the annoyance of some, and Robert and I moved to Melbourne, leaving Canberra, much relieved, and with a new endeavour in mind. Packers and removalists had been selected by administration and we drove ourselves to Melbourne. Our goods and furniture would be arriving two days later.

We had a temporary address where we waited to receive our belongings. After four days a van arrived with the furniture and personal effects with three large boxes missing, which were never retrieved. After enquiries made over six months conducted by the removalists, it appeared that the contents of the van were removed halfway and some boxes 'must have been left on the roadside (*sic*)'. We lost expensive camera equipment, my music books, personal papers, photographs, albums and books. Finally, we were given $200 compensation eighteen months afterwards – hardly a propitious start to my duties at headquarters.

Domestically, we were settled in a pleasant flat in the suburb of South Yarra, close to Fawkner Park, which inspired me to purchase another bicycle enabling me to ride to work each day. Our great delight of this posting was the beach at St Kilda on Port Phillip Bay. During the summer months we swam daily. This was exhilarating; we started to feel like Melbournians and I must admit this feeling has become even stronger with the years.

Life in the new office at Melbourne headquarters, regrettably, presented familiar problems. I was now dealing with the Soviet satellite countries, Hungary and Poland, about which very little research had been done. The subject was more or less in its infancy with files opened but without much useful content.

I soon realised that quite a number of migrants from eastern European countries were employed in areas of access in Canberra and other places. Furthermore, at this time representatives from East Germany, Hungary, Poland and Czechoslovakia had established consulates in Sydney, and satellite business firms were operating around Australia. Naturally, contacts were made with locals and, perhaps more importantly, with recent migrants from these countries. The latter category, especially individuals with access in the workplace to classified information, needed to be addressed – in particular, those individuals who regularly travelled to their homelands on holidays and family visits.

The security services of communist eastern Europe would certainly not allow such comings and goings without first trying to cash in on information they might be able to extract about specific areas of interest, such as political and technological developments, especially chemical, industrial, or anything classified, in Australia. Projects involving cooperation with the United States or Great Britain were obvious targets, while local inventions also attracted more than a cursory interest.

Any refusal by an Australian migrant from eastern Europe to cooperate and provide required details could result in unpleasant repercussions for his family members back home. These communist regimes were known to be brutal in this regard.

Experience overseas indicated that the KGB worked closely with its satellite spy agencies across Soviet-occupied central and eastern Europe, where success was sometimes more easily achieved. In the 1980s we received first-hand information that confirmed Moscow had pursued intelligence-collection by using their Warsaw Pact allies' strengths in certain areas and that overt supervision was less except in penetration operations. Furthermore, the East German, Polish and Hungarian secret services augmented their budgets by selling to the KGB information they had gained.

Once again, and to my great disappointment, ASIO's experience in this area was sadly deficient. The organisation lacked resources and trained staff; but, worst of all, it did not even seem motivated to tackle the problem. It was a depressing prospect that I shared with several other colleagues who were as perplexed as I was at the time. Some left, others remained and some tragically died. Stress had become commonplace and it became a case of the 'flea pushing the elephant', with very little positive work achieved overall.

Although counter-espionage work on the Soviet presence in Australia demanded a high share of scarce resources, other operational areas were draining resources, especially in what was basically police work. Pernicious 'empire-builders' within ASIO appeared oblivious to the 'combined Soviet bloc espionage offensive' in the chilliest days of the Cold War.

The Cold War meant little to the Australian public, but was reportedly taken very 'seriously' at ASIO headquarters, especially in the early 1980s, when a Soviet pre-emptive nuclear strike against the United States was considered more than a possibility,[1] and especially after an air tragedy on September 1, 1983, when a Soviet fighter pilot fired a heat-seeking air-to-air missile at a Korean Air Lines civilian airliner flying over the Sea of Japan, killing all 246 passengers and 23 crew members on board. Tensions between the United States and the Soviet Union escalated to perilous levels not seen since the 1962 Cuban Missile Crisis.

These ominous international developments occurred at a time when the Australian government was rigorously cutting public expenditure. 'Razor gangs' sliced through meat, muscle and sinew to the bone, compelling senior management to neglect active coverage in certain areas in favour of a 'watching brief', which meant in practice absolutely nothing. Another development which impeded our efforts was the growing expansion in Australia's intelligence agencies of an 'administrative class' to whom intelligence work meant very little.

Some months before my retirement, ASIO received from London a message about an intelligence officer from Hungary's secret police, the AVH, who had escaped from Hungary and was in the UK. Our UK counterparts had looked after him since his arrival and he had been interviewed and proved to be cooperative. We were approached, as his final destination was to be Australia. The necessary arrangements were made and this former AVH officer, with his wife and young daughter, were met and welcomed in Sydney where our Sydney office took over domestic arrangements.

Because this family was Hungarian, and Hungary was my responsibility, I was tasked to visit Sydney and carry out the necessary interviews. On arrival in Sydney, I was asked to accept a young female trainee to sit in during the interviews. I thought this a very good idea as the woman would also serve as a witness should the need arise.

On the day of the first interview, the Hungarian man came alone, introduced himself very politely, was quite demure and ready to answer any questions. The interview went well. He gave a long account of his experiences and gradually became more emotional to the point of breaking down at the thought of it all. He also warned of the unscrupulous methods used by the AVH on ethnic Hungarians returning to their homeland on business or holidays.

We resumed our interview the next day, and again several days afterwards. Everything was recorded. I duly returned to Melbourne and prepared a report on the case. However, the Hungarian defector's testimony was never commented upon nor did anyone ever listen to the recordings. They were placed in a drawer and may still be there today, for all I know. It was certainly not sighted or acknowledged by the head of ASIO's counter-espionage department.

At that time ASIO had very little insight into the workings of the AVH, a dreaded body that terrorised the Hungarian population during the Cold War and tortured innocent victims KGB-style. The level of interest in our office was minuscule, despite the fact that it had been proven beyond doubt that this defector was an intelligence officer possessing valuable first-hand information about the AVH.

On my return from Sydney, I suggested that he be brought to Melbourne to give a talk to the head office staff. This, I understand, was arranged soon afterwards. The testimony he gave revealed much of value. He responded well to questions and did not hold back or hesitate. The material I brought back from Sydney, however, was never referred to while I was at headquarters. Nobody, it seemed, was interested. Perhaps, if one were pushed to speculate, it would have been different had the task been carried out by a male member of staff.

Among the Melbourne ASIO staff was one particular colleague, 'Marley', with whom I did not get along, but who nonetheless was inexplicably regarded well by some senior officers. He presented as a well-dressed, educated, often well-mannered man, which blinded those who should have known better to his profound deficiencies in handling staff and accurately recording notes. He continually caused friction in the office and differences of opinion. Like most other women, I found my encounters with him difficult and usually unproductive. He used to address the few younger female officers and me as 'my dear lady' in the process of talking down to us. I suspect he thought I was highly eccentric, strange or, more likely, mad.

Amidst all the confusion and goings-on, I had a good friend in ASIO's Melbourne headquarters, Chris, with whom I could discuss my worries, fears and doubts. He was a fine man with a distinct knowledge of the many unhappy situations and shortcomings within our organisation. He witnessed many injustices perpetrated against committed and gifted members of staff, including himself. He suffered from stress and overwork, resulting in declining health and, finally in 1986, was medically discharged without financial compensation. This gentleman suffered years of unnecessary financial pain, not to mention physical handicaps, which have increased over the years. There were a number of other very disappointed and hard-done-by members of staff who left without due reward and recognition. This has not helped ASIO's reputation. It was a great shame that this was allowed to occur. The age of the disposable employee had arrived.

Much of my work cannot be disclosed, but what I can say is that discrimination in all areas of ASIO was rife – and manifested itself overtly by the rates of pay and ranks afforded to women. This was a disgrace and had to change and, I understand, eventually did.

I learned later that the 'First National Agenda for Women' was launched in 1988 by the Hawke government on a campaign which declared: 'A Choice, A Say, and A Fair Go'. The agenda was established to provide Australian women with 'economic security and independence, freedom from discrimination and equality of opportunity' and to ensure that their needs were fully considered in government business – a far cry from the raw deal I had been given.

The Department of Finance was cool towards the idea, stating its concern it would 'likely build up unrealistic expectations'. Other fears raised were that some women's organisations might argue that the plan did not go far enough.

Looking back, I could never have survived on my salary in Canberra had I not received a bequest from an aunt who passed away in London. Probate was granted after our arrival, which enabled us to keep our heads above water.

Brigadier Spry had written to me before my arrival, confirming my status and salary. This status was, as I later discovered, three grades higher than was subsequently entered in my file, which meant that my pay was commensurately downgraded. The file entry was signed by the administrative officer, not by Spry and had presumably been altered.

I kept Brigadier Spry's original letter to me, which eventually proved valuable to restore my grading and salary and to qualify me for a reasonable pension adjustment after my retirement, which was severely diluted by the legal fees I had to pay to get it.

I was due to leave the organisation on my retirement in February 1983, but I was keen to seek other employment. An important preoccupation for me now was my pension. To what was I entitled? I had my doubts as I knew I would be on a lower rate than most due to my age on arrival in Australia and length of service. My 15 years in The Hague did not count, so I needed to know the facts. I visited the Australian Pensions Office in Canberra to inquire. To my horror, nobody knew me. According to their records, I did not exist. Worried, I returned to ASIO's administration officer, who expressed outrage that I had taken it upon myself to visit the Pensions Office in Canberra to make inquiries. He told me I had another name in official records, a 'cover name' provided by ASIO, which he then reluctantly supplied so I was able to return to Canberra to be identified.

The shock of hearing what my pension amounted to almost blew me back to the administration department to question the truth of its statement. The administration officer was not blessed with any measure of diplomacy or tact and started explaining the very complex system between the male and female salary structures and pension entitlements. At this point I sought further advice from Phillips Fox solicitors in Melbourne. I then experienced a terrible period of worry and anxiety, fuelled by strong rumours from other ASIO personnel who had been short-changed, being deprived of large sums of money to which they believed they were entitled. When my solicitor inquired of ASIO what my function had been, the female personnel officer there told him I was a 'translator'. This was quite incorrect. I never worked in that capacity in ASIO in Australia. My duties were entirely focused on counter-espionage.

For twelve years my solicitor fought a Herculean battle on my behalf against every government instrumentality that might have an answer, but without success – that is, until the Inspector-General of Intelligence and Security, Roger Holdich, was appointed in the early 1990s. This important turn of events came at just the right time to save me! This fair-minded gentleman examined all my letters of appointment and the papers I had provided. He made numerous inquiries wherever he could, including in the UK, and interviewed my former colleagues.

He brought down a judgement in my favour, whereupon I was awarded a lump sum to compensate for losses suffered. This money was paid direct to my firm of solicitors who deducted all the expenses and legal fees accrued over the past twelve years. This devoured most of my entitlement! This arrangement at least enabled me to retain my home, which would otherwise have been sold to cover outstanding legal fees; but I was left with only a minimal monthly payment after 30 years of loyal service to ASIO.

This is certainly not the way intelligence officers retire in other, civilised countries. I was not allowed to contribute to the superannuation fund until 1974, five years after my arrival. Then I could only afford a minimal fee from the minimum salary I was earning under 'women's conditions of service'. I trust female officers today receive a much better deal – a far cry from my torrid experience. Perhaps I was a pioneer, although some would say I was also a victim of the poor progress made by women under several governments.

I still retained a passion for the work in which I had been involved for so long and a deep and lasting respect for many of my former colleagues. The founding principles of ASIO are as relevant today as ever, and ASIO itself deserves to be a great and important organisation. The existence of a reliable and trustworthy domestic security and counter-intelligence service is vital to any nation, irrespective of which political party holds government.

Hated by one major political party and barely tolerated as a functional necessity by the other, ASIO has often been deprived of the national respect to which it was entitled from its inception and has never been regarded, in the ringing words of Brigadier Sir Charles Spry, as Australia's 'fourth line of defence'. My experience of Western European security services was very different. These services held the trust and confidence of their respective nation, but, most importantly, also of their government of the day. This was sadly lacking in Australia.

My view is that the need for ASIO remains vital to our present situation. There have been many changes of directors-general since 1983, and most of the 'old guard' have thankfully retired or are no longer with us. Now, recruitment is strictly controlled and only the best are selected. Some of our bright young officers who joined with a distinct career in mind sadly left over time before the many appropriate changes were put in place.

The best thing I can say now is that all that went before lies behind us. I would hope that we now have an intelligent group of dedicated, hard-working men and women who realise the importance of their work and purpose for the protection of the nation and its inhabitants. In this troubled age of international terrorism we all need a reliable, competent and gifted team of officers ready to meet today's challenges under truly professional leadership.

I was relieved, delighted and very comforted to read early in 2015 the following job advertisement in *The Australian*, which read as follows:[2]

> ASIO is looking for talented people to fill a number of critical roles in the collection and analysis of intelligence. As an Intelligence Officer you will identify and investigate patterns and anomalies, solve complex problems and produce high-quality advice for government....
>
> Selected applicants will undergo an extensive security vetting process.

I am sure this will enhance the confidence in our nation's very important security service. If only I was younger, I would apply immediately....

14

Soviet penetration of Australian security: the evidence

> A nation can survive its fools, and even the ambitious; but it cannot survive treason from within. An enemy at the gates is less formidable, for he is known and carries his banner openly, but the traitor moves amongst those within the gate freely, his sly whispers rustling through all the alleys, heard in the very halls of government itself; for the traitor appears not a traitor; he speaks with accents familiar to his victims, and he wears their face and their arguments; he appeals to the baseness that lies deep in the hearts of all men. He rots the soul of a nation, he works secretly and unknown in the night to undermine the pillars of the city; he injects the body politic so that it can no longer resist. A murderer is less to be feared.
> — *Attrib. to Marcus Tullius Cicero 106BC – 43BC*[1]

Australia's national security repeatedly compromised

On at least three occasions since the war Australia has been barred from intelligence-sharing with its principal allies, Britain and the United States. These periods were approximately as follows: in the late 1940s; in the early to mid-1970s; and in the early 1980s. We shall examine each of these periods in turn.

After World War II, the Americans and the British had shown increasing reluctance to share their secret intelligence with Australia. Technical operations and Soviet defectors had revealed conclusively that high-level penetration agents, or 'moles', operating in Australia, were betraying classified intelligence to Soviet intelligence officers. As a result of this, Ben Chifley's Labor government was persuaded by Australia's allies to set up a professional security and counter-espionage service along the lines of Britain's MI5. In 1949, the Australian Security Intelligence Organisation (ASIO) was established, albeit with strong opposition from the Left.

The Venona Project

When I was still working in the Netherlands, Brigadier Spry informed me of the 'Venona Project', a secret decryption by U.S. and British signals intelligence agencies of Soviet radio messages transmitted during the 1940s. 'Venona' was the code-name for data collected by the United States Army Signal Intelligence Service (USASIS) near Washington DC in Virginia at Arlington Hall. British code-breakers at the UK's Government Communications Headquarters (GCHQ) – the successor of 'Station X' at Bletchley Park – used a different code-name: 'Bride'. This joint project was responsible for intercepting and decoding some of Moscow's encrypted radio communications with its intelligence officers around the world. It was one of the most remarkable code-breaking triumphs of the early Cold War.

The Venona decrypts revealed that Moscow had spies in almost every department of the U.S. administration, and, what was most alarming of all, in the top-secret Manhattan Project with access to information on America's development of nuclear weaponry. Venona in due course would also identify two ace British spies: Donald Maclean (codename *Homer*) in the British Foreign Office, and later Kim Philby (codename *Stanley*) in Britain's Secret Intelligence Service, MI6.[2]

The Venona material also demonstrated beyond doubt that the Soviet Union was conducting major espionage operations in Australia, both during, and after World War II. According to Richard Aldrich, a professor of international security at the University of Warwick, 'the KGB Moscow-Canberra cables proved to be the most successful part of the Venona operation'.[3] Even so, according to a pioneering study by two Canberra academics, Desmond Ball and David Horner,

Breaking the Codes: Australia's KGB Network, 1944-1950, of the nearly 5,000 encrypted messages sent between Moscow and Canberra from 1943 to 1948, only five per cent of them have been deciphered. Many Australians who were spying for the USSR were referred to in these messages, but remain unidentified to this day.[4]

British author Nigel West has written: 'During the first months of ASIO's existence, inquiries prompted by the existence of VENONA texts identified more than a dozen spies, and led ASIO to begin offensive operations.'[5] The Australian suspects became known as the 'Venona Twelve'.[6] The nine principal spies were all members of the Communist Party of Australia (CPA).[7] Professor Aldrich writes:[8]

> Thereafter, ASIO was almost entirely focused on what it called 'The Case'....
>
> The 'Venona Twelve' kept ASIO's staff of close to two hundred busy well into the 1950s. Each new suspect opened a world of further associates and contacts who required separate examination. The task was difficult, since the Communist Party of Australia had long expected to be banned, and had built up a substantial underground organisation.

Soviet espionage in Australia's Department of External Affairs

One Australian government department that was well and truly penetrated by a Soviet spy-ring during and after World War II was the Department of External Affairs.

Some of the suspected Australian spies identified by the Venona decrypts are as follows:

Walter Seddon ('Wally') Clayton (code-name *Klod*, or 'Claude').
Wally Clayton, a member of the central committee of the Communist Party of Australia, was the controller of the spy ring. The Soviet

KGB had recruited him in order to obtain classified documents received by the Australia government from its American and British allies. This Clayton managed to achieve by running a number of ace agents in the Department of External Affairs who supplied him and his Soviet masters with invaluable material. ASIO, under the then Colonel Spry's direction, did a very professional job in uncovering this particular network.

The CPA boasted a membership of around 20,000 members in 1950. ASIO needed to identify those members who held positions in government service. Everything that ASIO did, from its inception in 1949 under Ben Chifley's Labor government up to the collapse of the Soviet Union 40 years later, must be seen in the context of the discovery of this highly successful and dangerous KGB spy-ring that had gravely compromised Australia's security. This was why ASIO came into existence.

By June 1949, ASIO was satisfied that it had identified Clayton as the KGB's 'principal spymaster', concluding that he must be the mysterious *Klod* referred to in Moscow's coded cables. In 1957, Clayton and his wife attempted to fly to the Philippines. ASIO, fearing that his ultimate destination was the Soviet Union, persuaded the then Prime Minster Robert Menzies to cancel his passport. For decades Clayton denied he had ever been involved in espionage; but in 1993 he privately confessed the secret work he performed for the KGB to Laurie Aarons, national secretary of the CPA. His confession only came to light in 2010 after his death.[9]

Dr Ian Frank George Milner (*Bur*)

Ian Milner – known as the 'Rhodes Scholar Spy' – was an academically gifted New Zealander who won a Rhodes Scholarship to Oxford before the war and graduated with first-class honours in philosophy, politics and economics. While at Oxford he became a communist. He migrated to Australia to take up an appointment in early 1940

From left: Dr Ian Milner, Jim Hill and Katharine Susannah Prichard

as lecturer in political science at Melbourne University. He joined a branch of the Communist Party of Australia, even though it was illegal to do so at the time.

In 1944 he joined the Department of External Affairs and was appointed to the Post-Hostilities Division. From the end of World War II until 1947, he stole, copied and passed on to Clayton important classified documents on British and American policies on eastern Europe, the Middle East, trade with the Soviet Union and the surrender of Japan. From 1947 until 1949 he was appointed to the Australian contingent at the United Nations Security Council, where his espionage attracted the attention of the U.S. In 1950, Milner, upon learning that an Australian high-level inquiry was afoot to investigate how a top-secret defence document to which he had access has ended up in Soviet hands, planned his escape. He and his wife Margot, who shared his communist beliefs, fled to communist Czechoslovakia, where he remained until his death in 1991.[10]

James Frederick ('Jim') Hill (*Turist* or 'Tourist')

Another postwar Department of External Affairs officer identified from Venona was Jim Hill,[11] a graduate of Melbourne University, with known communist sympathies. His lawyer-brother, Ted Hill, had been identified by the Commonwealth Security Service in 1943 as a key member of the party's 'inner circle', and in 1949 had became secretary of the CPA's Victorian branch.[12]

During his time in External Affairs, Jim Hill passed on to Clayton classified documents from both Australia's Department of External Affairs and Britain's Foreign Office.[13] In the late 1940s he was posted to London. In 1950 he was questioned about his activities by MI5 on the premises of Australia House. According to his interviewer, Hill was 'very badly shaken' by the ordeal, but insisted he had never stolen classified documents. Hill faced three further interviews with MI5, each time refusing to admit anything. He returned to Australia, where he was transferred to the Attorney-General's Department. Believing he was still under a cloud, he later resigned from the public service altogether.[14]

Katharine Susannah 'Katie' Prichard (*Academician*)

Born in Fiji in 1883, Katie Prichard grew up in Australia, became a journalist and established herself as a successful novelist. In 1921 she was a founding member of the Communist Party of Australia, a cause to which she devoted the rest of her life. In 1933, while she was overseas touring the Soviet Union, her war-hero husband Hugo 'Jim' Throssell, who had remained behind in Australia, committed suicide owing to the collapse of his business during the worldwide Depression.

In 1934, Prichard published a pamphlet, called *The Real Russia*, in which she extolled what she thought were the heroic qualities of Stalin's Soviet Union.[15]

She performed a number of important roles for Soviet intelligence, among them working as an agent of influence, talent-spotter and courier. She provided vital operational support to the Clayton network.[16] She died in 1969, survived by her and her late husband Hugo Throssell's only son, Ric.

Richard 'Ric' Throssell (*Ferro*)

Katie Prichard's only son, Ric Throssell, became a diplomat, joining Australia's Department of External Affairs in 1943. His first posting was to Moscow. In the late 1940s he became an adviser to the Minister of External Affairs, Dr H.V. Evatt, when Evatt held the position of President of the United Nations General Assembly. The KGB's Moscow Centre valued Throssell as an agent, advising its KGB 'residency' in 1953 that he had 'transmitted valuable information to the Communists, and they to us'.[17] As a result of his being identified by ASIO as one of the 'Venona Twelve', Throssell not surprisingly found his diplomatic career impeded by the refusal of ASIO to grant him security clearances.

In 1989, he recounted some of his eventful life in his autobiography, *My Father's Son*. A decade later, after the death of his second wife Dorothy, he took his own life, as his father had done in 1933.[18]

The Minister and his Departmental Secretary

So far we have looked at the activities of identified spies in the Department of External Affairs who stole secrets for Moscow. We have not yet examined two important individuals who may have inflicted even more lasting damage to Australian security: the department's Secretary from 1947 to 1950, Dr John Burton, and the Labor government's Minister for External Affairs (and Attorney-General) from 1941 to 1949, Dr H.V. Evatt.

Dr John Wear Burton

In introducing Dr Burton as a guest on his ABC Radio National *Late Night Live* programme in 2004, Australian left-wing broadcaster and writer Phillip Adams said:[19]

John Burton was probably the most controversial and visionary public servant of the 20th Century. Branded a 'pink eminence' of the Labor Party by conservative critics, he was clearly one of the most important intellectuals and policy-makers associated with the Curtin Labor Government of the 1940s. As a close associate of 'Doc' Evatt and head of the department of External Affairs (now Foreign Affairs) he did more to shape Australian foreign policy towards Asia and the Pacific than any other person before or since.

Dr John Burton

Two Australian diplomats who worked closely with Dr Burton in the 1940s, developed a strong aversion towards him.

One of them was Paul Hasluck, a future Liberal politician who himself served as Minister for External Affairs from 1964 to 1969. He was particularly trenchant about Dr Burton's personal management style. From 1941 until 1947 Burton, as well as being a Department of External Affairs official, had been personal secretary to Dr Evatt. In March 1947, aged only 32, he was promoted ahead of more senior diplomats to be the department's Secretary, a position he held until June 1950. This was too much for Hasluck who, on March 25, 1947, wrote to a colleague, commenting:[20]

> I have lost confidence in the Administration itself when by Burton's appointment Cabinet set its approval on a whole system of petty intrigue, tale-bearing, favouritism and personal attachment to the Minister which, as an Australian citizen, I consider contrary to public service principles.

A colleague of Hasluck's, Coral Bell, who served in the Department of External Affairs from 1945 until 1951, detected something altogether more sinister about Burton's character. (Dr Bell would later go on to a distinguished career as a university academic, working with Arnold Toynbee at Chatham House, teaching at the London School of Economics and Sussex University, and later returning to Australia in 1977 as visiting fellow at the Defence Studies Centre at the Australian National University).[21]

During her first three years in the Department of External Affairs she became acquainted with a number of members of the department who were spying for the Soviet Union, including Jim Hill and Ric Throssell. She was later amused to learn that the KGB's codename for the department was 'Nook', a sheltered place. 'But who was doing the sheltering?' she asked. 'To my mind, [it was] Burton.'[22]

Dr Bell recalled foreign diplomats roaming freely around the offices when staff officers were absent during their lunch hour. Security was non-existent as the erratic Minister for Foreign Affairs, Dr H.V. Evatt, in her words, 'despised security'. In 1946 Bell was transferred to the United Nations division of this department, headed by Burton, It was here that she became acquainted with Hill and Throssell. The pair used to be joined at lunch by Fred Rose, who worked in the Department of Territories and Post-War Reconstruction, but also clandestinely for Soviet intelligence (his codename was 'Professor').

At one of these lunches, some time in late 1947, Throssell turned to her and said: 'Some of us think that the Soviet Union ought to see these documents.' The 'documents' to which he was referring were confidential British Foreign Office dispatches and telegrams, which were circulated to British Cabinet ministers and to the foreign affairs departments of trusted Commonwealth countries. Bell recalled: 'I assumed he was joking, so I laughed merrily, and said something to the effect that it sounded like a splendid way to get oneself into jail.'

Bell was certain that Throssell must have told Burton of her response and that Burton 'acted fast' to move her to another section of the department. She told Professor Desmond Ball, in the course of interviews he conducted with her in late 2010 and early 2011:[23]

> A (week or two) after that carefree mention of jail, I had found myself transferred out of Dr Burton's UN division to the Southeast Asia division, so I saw less of the others. And again, only a few months after that, in 1948, I was 'posted' to the Australian office in New Zealand, so I never saw any of them again.

In 1951 she resigned from the Department of External Affairs and migrated to Britain to embark on her distinguished academic career.

For the rest of her life it was Bell's honest opinion that Burton was deeply involved with Soviet intelligence. She speculated that Burton could well have been the principal agent reporting to Colonel Viktor Sergeivich Zaitsev,[24] the GRU (Soviet military intelligence) *rezident* in Australia from March 1943 to April 1947.[25] Before he was posted to Australia, Zaitsev had been posted to the Soviet embassy in Tokyo, where he had provided undercover operational assistance for the legendary Richard Sorge, one of the Soviet Union's most famous spies.[26] Recent re-assessment of that period indicates that Zaitsev was a top-class intelligence officer, with many contacts in Canberra, and an active recruiter of agents.[27]

A few years ago, Rob Foot made a careful study of the career and person of Dr Burton. He concluded:[28]

> ... [T]he strong likelihood is that Burton was an active agent for the Soviet Union at least during the time he held senior office in the Department of External Affairs, including the secretaryship, and a highly effective agent of influence thereafter. In the former role, his activities led directly to a breakdown in Australia's relationship with the USA.

Dr Herbert Vere 'Bert' Evatt

During the entire period of 1941-1949, when Labor was in government, first under John Curtin, then under Ben Chifley, the Minister of External Affairs and Attorney-General was the intellectually brilliant but volatile Dr H.V. Evatt. His life and career have been analysed in a path-breaking two-part article by Dr Andrew Campbell, an intelligence analyst who once worked for the Australian government's Office of National Assessments (ONA).[29]

Evatt counted a number of leading Australian communists among his closest friends and advisers and scarcely bothered to conceal his own pro-communist sympathies. In 1934, Evatt, then a High Court judge, behaved in an extraordinarily partisan manner when he defended a visiting Czech Comintern operative, Egon Kisch, whom the Lyons government was trying to deport as an undesirable alien.[30]

Evatt was particularly close to the Australian communist author, Katharine Susannah Prichard, who, as we have seen, was identified from the Venona decrypts as a Soviet spy. In December 1941, he personally assured her that, in his capacity as federal Attorney-General, he had ordered Commonwealth Security officers to halt their surveillance of her.[31]

In 1945, Evatt, John Burton, Paul Hasluck and other officials of the Department of External Affairs travelled to San Francisco to attend the inaugural conference of the United Nations. During the conference, Evatt leaked a secret British government document to the Soviet foreign minister, Vyacheslav Molotov. Hasluck recalled that the British quickly identified Evatt as the culprit, and the following morning he was very publicly reproved by the British Foreign Secretary, Anthony Eden, and the Dominions Secretary, Lord Cranbourne.[32]

During and after World War II, when Evatt was Minister for External Affairs, not only was his department, as we have seen, penetrated by Soviet agents, but so was his private office. Among his personal staff

John Burton, left, with Australian Minister for External Affairs Dr H.V. Evatt at a meeting of the United Nations

were at least four operatives reporting to the Soviet KGB: Frances Bernie (code-named *Sestra*, or 'Sister'), his personal secretary Allan Dalziel (*Denis*) and two other staffers Fergan O'Sullivan (*Zemliak*) and Albert Grundeman.[33]

In the 1949 general election, the Chifley Labor government was defeated and replaced by a Liberal-led government under Robert Menzies. In 1951, Dr Evatt replaced Chifley as leader of the Labor opposition. During the early 1950s, as Dr Campbell has shown, ASIO repeatedly briefed Evatt on the grave security risk posed by some of his key staffers, who had been discovered to have had clandestine links with Soviet intelligence officers.[34]

A prominent official of the New South Wales branch of the Labor Party, Frank Rooney, in 1953 presented Evatt with evidence that his press secretary Fergan O'Sullivan (*Zemliak*) every evening was phoning the Sydney headquarters of the Communist Party of Australia. Rooney recalled Evatt's 'extraordinary' reaction to the news and observed how Evatt's hands were trembling as he gave him a cigarette. Evatt refused to discuss the matter any further, and on the next day 'conducted himself as if nothing had happened'.[35]

In April 1954 came the dramatic defections to Australia of Vladimir Petrov and his wife Evdokia, both of them officers of the Soviet KGB. First, Petrov defected on his own on April 3, probably sooner than he had planned. He had discovered, to his alarm, that the contents of his safe at the Soviet embassy had been tampered with,[36] and feared that the KGB had somehow learned of his intentions.

Moscow then dispatched two thuggish 'couriers', named Zharkov and Karpinsky, to Australia to seize Petrov's wife, Evdokia, and bring her back to Russia and doubtless a terrible fate. On April 19, Sydney's Mascot Airport was the scene of rowdy anti-communist demonstrations by Australian migrants from the 'captive nations' of Soviet-occupied central and eastern Europe as the two KGB heavies, armed with guns, dragged the visibly distressed Mrs Petrova across the tarmac to a waiting aircraft.

Melbourne academic Robert Manne has vividly described how the brutal abduction and manhandling of Mrs Petrova on Australian soil 'was itself startling enough to awaken the tranquil democracy of mid-1950s Australia'. He wrote:[37]

> The nation saw an attractive young blonde woman, weeping and vulnerable, one foot bare, being dragged across the tarmac by two formidable, scowling Slavic gorillas. A durable visual image of what most Australians still believed the Cold War to be about – the struggle between the forces of Evil and Good – penetrated the national consciousness.

Evdokia Petrova at Sydney's Mascot Airport, being dragged across the tarmac to a waiting plane by two armed Soviet diplomatic couriers (April 19, 1954)

It was only when the aircraft landed at Darwin to refuel that the acting administrator of the Northern Territory, Reginald Leydin, and a squad of armed policemen were able to confront the guards on the grounds that they were carrying firearms aboard a civilian flight, and to offer Mrs Petrova asylum in Australia with her husband, which she accepted.[38]

Prime Minister Menzies announced the setting up of a royal commission to investigate Vladimir Petrov's testimony about Soviet espionage, both in Australia and overseas.

Evatt thereupon reacted by accusing Menzies and ASIO of having conspired to time the defection to help damage Labor's prospects

Dr H.V. 'Bert' Evatt (Picture: National Archives of Australia)

of winning the election that year. He appeared before the Petrov royal commission as counsel to defend two of his staff, Dalziel and Grundeman, from what he claimed was ASIO-fabricated evidence, and also to repeat his accusations that the Petrov defection has been manipulated by Menzies for political ends.[39]

In October 1954, Evatt launched a sensational attack on the anti-communist Industrial Groups within his own party. He accused them of disloyalty to Labor ideals. In March the following year, at a Labor Party conference in Hobart, Tasmania, Evatt, with the help of left-wingers such as Clyde Cameron, expelled from the party countless moderate members of long standing, many of whom would later form the Democratic Labor Party (DLP). The political turmoil that ensued, and which kept Labor out of office federally for a further seventeen years, became known as the Great Labor Split.

On October 21, 1955, after the final report of the Petrov royal commission had been presented to parliament, Evatt rose to deliver an extraordinary speech, which further damaged his credibility. He announced to the House of Representatives that he had personally written to Soviet Foreign Minister Molotov, inquiring whether the Soviet Union had stationed any spies in Australia, and that he wished to table the reply he had received in which Molotov had (not surprisingly) reassured him that there were none! This naïve statement was greeted by Parliament, first with stunned silence, then with derisive laughter.[40]

Soviet agents of influence in the Labor Party

Many senior Labor figures, such as former New South Wales premier and Foreign Minister Bob Carr,[41] have since come to regard Evatt's public career as having greatly harmed the party.

Bill Hayden, who was leader of the Labor Party from 1977 until 1983, commented in his autobiography on 'Evatt's enormous capacity for crafty self-serving conduct, the flaws in his political judgment, and the general problems of a perhaps faltering personality'. He concluded that Evatt 'was the cause of Labor's greatest and longest running disasters, and he should be held accountable for that'.[42]

Evatt's actions saw the expulsion of a whole generation of democratically-minded, anti-communist members of the Labor Party. As a result, many communists and other militant leftists were able to rise to prominent positions in the Labor Party.

Dr James Ford 'Jim' Cairns

Australia's one-time Labor Deputy Prime Minister, Dr Jim Cairns, was a top-ranking office-bearer of a Moscow-funded front organisation and a long-standing Soviet agent of influence over a period of twenty-five years.

First elected to the House of Representatives in 1955, Cairns became a popular leader of Australia's pro-communist Left, and in 1968 came within a handful of votes of toppling Gough Whitlam as leader of the Australian Labor Party. In the late 1960s and early 1970s

Labor's Dr Jim Cairns

he succeeded in mobilising huge public protests against Australia's involvement in the Vietnam War. He served as Deputy Prime Minister and federal Treasurer in the Whitlam Labor government (1972-75). He died in 2003, aged 89, still revered by many on the political Left.

During much of his career, Cairns was prominent in the so-called World Peace Council, a Soviet front organisation set up by Joseph Stalin in 1949 to urge Western democracies unilaterally to disarm. In the 1950s the governments of the United Kingdom, Austria and France barred WPC delegates from holding conferences in their respective countries. The WPC unswervingly defended Soviet military aggression in eastern Europe and elsewhere as somehow serving the cause of 'peace'.

Cairns was co-founder and first chairman of an early WPC offshoot, the Australian Peace Council, which he helped publicly launch in Melbourne's Town Hall in April 1950. He continued to play a leading role in the APC's post-1959 incarnation, the Australian and New Zealand Congress for International Co-operation and Disarmament. On May 8, 1970, he made history when he led a huge Australia-wide anti-war protest, which became known as the Vietnam moratorium. On that day, 75,000 protesters occupied the streets of Melbourne, bringing the city to a standstill.[43]

Cairns's political agenda, however, was not a pacifist one, but solely directed against the foreign policy of the United States. He specifically and repeatedly spoke in favour of the eventual victory of communist forces in Indo-China – which eventually occurred in April 1975, with tragic consequences for the people of Cambodia and Vietnam.

In 1973, when he was a senior Cabinet minister in the Whitlam government, Cairns sponsored a visit to Australia of representatives of communist North Vietnam. On April 26 — the day after Anzac Day — Cairns was photographed with his guests in the Sydney Town Hall, surrounded by Viet Cong flags and a huge picture of communist dictator Ho Chi Minh.

In 1974, official letterhead stationery of the Australian WPC described Cairns both as President of the Committee of World Peace Councillors in Australia and as Deputy Prime Minister.[44]

On April 8, 1975, Cairns told the Australian Parliament: 'It now seems inevitable that the Saigon [South Vietnamese] and Phnom Penh [Cambodian] governments would fall. That is the best solution….'[45] Western Australian historian and author Dr Hal G.P. Colebatch has commented:[46]

Senior Cabinet minister Dr Jim Cairns, photographed with representatives of communist North Vietnam in the Sydney Town Hall, surrounded by Viet Cong flags and a picture of dictator Ho Chi Minh (April 26, 1973)

In an interview published in the *Age* [Melbourne] on May 2, following the fall of Saigon and Phnom Penh, Dr Cairns said he greeted the end of the war with relief. He commented on the likely fate of anti-communist Vietnamese along the lines that they would be dealt with as 'collaborators' and that many people believed that reprisals against them would be justified.

Terrible reprisals indeed followed for millions of South Vietnamese, who for decades had fought to prevent their country falling victim to the communist North. Over a million of them were forced to flee their country.

In neighbouring Cambodia, communist repression was even more ferocious. Between April 1975, when the communist Khmer Rouge came to power, and 1979, when they were ousted, between a fifth and a third of the Cambodian population was either murdered or starved to death.[47]

Cairns viewed these unfolding tragedies with equanimity and never once expressed any misgivings about the cruel nature of communism or about the Soviet Union's responsibility for promoting its spread throughout the world.

In 2010, a prominent anti-communist Labor figure, former New South Wales premier and Foreign Minister Bob Carr, remarked of Cairns:[48]

> In acres of speeches and writings on foreign policy by Cairns, a single criticism of the Soviet bloc would be a discovery of gem-like value. Perhaps not a dual ticketholder, he wore the appellation 'fellow traveller' like a second skin.

Albert 'Bert' James

Bert James served as a federal Labor parliamentarian for two decades, during which time he was also a secret KGB informant, according to information that first came to light in 2014.

A former policeman, James was Labor member of the House of Representatives electorate of Hunter in the state of New South Wales from 1960 until 1980 – a seat previously held by Dr Evatt. The revelation of his activities as a Soviet agent of influence and KGB informant came from a high-ranking KGB intelligence officer and senior archivist, Vasili Mitrokhin, who defected to the United Kingdom in 1992. His testimony about James was released by the Churchill College archives centre at Cambridge University in July 2014.

Bert James MP
(Photo credit: Peter Stoop)

During his two decades in federal parliament, James expressed strong public opposition to the foreign policy of the United States and admiration for Fidel Castro's communist dictatorship in Cuba.

According to *Sydney Morning Herald* reporter Philip Dorling:[49]

> Australian Security Intelligence Organisation records, mainly phone intercept transcripts, reveal James was in regular contact with the Soviet embassy in Canberra in the early 1970s, dealing with third secretary Alexander Ekimenko who was suspected by ASIO as being a Russian intelligence officer, and was a regular recipient of Soviet hospitality.
>
> In an oral history recorded in 1984, James declared that 'the greatest threat to world peace is USA imperialism' and claimed that the U.S. Central Intelligence Agency had tried to remove Prime Minister John Gorton from office.

Bert James died in 2006.[50]

Arthur Gietzelt AO

For decades after World War II Arthur Gietzelt was a leading figure of the Australian Labor Party's left wing and of the Federated Clerks Union. From 1941 to 1945 he had served in the Australian army in New Guinea.[51] After the war his communist affiliations came to the notice of the Returned Soldiers' League (RSL), which promptly expelled him.[52] In 1956 he was elected to the Sutherland Shire Council in southern Sydney, serving as a councillor for fifteen years, during nine of which he was mayor. In 1971 he was elected Labor senator for New South Wales, a position he held for twenty years. He was Minister for Veterans' Affairs from 1983 until 1987 in the Hawke Labor government.

A former Labor senator for NSW – later a national president of the ALP, Stephen Loosley AM – has recorded in his recently-published memoirs:[53]

> Gietzelt was what was known as a double ticket holder. Put simply, he was a senior member of the Communist Party of Australia and also had a ticket in the ALP, all while occupying senior public office.
>
> When you were admitted to the inner councils of the Labor machine, you were quietly advised of communist influence in the senior reaches of the Left (faction). There was no doubt about this. The Australian Security Intelligence Organisation guaranteed the accuracy of the assessment.

Mr Loosley recalls how Paul Keating, who was Labor prime minister from 1991 to 1996, used to describe Gietzelt as a 'black widow spider' who was 'seemingly not a menace, but poisonous all the same'.

Hitherto classified ASIO files revealed a few years ago that for four decades after the war Gietzelt had been a 'full-time paid member' and secret operative of the Communist Party of Australia and in regular touch with the Soviet embassy. According to records of ASIO and its predecessor, the Commonwealth Investigation Service, Gietzelt received substantial financial subsidies from the CPA and participated in CPA conferences.⁵⁴

In the early 1970s U.S. diplomats based in Canberra sent secret cables to Washington warning that Gietzelt's communist activism posed a national-security risk to the Whitlam Labor government when it was in power.⁵⁵ Gietzelt did little to allay these concerns when he penned an extraordinary article denouncing the United States and calling upon the Australian

The Hon. Arthur Gietzelt AO

government to expropriate all land owned by American corporations, close down all U.S. intelligence-gathering facilities on Australian soil, lobby to have the U.S. expelled from the United Nations and bar entry to Australia of any American citizen who did not support the aims of the left-wing 'peace' movement.⁵⁶

A decade later, during the 1983 election in which Labor's Bob Hawke defeated Malcolm Fraser's Liberal-National coalition government, ASIO compiled a dossier on Gietzelt, alleging that he 'has been, and possibly remains, a secret member of the Communist Party', and speculating that he could be 'under some form of control by the Soviets'.⁵⁷

Gietzelt retired from parliament in 1989. In 1992 was made an Officer of the Order of Australia 'in recognition of service to the Australian Parliament and to local government'.⁵⁸ He died in 2014.

Bob Carr has praised ASIO's professionalism in never succumbing to the temptation to use its files on Gietzelt for political ends. He writes: 'I'm struck by ASIO's restraint. After all, a leaked copy of Gietzelt's ASIO file could have killed Labor's chances at any number of elections.'⁵⁹

Lee Rhiannon (née Brown)

Jim Cairns, Bert James and Arthur Gietzelt have long departed public life and are deceased. However, another left-winger of a younger generation who was very active in communist politics during the Cold War, Lee Rhiannon, is still very much with us and is currently the Greens Party senator for New South Wales.

Born in 1951 as Lee Brown, she is the daughter of Bill and Freda Brown, both of them veterans of the communist movement.

She first came to ASIO's attention in early 1970, at about the time she was preparing to sail from Sydney to Southampton aboard a Soviet cruise ship, the MS *Shota Rustaveli*. ASIO intercepted a call to her family home from a Soviet embassy official, Vladimir Alekseev, on behalf of his colleague, Ivan Stenin. Both Russians were known to be high-ranking KGB spies. ASIO believed that Alekseev was the KGB *rezident* – that is, the most senior Soviet intelligence officer in Australia. In the course of his phone call, Alekseev told Mrs Freda Brown that he would rendezvous with her daughter aboard the Soviet vessel.[60]

At this time, the Communist Party of Australia was in considerable turmoil, with its membership sharply divided over the 1968 Soviet Union's crushing of the Prague Spring, a brief period of comparative freedom during which Alexander Dubcek had attempted to soften communist rule in his country and introduce 'socialism with a human face'. A majority of CPA members condemned the Soviet-led invasion. Hard-line Moscow loyalists, however, broke away and formed the rival Socialist Party of Australia (SPA), which was controlled and funded by the Soviet embassy in Canberra.[61] Bill, Freda and Lee Brown all chose to become members of the SPA.

Writer and broadcaster Mark Aarons, a former long-standing friend of Rhiannon, who, like her, grew up in the communist movement but who remained in the CPA, recalls:[62]

Lee joined the SPA, attending its founding congress. She became a senior office-bearer of the youth wing, serving on the central committee's youth subcommittee; attended Australia-Soviet Friendship Society meetings; and developed close relations with Soviet, Czechoslovak and East German communist youth groups. In 1977, Rhiannon led an SPA delegation to Moscow at the invitation of Leonid Brezhnev's neo-Stalinist regime....

She also edited the SPA's Soviet-funded journal, *Survey*, from 1988 until 1990, when it folded up at about the time the Soviet Union itself collapsed.

A journalist of *The Australian* newspaper, Christian Kerr, writes:[63]

... [Rhiannon's] activities earned her an ASIO file that runs to five volumes and more than 800 pages for the nine-year period 1969 to 1978....

But Rhiannon has refused to recant her support for the Soviet Union during a period marked by intervention in Poland to suppress the independent Solidarity trade union, heightened persecution of Soviet Jews and gross abuses of psychiatry as a tool of political repression.

Since 1999, Rhiannon has been a parliamentarian representative for the radical left-wing Greens Party, first as a member of the New South Wales upper house, the Legislative Council, then, since 2011, as a senator representing NSW.

Expulsion from parliament

Known pro-Soviet activists and agents of influence, such as Bert James, Jim Cairns and Arthur Gietzelt, should never have been allowed to sit in parliament, let along serve as government ministers. Australia's Constitution (section 44) clearly states: 'Any person who ... is under any acknowledgement of allegiance, obedience, or adherence to a foreign power ... shall be incapable of being chosen or of sitting as a senator or member of the House of Representatives.'

The above parliamentarians, had the public been aware of their allegiance to a hostile foreign power while they were holding elected office, should have been stripped of office, expelled from parliament and their pension rights revoked.

Clandestine Soviet funding of the Communist Party of Australia

While pro-Soviet parliamentarians were active in the ranks of the Labor Party, the Soviet Union did not neglect to support the Communist Party of Australia. Mark Aarons, a former CPA member and son of Laurie Aarons, who was the party's general secretary for decades, has recorded in his 2010 book, *The Family File*, some of the many substantial payments Moscow made to the CPA in the 1960s, for example: $US168,000 in 1961, $US80,000 in 1963, $US130,000 in 1965, $US130,000 in 1966 and an undisclosed amount in 1967 – a total in excess of $508,000, which was a considerable sum in those days.[64]

As we have seen previously, Moscow, following the CPA's split after 1968, re-directed its funding to the hardline Soviet-aligned breakaway group, the Socialist Party of Australia (SPA).

Soviet intelligence officers on Australian soil

During all this time, what was the Australian Security Intelligence Organisation doing to prevent spies from operating successfully in our country? The answer is simple: nothing tangible. Our operations, some carefully planned and scheduled, were frequently botched, halted or cancelled with all sorts of clever excuses and rationalisations. During my time of service we had at least half a dozen Soviet intelligence officers who deserved to be given PNG *(persona non grata)* status and expelled.

Here are the identities of some of them:

Ivan Stenin, second secretary and press liaison at the Soviet embassy in Canberra,[65] was identified as the KGB station chief in Canberra soon after his arrival in 1965. He was a short, inconspicuous type, sighted on several occasions with our Canberra deputy regional director, John Elliott. These meetings were not authorised by ASIO, but continued for the duration of Stenin's posting in Canberra. Several operations of ours during this period were planned but failed.

Geronty Pavlovich Lazovik arrived in the early 1970s. He was a suave, highly-skilled agent-runner. He specialised in cultivating Labor politicians, political staffers and policy-makers.[66] With all the adverse evidence ASIO had collected on him, I had hoped he would be a perfect candidate for PNG status. But this could not be implemented in the then prevailing political climate. Lazovik developed a wide range of contacts in government circles and, according to a former ASIO officer, was rewarded on his return to Moscow for 'allegedly recruiting a top agent in ASIO, Defence or [the Department of Foreign Affairs]'.[67]

Vladimir Aleksandrovich Alekseev was a highly-skilled, trained and experienced KGB operative who was also a frequent visitor to the MS *Shota Rustavelli*, a Soviet cruise ship often berthed in Sydney harbour. On-board meetings, such as his 1970 rendezvous with Lee Rhiannon mentioned earlier, made surveillance impossible. Declassified ASIO files of the late 1960s and early 1970s described Alekseev as 'running two Australian politicians as agents, using tradecraft of a fairly high order'.[68]

Vladimir Yevgenyevich Tulayev took over from Alekseev as an energetic, ill-mannered but intelligent KGB operative, who dressed well and, according to ASIO files of the time, was 'aggressively involved in intelligence operations in Australia'.[69]

Gennadiy Nayanov was the KGB *rezident* (chief) at the Soviet embassy in Canberra in the late 1970s.[70]

Yuriy Ivanovich Stepanenko was identified by ASIO as a senior officer of Soviet military intelligence, the GRU. He fell victim to stomach cancer during his posting and suffered poor health.[71] There were frequent sightings of our deputy regional director, John Elliott, with this officer.

ASIO's failures

ASIO was unable to successfully secure PNG status for any of the above-named Soviet intelligence officers. Australia's Labor Prime Minister from 1972 to 1975, Gough Whitlam, suspended many ASIO investigation for fear they could cause 'diplomatic embarrassment'. To make matters even worse, his government suspended ASIO phone taps on the Soviet embassy

During my fourteen years of service in ASIO, not a single KGB or GRU officer was expelled. This was despite all the elaborate investigations which took ASIO personnel hours of painstaking work, study and research to identify threats to Australia's security.

The Soviet intelligence officers listed above were constantly active in the Canberra community, and ASIO prepared reports for presentation to the Department of Foreign Affairs recommending PNG status on security grounds. Not one of these recommendations was acted upon. The DFA did not want to know! Its European section, which dealt with the USSR, strongly opposed many of ASIO's attempts to restrict the number of Soviet officials in Australia. The DFA came to be known by many as a 'hot bed of cold feet'.

The crisis in ASIO in the 1980s

The fruit of this inaction was a bitter harvest for Australia and its allies.

Andrew Fowler, of the Australian Broadcasting Corporation (ABC)'s investigative unit, in an ABC TV *Four Corners* documentary he produced in 2004, called 'Trust and Betrayal', summed up well what I've attempted to convey in this book. He described how, starting in the 1970s, 'one ASIO operation went wrong after another'. He said: 'By the early 1980s, it became increasingly obvious to many in ASIO that someone in the organisation was leaking to the KGB.'[72]

Those in charge of ASIO during this time failed in their most basic duties as intelligence officers. By their inaction they tacitly aided the enemy by default. Writing this is not easy, but that is what happened.

I was brought up and trained to be loyal. In Britain I had served my country with the King's Commission. I had hoped to serve my adopted country, Australia, in a similar fashion, but was often thwarted from doing so by my superiors. In fact, with the way in which ASIO remunerated me, I was in the 'security risk' category, receiving a salary which was barely enough to exist on. Private means enabled me to survive. The Russians did not approach me for obvious reasons – I was known to them as a loyal subject of the Crown and a loyal citizen of Australia.

The struggle against forgetting

During World War II, the Soviet Union under its dictator Stalin was accepted by Britain and the United States as a necessary ally in the titanic European-wide struggle to resist and defeat Hitler's Nazi regime. The full story of the savagery of communism was largely unknown in the West, until it was more comprehensively revealed and chronicled after the war.

Seizing power in October 1917, Lenin's Bolsheviks abolished Russia's parliament and set up a dreaded secret police, the Cheka, an early forerunner of the KGB. Lenin mercilessly persecuted his political enemies and unleashed a reign of terror on the Russian population.[73] Lenin's successor, Joseph Stalin, in the late 1920s sought to establish a perfect communist society by confiscating land from peasants and seizing all their agricultural produce. Millions of peasants resisted Stalin's coercive policies. As a result, millions of them were shot or simply starved to death. In the mid-1930s Stalin ordered a witch-hunt against real or imagined enemies of his regime and had them shot or sent to Arctic slave labour camps. Millions more innocent people perished.[74]

There is no excuse for people to remain ignorant of the terrible human cost of communism. A person who witnessed it all at first hand was Russia's Nobel Prize-winning author, Aleksandr Solzhenitsyn, who had been an inmate of Stalin's slave labour camps. After he survived a KGB assassination attempt in 1971, he was finally expelled from the Soviet Union in 1974. He thereupon set about publishing in the West a three-volume indictment of communist rule, entitled *The Gulag Archipelago*.[75]

With the abundance of information about the reality of communism so widely available, it is incomprehensible that so many misguided Western intellectuals persist in, if not explicitly defending this ideology, promoting it in more or less clandestine ways.

Similarly, it is lamentable and quite alarming to recognise that a great number of people born after the late 1970s have grown up ignorant of the 'Cold War' through which my generation lived. This dangerous historical amnesia was well summed up in an editorial column of *The Australian* in 2010:[76]

> Unfortunately, the myopic, left-leaning view of 20th-century history presented in many universities and schools has left even educated Australians, like citizens of other democracies, ignorant of the realities of the Cold War. For all the derision heaped upon U.S. senator Joseph McCarthy, for example, there is no moral equivalent between McCarthyism and the KGB and its associates, which murdered at least 25 to 30 million 'enemies of the state' – mostly ordinary people – and

persecuted many more in Russia, Eastern Europe and the Baltic states.

I feel strongly about all this – our failure to tackle the Soviet threat to Australia's national security during the Cold War, and the younger generation's ignorance of how close the free world came to losing its freedom during this period.

Australia alone and isolated

My experience working in ASIO contradicted all I had been taught in Britain and Europe. The organisation's understanding of professional intelligence-gathering, not to mention work ethic, left much to be desired. Important intelligence leads, instead of being actively followed up, were often dropped prematurely, either out of lack of interest or because of pressure from above. Following on from Justice Hope's recommendations in his review of ASIO, Justice (later Sir) Edward Woodward (now sadly deceased) was appointed and faced the great problems of re-organising and re-modelling ASIO, which took many years after the retirement of 'the old guard' to which I had belonged.

It is a sad fact that I have to record here that nothing of real importance was achieved by ASIO during my fourteen years of service in Australia, but sadder still is that the organisation possessed the staff and resources to have been able to unmask spies and ensure they were brought to justice and given appropriate sentences for their treachery.

There are no excuses for this endemic failure. The evidence lies in the fact that this book has provided abundant evidence, from numerous sources as well as from my personal recollections, of the presence in Australia of spies reporting to the Soviet KGB and GRU. We even know some of their code-names. These persons were traitors and their trade was treachery. They held senior positions in government departments and earned good salaries and pension entitlements, while all the time knowingly and wittingly deceiving the nation.

Yet, to date, no exposure has ever seriously been contemplated, let alone a trial. They all went to their comfortable retirements as 'innocents' and were never jailed. Why no arrests? Why no trials? The secret intelligence services of our British and American allies were well aware of Australia's compromised national security and prudently excluded the country from much intelligence-sharing. During my time in Canberra, I was told by the then CIA head-of-station at the U.S embassy: 'We are not joining your operations – you are penetrated. We *know*.'

Not that this surprised me, but it did bring home to me the fact that Australia had lost some powerful support that it badly needed. As a result, we in Australia stood alone and isolated.

As we shall see in the next chapter, Australia during the Cold War was warned by its allies time and again that its security had been compromised by Soviet espionage.

The question that confronts us today is this: how can a country that has been warned by so many overseas governments, so many times, about its unsatisfactory and negligent security practices expect to be able to withstand the challenges posed by the rising powers such as China, a resurrected Russia under Vladimir Putin, or the present-day spread of militant Islamic terrorism?

ASIO penetrated from its early beginnings?

As we shall see in the next chapter, evidence has emerged in recent years suggesting that ASIO was penetrated from its early beginnings. Judging by the number of Soviet intelligence officers present in Canberra when I arrived in 1969, I would have to conclude that there was something seriously deficient and wrong with the way ASIO operated. Its ineptitude, unawareness or, more likely, sheer lack of interest in the massive problem it faced at the time made the activities of traitors within the organisation relatively easy.

In 2014, the national daily newspaper, *The Australian*, published an excellent article by Cameron Stewart, with the telling headline, 'ASIO fears its historians will shed too much light on dark past of Soviet infiltration'.[77]

A quote from Winston Churchill comes to mind: 'The further backwards you look, the further forward you can see.'[78]

15

THE LAST SECRETS OF THE COLD WAR

> There are two maxims for historians which so harmonise with what I know of history that I would like to claim them as my own, though they really belong to nineteenth-century historiography: first, that governments try to press upon the historian the key to all the drawers but one, and are anxious to spread the belief that this single one contains no secret of importance; secondly, that if the historian can only find the thing which the government does not want him to know, he will lay his hand upon something that is likely to be significant.
> — **Sir Herbert Butterfield**, Cambridge historian.[1]

The findings in the case of ASIO's Russian language interpreter George Sadil, mentioned in Chapter 12 above, have never been released, nor has any meaningful statement been made on the contents of the abortive trial. More serious still, clear and unmistakable evidence has emerged since the early 1990s that a number of ASIO officers, some of them reportedly of senior rank, were responsible for having betrayed Australian, British and particularly U.S. secrets to Moscow over a number of decades. In the mid-1990s some of the suspects were discreetly retired, with full superannuation rights, and the whole matter hushed up by the Australian government.

Evidence for this major spy scandal comes from three principal sources:

1. An admission on Australian television in 2004 by the secretary from 1989 to 1994 of the Attorney-General's Department, which oversees ASIO;

2. The testimony of three high-ranking former Soviet KGB officers who defected to the West: former Major-General Oleg Kalugin, a longtime head of KGB operations in the United States; former Colonel Oleg Gordievsky, a longtime KGB bureau chief in London; and former Major Vasili Mitrokhin a longtime senior KGB archivist.
3. The results of an Australian Federal Police top-secret probe of ASIO, launched in late 1992, called Operation Liver.

The Australian government Attorney-General's department

The ASIO spy scandal was the subject of a 2004 Australian Broadcasting Corporation *Four Corners* television documentary entitled 'Trust and Betrayal'. The result of three months' research by Andrew Fowler of the ABC's investigative unit, the program revealed that, in the 1980s and early 1990s, both the United States and Britain had cut off the flow of secret intelligence that they were willing to share with Australia.

In the course of the *Four Corners* documentary, an Australian government official, Alan Rose, recalled how, during his time as secretary of the Attorney-General's Department from 1989 to 1994: 'We weren't being taken fully into the Americans' confidence. We weren't being trusted in a way which ought to exist between organisations with a common goal.' The reason, said Rose, was that the U.S. lacked confidence in ASIO's 'ability to ... guarantee the security of U.S. information'.

Fowler asked Rose: 'How far up the chain of command in ASIO do you think the moles went?' Rose refused to be drawn into naming names, but admitted that the suspects were of much higher rank in ASIO than the Russian interpreter, George Sadil. He said that, given the fact that ASIO's security had been compromised over a very long period, there was a 'concern amongst many people' that serious security breaches had occurred at 'senior and responsible levels within the organisation and not just individuals who had the capacity to access and remove documents and material out of internal systems'. He said that those responsible for stealing secrets for Moscow were of such high rank that they were 'clearly able to influence the direction of the organisation's activities'.[2]

Three senior Soviet KGB officers who defected to the West

Independent corroboration of deep-cover Soviet penetration of ASIO has come from three former senior officers of the KGB.

1) Major-General Oleg Kalugin

For many years Oleg Kalugin worked for the KGB from the Soviet embassy in Washington DC. In 1974, when he was only 40, he was promoted to the rank of general and returned to Moscow to become head of the KGB's foreign counter-intelligence operations. In 1990, the year before the collapse of the Soviet Union, Kalugin was forcibly retired from the KGB, on account of his increasingly vocal criticisms of the spy agency.[3] In 1995 he moved to the United States, where he has lived ever since.

To date he has refused to reveal the identities of any Soviet spies except those already known to Western intelligence organisations. However, he has been prepared to go on the public record to describe, but not name, one high-level penetration agent in ASIO who, from the late 1970s onwards, supplied the KGB with high-grade secret intelligence, not only from Australia, but from Australia's major allies, the United States, Britain and Canada.

Kalugin described the significance of the KGB's intelligence coup on ABC's *Four Corners* programme. 'Once we penetrate ASIO,' he

From left: Oleg Kalugin, Oleg Gordievsky and Vasili Mitrokhin

said, 'we have actually some penetration and sometimes very deep penetration of the CIA or the FBI and the British MI5 and MI6. That's precisely what happened.' As a result of this achievement, the head of the KGB in Australia was awarded a special medal.

Andrew Fowler of the ABC's investigative unit said on the same programme exactly what I've recorded in this book from my own first-hand observations: 'Over the next decade, one ASIO operation went wrong after another. By the early 1980s, it became increasingly obvious to many in ASIO that someone in the organisation was leaking to the KGB.'

Kalugin said of this particular mole in ASIO: 'He had a good access. Everything about Australia, the United States, mutual cooperation, political plans, agents planted in the Soviet Embassy, surveillance squads, I mean, everything. ... We were aware of practically all steps taken or planned by ASIO against Soviet targets in Australia.'[4]

2) Colonel Oleg Gordievsky

Colonel Oleg Gordievsky was a longtime KGB bureau chief in London, who defected to Britain in 1985, after having secretly worked as a British penetration agent within the KGB for the previous decade. He headed the political section of the KGB which was responsible for English-speaking countries, including Australia and New Zealand.[5] He has readily confirmed Kalugin's account of the KGB's penetration of ASIO: 'It was clear to me that Kalugin and his security department did have sources in the Australian Security Intelligence Organisation.'

Commencing in 1986, the year after his defection, Gordievsky made two trips to Australia and four to New Zealand, where he met 'top-level political leaders' such as Bob Hawke and David Lange.[6] He was especially concerned about New Zealand, which, he said, 'had been under massive propaganda and ideological attack from the KGB and the [Soviet Union's] Central Committee, and the ruling Labour Party had seemed unaware of the extent to which the fabric of their society was being damaged by subversion'.[7]

3) Major Vasili Mitrokhin

To date, by far the most significant disclosure of the KGB's penetration of ASIO has come from a third Soviet defector, Vasili Mitrokhin. Like Kalugin and Gordievsky, he worked for the foreign intelligence arm, or First Chief Directorate, of the KGB. For years he was a senior archivist for the spy agency. In 1972 he was given sole responsibility for supervising the moving of some 300,000 top-secret files from the overcrowded KGB headquarters at the Lubyanka in Moscow to a new location south-east of the Russian capital. This laborious task, which necessitated his personally checking and sealing each file, took twelve years for him to complete.[8]

On examining the archives' contents he grew more and more horrified as he learned about the vast scale of the KGB's repressive treatment of the Soviet population. He recalled: 'I could not believe such evil. It was all planned, prepared, thought out in advance. It was a terrible shock when I read things.'[9]

From 1972 until 1984, while cataloguing the KGB files, Mitrokhin secretly made meticulous hand-written records of them and smuggled them home. During the weekends he travelled to his country dacha where he typed up his notes and hid them under the floor in trunks, suitcases and even a milk churn. He retired from the KGB in 1984, aged 62.[10]

In 1991, the Soviet Union broke up and countries such as the Baltic states and Ukraine broke free from Russian control. In March 1992, Mitrokhin headed to the newly-freed republic of Latvia with the intention of defecting to the West. He dressed himself shabbily to avoid attracting the attention of Russian border guards and hid some samples of his secret archives in the bottom of a battered case on wheels.[11]

He walked into the American embassy in Riga, Latvia's capital, and requested asylum; but the Americans, overwhelmed with hundreds of other Russian asylum-seekers, failed to recognise Mitrokhin's importance and turned him away. He tried the nearby British embassy, where he had better luck. The British immediately realised the significance of Mitrokhin, whereupon the UK Secret Intelligence Service, or MI6, devised a means to smuggle Mitrokhin, his family and the rest of his archives – which filled six trunks – out of Russia. On September 7, Mitrokhin and his family finally set foot on British soil.[12] For the rest of his life in Britain he lived under police protection and with a false identity.

The six trunks of files Mitrokhin brought with him to the West contained 'details not of a few hundred but of thousands of Soviet agents and intelligence officers in all parts of the globe'.[13] It was a huge haul of secret intelligence. America's FBI described it as 'the most complete and extensive intelligence ever received from any source'. The CIA called it 'the biggest CI [counter-intelligence] bonanza of the post-war period'.[14]

In 1995, Mitrokhin commenced collaboration with Christopher Andrew, a Cambridge professor who specialises in the history of secret intelligence, to publish in English two volumes from his archives. The first volume, on the KGB's operations in Europe and the West, appeared in 1999. The second volume, about the KGB's operations in the developing world, appeared in 2005, a year after Mitrokhin's death aged 81.[15]

Nevertheless, to date, much of Mitrokhin's archives has remained unpublished. In particular, nothing of significance on Australia or New Zealand appeared in either of the volumes Mitrokhin co-wrote with Professor Andrew; yet, as we shall see, Mitrokhin brought to the West considerable information on KGB operations in both these countries.

In July 2014, a few new tantalising slivers of information appeared from the unpublished Mitrokhin archives after some of them were declassified and made available to the public for the first time at the Churchill Archives Centre in Cambridge.[16]

The *Sydney Morning Herald*'s Philip Dorling reported on a couple of items concerning Australia:[17]

> The KGB's priorities in Australia included information on Australian politics, international affairs in Asia and the Pacific, and 'infiltrating the embassies of England, USA, the Australian Ministry of Foreign Affairs ... [as well as] counterintelligence operations to infiltrate intelligence and counterintelligence agencies'.
>
> Mitrokhin's papers show the KGB exploited academic exchanges with Australia to infiltrate agents into Australian universities, including Leonid Stupin, agent 'Gatsky', a Soviet academic who taught Russian at the Australian National University from 1968-70.

In the same article, Dorling revealed, as we saw in Chapter 14 above, that a long-serving federal Labor MP from New South Wales, Albert James, had been a KGB informant.

Simultaneously, Phil Kitchin, of New Zealand's *Dominion Post*, reported the discovery in the Mitrokhin archive of new evidence that cleared up a forty-year-old New Zealand Cold War spy mystery. In 1974, a high-ranking and long-serving government official, William 'Bill' Sutch, had been arrested in 1974 while meeting a KGB officer in a park in New Zealand's capital, Wellington. He was charged with 'obtaining information helpful to the enemy'; but, after a sensational five-day trial, he was acquitted. The documents from the Mitrokhin archives released in 2014 provided evidence that the KGB had in fact recruited Sutch in 1950, and that Sutch went on to spy for Moscow for a quarter of a century.[18]

New Zealand's Bill Sutch

These 2014 partial disclosures from the Mitrokhin archives concerning Leonid Stupin, Albert James and William Sutch, however, were all about individuals long dead. Yet we know that, when he defected to Britain in 1992, Mitrokhin brought with him a great deal of secret intelligence on the KGB's penetration of ASIO. This was confirmed by the British government's Intelligence and Security Committee, which in 2000 disclosed:[19]

> As soon as Mr Mitrokhin's material reached the UK, the SIS [Secret Intelligence Service, or MI6] passed that relating to the UK to the Security Service [MI5] in unprocessed form for them to take matters forward and investigate. ... Material relating to Australia was passed to the Australian Intelligence Security Organisation [ASIO] in September 1992.

December 1992: Operation Liver launched

The then Keating Labor government in Australia, under pressure from the British and American security services, ordered an intensive investigation of ASIO. In December 1992, the Australian Federal Police launched a top-secret probe, codenamed Operation Liver.[20] Headed by AFP Commander Alan Mills, it was carried out in the utmost secrecy, and nothing of its findings has been revealed to the public, although some information has trickled out from time to time.

The 1994 Cook Report

So sensational were the findings of the Operation Liver probe that the Keating government appointed a senior intelligence specialist and diplomat, Michael Cook AO, to write a full report on the suspected KGB penetration of ASIO. (Cook had been Director-General of the Australian government's Office of National Assessments from 1981 to 1989, and had served as Australian ambassador to Washington from 1989 to 1993.) The review was completed in 1994; but, as the ABC investigative unit's Andrew Fowler has observed, 'the contents of the Cook report remain a closely guarded secret'.[21]

Canberra's cover-up

However, Australia's *News Weekly* magazine in 1999 reported the following results of the molehunt:[22]

> According to disaffected Canberra-based ASIO sources, in the mid-1990s a number of ASIO officers were silently retired (with full superannuation rights). They had been linked to a KGB penetration operation that spanned decades and which involved Australian, British and particularly U.S. secrets.

According to an investigation conducted into ASIO, the agency contained over ten suspected KGB penetrations – a chilling number given the size of ASIO.

Significantly, their activities were only discovered by accident during the course of another investigation!

However, this was hushed up, the sole concern – or fear – was to conceal the truth of KGB penetrations from the Americans.

Australia's veteran political commentator Laurie Oakes commented on the affair:[23]

> If there were, in fact, 10 ASIO [officers] suspected of working for the Soviets, it is of major importance. And it undoubtedly would freak out the Americans. Not surprisingly, the allegation is difficult to check, but I have been told there *was* a federal police investigation which uncovered something embarrassing, and several ASIO officers *were* pensioned off in mysterious circumstances. ...
>
> Since the *News Weekly* article appeared, further allegations have circulated about the same issue. It is said, for example, that both sides of politics were involved in the decision to cover up the suspected KGB penetration of ASIO. The claim is that the then Labor government provided a secret briefing to the Coalition leadership on the federal police investigation and the possible consequences for intelligence-sharing within the U.S. alliance if details reached the CIA – and it was agreed the whole thing should be dealt with as silently as possible. According to a former spook, the ASIO operatives under suspicion went quietly and the federal police investigation was rolled up.

Surely the Australian people have a right to know if real spies were operating, and for how long, in our government departments, instrumentalities and intelligence agencies. They should have been exposed, prosecuted and served lengthy prison terms, and not quietly let off the hook and allowed to retire with full pension rights.

Why has the Australian government never considered taking action against these individuals? And why the cover-up? The public deserves better than this.

Mitrokhin's revelations about ASIO, as well as the results of Operation Liver and the contents of the Cook report deserve to be edited, published and, where possible, acted upon. There is no need to worry about what our American and British allies might think. They would know this already! They have lived with our 'problem' for far too long.

16

MI5's Roger Hollis and the Founding of ASIO

The security problems which beset ASIO during the Cold War may have originated as far back as the 1940s, when the organisation was in the process of being set up.

As we saw in chapter 14, after World War II the United States and Britain had placed an embargo on intelligence-sharing with Australia,

Roger Hollis

after it had been discovered that many Allied secrets were being betrayed to Soviet intelligence officers stationed in Canberra.

As a result of this, the postwar Labor government of Ben Chifley was put under considerable pressure by its U.S. and British allies to tackle Australia's security problem by setting up a professional security and counter-espionage service.[1] To help persuade both Australia and New Zealand to improve their security, Britain's Labour Prime Minister, Clement Attlee, in February 1948 sent no less a person than the Director-General of Britain's own Security Service MI5, Sir Percy Sillitoe, to advise the two countries' respective governments. Accompanying Sillitoe was MI5's then head of protective security, Roger Hollis.[2]

Later in his career, Hollis was to serve as MI5 Director-General from 1956 to 1965, earning a knighthood along the way, but also coming under suspicion from some quarters that he himself was a Soviet agent, working clandestinely to undermine British security. If this accusation was true, then his role in helping set up ASIO would likely have seriously compromised the organisation's operational effectiveness from its inception.

After his early 1948 trip to Australia and New Zealand with Sir Percy Sillitoe, Hollis paid two further visits to Australia – one of them from July to September 1948; the other from January to March 1949.[3] Both Cambridge historian Christopher Andrew's authorised history of MI5 and Australian defence historian David Horner's official history of ASIO clearly establish that Hollis was no mere backseat adviser on Australian security but played a prominent hands-on role, laying down very specific instructions on how ASIO should be run.[4]

David Horner in particular describes how the 'final impetus' for creating ASIO 'came when Roger Hollis returned to Australia', on January 24, 1949. Horner writes:[5]

His principal mission was to provide the Australian Government with advice on the establishment of the new security organisation, including its charter, responsibilities, organisational structure and senior appointments.

The new service was duly inaugurated on March 16 by a charter signed by Prime Minister Chifley and presented to the organisation's first Director-General, Mr Justice Geoffrey Reed.[6]

The question of Hollis's allegiances has been the subject of much acrimonious debate in Britain and the United States over the years. The public first learned about the controversy in early 1981, when veteran Fleet Street investigative journalist Chapman Pincher first aired it in his book, *Their Trade is Treachery*,[7] prompting the then Prime Minister Margaret Thatcher to rebut the allegations in the House of Commons.[8]

The Hollis affair erupted again in 1985, when a renegade former MI5 officer, Peter Wright – the principal source of Pincher's allegations against Hollis – attempted to publish his controversial tell-all memoirs, *Spycatcher*.[9] The British government attempted, unsuccessfully, to suppress the publication of Wright's book, as its contents clearly contravened Britain's Official Secrets Act.

Several secret MI5 files from the Cold War, which have recently been declassified, have, however, renewed speculation about Hollis. As recently as April 2015, the Washington-based Institute of World Politics hosted a special conference of intelligence specialists, called 'British patriot or Soviet spy? Clarifying a major Cold War mystery', to try to establish whether or not Hollis had been a Soviet agent.

Roger Hollis at Oxford and in China

Roger Hollis was born in 1905 in Somerset, England, the third of four sons of an Anglican theologian who became bishop of Taunton.

Agnes Smedley, left, and Arthur Ewert

A quiet and diligent student, he won a classics exhibition to Worcester College, Oxford, where he enrolled in the autumn of 1924.

During his time at university he abandoned his Christian faith and, according to an Oxford contemporary (and future MI5 colleague) Dick White, soon gained a reputation for wasting his time on 'wine, women and golf', perhaps as a reaction to his closeted religious upbringing.[10] Among his early acquaintances were three noted communist sympathisers, Cecil Day-Lewis, Claud Cockburn and Maurice Richardson.[11] In the spring of 1926, a year before he was due to take his final exams, Hollis was abruptly 'rusticated' (that is, expelled) from Oxford.[12]

In 1927 Hollis travelled to Hong Kong, then a British colony, where he worked as a journalist. The following year he moved to China itself, living in Shanghai, where he worked first for the *Shanghai Post* and later for the British-American Tobacco Company. In late 1930 he transferred to Beijing, but frequently returned to Shanghai.[13]

During his time in China, Hollis was known to have formed friendships with leading communist sympathisers there. One of them was the feisty American feminist, author and communist activist Agnes Smedley.[14] Another was Rewi Alley, a New Zealander with strong Marxist leanings, who worked as a factory inspector in Shanghai from 1927 to 1938.[15]

Hollis's most significant known communist contact during this period was Arthur Ewert, a German-born senior official of the Soviet Comintern, whose chief task it was to recruit communist agents from the English-speaking world.[16] A British army officer and Chinese language interpreter in Shanghai, Captain Tony Stables, knew Hollis when in China and shared a flat with him in Beijing intermittently during 1930 and 1931. He recalled seeing Hollis in the company of both Agnes Smedley and Arthur Ewert.[17]

The Shanghai spy ring

Smedley, like Ewert, was herself a formidable and militant communist activist. In January 1930 there arrived in Shanghai a gifted and highly-trained officer of the Soviet Red Army's military intelligence directorate, the GRU, Richard Sorge. Soon after meeting Smedley, he sought her help in recruiting agents for espionage work. This she willingly did. She also became his mistress.[18]

Another of Sorge's protégées was a German communist, Ursula Ruth Hamburger (née Kuczynski), later better known by her codename Sonia. Both Sorge and Sonia were destined to become two of the most successful spies of modern times.

It is not known if Hollis, during his years in China, was acquainted with either Sorge or Sonia. It has, however, been alleged in a book published in 1996 that he had an affair with Luise Klas,[19] the wife of Sorge's successor as GRU station chief in Shanghai, Karl Rimm,[20] and furthermore had been recruited as a GRU agent.[21] These allegations consist of mainly hearsay evidence and therefore should not be regarded as decisive for evaluating Hollis's career. However, they do merit further scholarly examination.

Richard Sorge, left, and 'Red Sonia' (Ursula Ruth Kuczynski)

In the summer of 1934 Hollis paid a visit to Britain, travelling part of the way on the Trans-Siberian Express and stopping off in Moscow.[22] In December of that year, back in China, he was diagnosed with tuberculosis and hospitalised. He left China for good in July 1936 and was back in England the following month.[23] In December that year he wrote to his future wife, Eve Swayne, describing himself as a 'staunch Conservative' and monarchist. However, Jack Swayne, a cousin of Eve's, who was also acquainted with Hollis, recalled: 'When Roger returned from China he was rather Red.'[24]

When Hollis applied for, and succeeded in being employed by Britain's Security Service, MI5, in 1938,[25] he did not divulge, as he should have done, his past acquaintance with known communists such as Claud Cockburn at Oxford or Agnes Smedley and Arthur Ewert in China.[26]

Sonia, the spy who haunted Britain

Sonia left Shanghai in December 1932 with the rank of captain in the Soviet Red Army's military intelligence directorate, the GRU.[27] After three months' training in Moscow on espionage, particularly on how to construct, operate and conceal a radio transmitter, Sonia was sent on two missions: first, to Japanese-occupied Manchuria, where she served as a link between Moscow and the local Chinese communist resistance; then to Warsaw and Danzig, where she ran a network of anti-Nazi spies.

In 1938, she returned to Moscow for more espionage training. During her time there she was awarded the prestigious Order of the Red Banner and promoted to the rank of major in the Red Army. She was then sent to Switzerland to set up a clandestine radio network. In Montreux she worked alongside Hungarian communist Alexander Rado, head of the so-called Lucy Ring, or *Rote Drei* ('the Red Three'), a highly successful GRU network which supplied Moscow with a flow of high-grade intelligence from the German High Command.[28]

In 1939, the Soviet GRU instructed Sonia to move to England. In order to secure British nationality, and thereby a British passport, she first had to divorce her German husband Rudolf 'Rolf' Hamburger and look for a British man to marry. Rolf agreed to the divorce, which was finalised that same year. Then, in early 1940, Sonia married an English communist and Spanish Civil War veteran, Leonard 'Len' Beurton, in Montreux.[29] She later wrote in her memoirs: '[A]lthough it was only a 'paper marriage', we wanted to choose an auspicious occasion. We decided on 23rd February, the birthday of the Red Army.'[30]

Meanwhile, in Britain, in October 1940, MI5 transferred most of its personnel and records from London to a safer location of Blenheim Palace (Churchill's birthplace) at Woodstock, about nine miles north of Oxford.[31]

In December Sonia left Geneva, accompanied by her two young children, travelling by bus from neutral Switzerland, through German-occupied France to the border of neutral Spain, and then on to Barcelona. There she took a train to Madrid and another one to Lisbon, where, after a few weeks' wait, she secured a steamship passage to Britain. The steamer sailed in a convoy with twelve others and made a long detour to Gibraltar. The voyage to England took more than a fortnight.[32]

Sonia's proximity to Hollis and MI5

She arrived in Liverpool in early February 1941, then went straight to Oxford. In early 1941, Sonia lodged at Glympton Rectory, near Woodstock, a small town adjacent to Blenheim Palace, where the major part of MI5, including the section headed by Hollis, had been evacuated. In April she moved to a furnished bungalow in Kidlington, halfway between Blenheim Palace and Oxford. In the autumn of 1942 she was moved to larger cottage in the Summertown district of Oxford.[33] CIA historian Benjamin Fischer has observed that Sonia's third home was 'less than a mile from where Hollis lived'.[34]

For the better part of a decade Sonia ran spies and transmitted secrets to Moscow. What is astonishing is that MI5 did so little, either during or after the war, to investigate Sonia's espionage activities (including coded radio transmissions), which were conducted under its very nose.

Atomic espionage

The spies Sonia ran on behalf of the GRU during her decade in Britain inflicted as much damage on Western interests as did the KGB's celebrated Cambridge spies discussed in chapter 6 above. She ran at least two atomic spies.

a) Klaus Fuchs

The most famous of them was the German-born research physicist Klaus Fuchs, who later worked in America's Manhattan Project on the

Atomic spies Klaus Fuchs, left, and Melita Norwood

construction of the first atomic bomb.[35] His betrayal of British and American nuclear secrets is estimated to have saved Soviet scientists at least two years' work in developing their own nuclear bomb.[36]

b) Melita 'Letty' Norwood (née Sirnis)

Another atomic spy, whose espionage only came to light in 1999 – a decade after the end of the Cold War – was Melita Norwood. She was not a scientist herself, but, thanks to her employment, first at the British Non-Ferrous Metals Association, then at the Tube Alloy Project, she had ready access to secret technical information on Britain's development of the atomic bomb.[37]

According to Soviet defector Vasili Mitrokhin, the Soviet Union at the outbreak of World War II valued Norwood even more highly than the better-known traitor, Kim Philby.[38] Cambridge historian Professor Christopher Andrew says that, on present evidence, she was not only 'the most important British female agent' working for Moscow at the time, but also 'the longest-serving of all Soviet spies in Britain'.[39]

c) 1943 Quebec Agreement

In 2002, the GRU revealed for the first time how in October 1943 Sonia pulled off the greatest espionage coup of her entire career. She transmitted to Moscow details of the top-secret Quebec Agreement of August 1943, when Britain's Prime Minister Winston Churchill and America's President Franklin D. Roosevelt pledged their respective countries to collaborate on the development of the atomic bomb, but not to share any information about it with any other country without prior agreement between them.[40] Only a very high-level penetration agent, whose identity remains unknown, could have provided Sonia with information of this calibre.

As a result of her string of espionage successes, Sonia became the only woman ever to be made an honorary colonel of the Soviet Red Army.[41] After her death in 2000, Russian President Vladimir Putin awarded her the posthumous title, 'Superagent of Military Intelligence'.[42]

A protective hand in MI5?

The most astonishing thing about Sonia's decade of espionage activity in Britain is that MI5 knew who she was and what she was. Her father, the German demographer and statistician, Robert 'René' Kuczynski, was well known for his communist sympathies. In 1928 MI5 had opened a file on him.[43] At the outbreak of World War II, when Stalin's Russia was the ally of Hitler's Reich, British authorities had interned him for a few months for spreading anti-British and defeatist propaganda.[44]

His daughter, Sonia, was also well known to MI5, her name having been recorded on its Central Security War Black List. MI5's watchers were ready and waiting to monitor her arrival when she disembarked in Liverpool, and under instruction to discover her destination.[45] Her first address, as we have seen, was adjacent to MI5's wartime headquarters at Blenheim Palace. Yet MI5 did nothing further about her.

Meanwhile, as the war progressed, Hollis assumed new responsibilities within MI5. He impressed his superiors with his warnings about the dangers of communist subversion and the Soviet threat, so much so that he came to be regarded as MI5's expert on the subject.[46] By April 1943, Hollis was head of MI5's F Division, which was responsible for monitoring subversive activities.[47] He was also appointed liaison officer on the subject with the Secret Intelligence Service, MI6.[48]

The following year, as we saw in chapter 6, Kim Philby was instrumental in setting up in MI6 a new body, Section IX, for the 'professional handling of any cases coming to our notice involving Communists or people concerned in Soviet espionage' and succeeded in making himself head of the new section. In Philby's own words, the Section IX was to be responsible for 'the collection and interpretation of information concerning Soviet and Communist espionage and subversion in all parts of the world outside British territory'.[49] As Philby's contemporary, Robert Cecil, later wrote of this manoeuvre: 'The history of espionage records few, if any, comparable masterstrokes.'[50]

It was not until 1999 that the public first learned of Hollis's role in the affair. An official historian of MI5, John Curry, writing in 1946, some years before Kim Philby was suspected of spying for the Soviets, wrote:[51]

> The formation of Section IX was the result of Mr Hollis' action in urging the importance of the question of the use of wireless for the transmission of messages between London and Moscow as raised by certain circumstances which had recently come to the notice of F Division.

Here again, Hollis gave the appearance of being zealous about tackling the threat of Soviet espionage. Indeed, his vociferous warnings about communist subversion are often taken at face value as ruling out any possibility he could have been a spy for Moscow. However, in numerous instances, as the late Chapman Pincher a few years ago copiously documented in his book, *Treachery: Betrayals, Blunders and Cover-Ups: Six Decades of Espionage: The True Story of MI5*,[52] Hollis repeatedly halted MI5 investigations and allowed Soviet spies to operate undisturbed. Moreover, he seriously misled Britain's American allies about the true extent of Soviet nuclear espionage.

a) 'No further action' on illegal radio transmissions

Concerning clandestine radio traffic, about which he expressed so much concern, Hollis did precisely nothing. During the war, Britain's Radio Security Service (RSS), with the assistance of hundreds of amateur radio enthusiasts, was responsible for intercepting illicit transmissions. RSS officers have testified that they repeatedly informed MI5 or MI6 of illegal transmissions, including ones from the vicinity of Oxford, where Sonia was operating, and urged that a detector van be sent to pinpoint the source. However, their logs were invariably returned to the RSS, by either MI5's Hollis or MI6's Philby, with the comment: 'NFA [No Further Action] or NFU [No Further Use].'[53]

b) Kuczynski family's communist connections

In December 1940, Hollis, in response to a U.S. embassy request for information on foreign communists living in Britain, provided the Americans with a list of 20 names, but omitted the names of Sonia's father, René Kuczynski, and two of her siblings, Jürgen and Brigitte, who were then living in Britain and who had been clearly designated in MI5 files as 'dangerous' communists.[54] About the Red Army intelligence officer Sonia, who arrived in Britain in early 1941, Hollis assured America's FBI, in a letter dated August 10, 1944, that she appeared to 'devote her time to her children and domestic affairs'.[55]

c) Nuclear spy Klaus Fuchs cleared six times

Hollis was responsible for clearing German-born nuclear physicist Klaus Fuchs six times,[56] despite warnings from his own colleagues that Fuchs could be spying for Moscow.[57] The consequence of Hollis's clearances was that Fuchs was able to steal not only Britain's nuclear secrets, but also America's after he was given clearance to join the designers of the world's first atomic bomb at Los Alamos in New Mexico in August 1944. Fuchs played a key role in the project, including editing a top-secret 25-volume encyclopaedia, summarising the latest developments in American nuclear technology.[58]

In 1946, the Canadians informed Hollis that, in the course of a probe into Soviet espionage, they had discovered the names and addresses of five Britons, one of them Klaus Fuchs, in the address book of a Canadian communist mathematician, Israel Halperin.[59] Hollis, however, declined to investigate any of the five British names.

In 1950, when Fuchs was belatedly arrested in Britain and confessed to espionage, the Canadians expressed their disbelief that MI5 could have failed to follow up the leads they had provided four years previously:[60]

> Surely when we had 150 to investigate, it was Britain's responsibility to investigate the five in their country including Fuchs.

In 1950, a British court sentenced Fuchs to fourteen years' jail. Meanwhile, Fuchs's GRU agent-runner, Sonia, quietly slipped out of England with her children and resettled in communist East Berlin.[61]

d) Other nuclear spies

In September 1950, not long after Fuchs's trial, another communist atomic physicist, Italian-born Bruno Pontecorvo, who had also betrayed British and American atomic secrets to Moscow, was discovered to be a communist. He managed to flee Britain, where he was living at the time, and defect to Russia, just as Donald Maclean and Guy Burgess would do a few months later. The Americans were furious and Britain's Prime Minister Clement Attlee was exasperated at this latest failure of MI5.[62]

Two other spectacular MI5 failures were not discovered until years after the end of the Cold War.

The Soviet Union's longest-serving female spy in Britain, Melita Norwood, had come to the attention of MI5 before World War II. Yet, according to her biographer David Burke:[63]

> Mrs Norwood ... was investigated on no fewer than ten occasions – in 1938, 1941, 1945, 1949, 1951, 1962, 1965, 1992, 1993 and 1999 – and each time walked away unscathed.

When her espionage became publicly known in 1999, her old GRU spy-handler, still living in Berlin, posted her a copy of her autobiography, *Sonya's Report*, with the inscription: 'To Letty. 'Sonya' salutes you!'[64]

In 2008 the Austrian-born physicist, Engelbert Broda, was discovered to have also been a major atomic spy for the Soviet Union.[65] Even though Broda had been known to MI5 as a communist as early as 1938,[66] the year he first set foot in the British isles, Hollis, who became his case officer, dismissed these concerns.[67]

Dr Paul Monk, a former senior intelligence analyst with the Australian Defence Intelligence Organisation (DIO), has said of Hollis's mishandling of these cases:[68]

> ... the number of proven Soviet spies and active agents who operated for years under Hollis's nose, when his chief task was detecting and neutralising such people, was more than thirty, excluding actual Soviet intelligence personnel working in the Soviet embassy. And the number of previously unidentified

Soviet agents that are being revealed as the Soviet archives open is steadily increasing.

All this, surely, demonstrates beyond reasonable doubt that there is a case to answer with regard to Hollis.

GRU secret agent *Elli*

In September 1945, a GRU officer and cipher clerk, Igor Gouzenko, who was stationed in the Soviet embassy in Ottawa, defected to Canada, bringing with him documentary evidence of extensive Soviet espionage in the country. As a result of his defection, nine Canadians, including a member of Parliament, Fred Rose, were jailed, and a British nuclear scientist, Alan Nunn May, was exposed as a spy and also jailed.[69]

MI6's Kim Philby recommended that his MI5 counterpart, Roger Hollis, fly to Ottawa to debrief Gouzenko.[70] The interview that followed was a curious affair. Gouzenko later recalled his encounter with Hollis: 'We were standing. We did not even sit down. It was very short. He just listened. He didn't write a word. Maybe he asked me one or two questions.' One of Gouzenko's most startling disclosures was his allegation that an MI5 officer, codenamed 'Elli', was working for the Soviet Red Army's intelligence directorate, the GRU, with such high-level access to intelligence secrets that his reports were sometimes taken directly to Stalin in the Kremlin.[71]

Hollis disregarded this particular part of Gouzenko's testimony and later derided Gouzenko as a source of information.[72] It was seven years later that Gouzenko gave the Canadian authorities a more detailed statement, in which he listed six features of the spy in MI5, 'Elli'.[73] The most cryptic of them all was the statement he had once heard from a Soviet colleague: 'This man has something Russian in his background.'[74] The investigative reporter Chapman Pincher, who for many years argued that Hollis was 'Elli', discovered in 1985 a book published by Hollis's older brother, which referred to the Hollis family's belief that they were descended from the Russian czar, Peter the Great.[75]

Hollis comes under increasing suspicion

By 1963, unmistakable leads were pointing to the existence of a Soviet penetration-agent in the senior ranks of MI5. According to the British intelligence specialist, Nigel West, 16 out of 21 senior MI5 counter-intelligence officers by then were convinced the mole must be either the then Director-General Roger Hollis or his deputy, Graham Mitchell.[76]

The most convincing evidence of MI5's endemic failure was the 'defector drought', as evidenced by the anomalous twenty-four year hiatus between the defection of Soviet aeronautics scientist Grigori Tokaev [Tokaty] in 1947 (discussed in chapter 5 of this book) and that of KGB officer Oleg Lyalin in 1971. West has noted that 'no British intelligence agency received *any* Soviet Bloc defector, whereas many opted for the CIA, a strong indication that potential candidates considered the security environment in England too dangerous because of high-level penetration' (the italics are West's).[77]

Many American intelligence specialists were convinced that MI5 was compromised and dysfunctional. A senior CIA officer stationed in London, Cleveland Cram, declared in 1963: 'Under Hollis, MI5 seems paralysed.'[78] In May 1965, Gordon Gray, a former National Security Adviser under President Eisenhower, and J. Patrick Coyne, a former FBI officer, arrived in Britain to conduct a surreptitious inquiry into the state of Britain's intelligence organisations. They reported very adversely on MI5's record and singled out Hollis for particular criticism.[79]

Roger Hollis – British patriot or Soviet spy?

The public first learned about the allegations against Hollis in early 1981, when Fleet Street investigative journalist Chapman Pincher first aired it in his book, *Their Trade is Treachery*.[80] The appearance of Pincher's book prompted Britain's then Prime Minister Margaret Thatcher to give a statement to the House of Commons, acknowledging that Hollis had indeed been investigated for espionage, but adding:[81]

> … no evidence was found that incriminated him, and the conclusion reached at the end of the investigation was that he had not been an agent of the Russian intelligence service.

Subsequently it was revealed that one of Pincher's main sources for his allegations against Hollis was a disaffected former senior MI5 officer, Peter Wright. A few years later, Wright went public with his own tell-all memoirs, *Spycatcher*, in which he recalled: 'For five years we bugged and burgled our way across London at the State's behest, while pompous bowler-hatter civil servants in Whitehall pretended to look the other way.'[82]

Wright was accused of being motivated by having been denied a decent pension by his former employers. The British government tried, unsuccessfully, to suppress the book's publication in Australia, where Wright was then living, stating that the author had clearly violated Britain's Official Secrets Act. The subsequent 'Spycatcher' trial in Australia made headlines around the world. Acting in Wright's defence was a young barrister, Malcolm Turnbull QC, now a Cabinet minister in the Abbott government, who led the case against the book being suppressed.

Britain's Security Service, MI5, has always maintained Hollis's innocence and has issued an official statements denying he was a Soviet mole:[83]

> It was claimed that Sir Roger Hollis, who was Director General of the Security Service from 1956-1965, was a

Russian spy. The Trend inquiry of 1974 cleared Hollis of that accusation. Subsequently, the evidence of the former KGB officer Oleg Gordievsky confirmed this judgement.

However, in relying on Soviet defector Gordievsky's testimony to clear Hollis's name, MI5 failed to point out that Gordievsky was speaking only about his personal knowledge of the spy service for which he had worked, the KGB. Gordievsky a few years later, in his autobiography, clarified what he had told MI5, and it certainly didn't exonerate Hollis. First, as a KGB officer, he would not have been in a position to know the secrets of the separate spy service, the GRU, which, he said, considered itself 'an organization apart' and was a 'more highly disciplined organization than the KGB'. He admitted he knew precisely nothing about GRU spies in Britain. He said: 'I never had any idea who its contacts were.'[84]

Other people have come to Hollis's defence, such as Professor Anthony Glees, who devoted a large section of his 1987 book, *The Secrets of the Service: A Story of Soviet Subversion of Western Intelligence* (1987), to refuting the allegations against Hollis.[85]

American intelligence professionals, however, have generally been far more sceptical. In a 1988, a British television documentary program hosted a mock trial of the late Sir Roger Hollis, hosted by a retired judge, Bernard Gillis QC. Witnesses for the prosecution included Ray Cline, the CIA's deputy director of intelligence from 1962 to 1966; Robert Lamphere, a former senior FBI officer, who knew both Hollis and Philby; and Charles Bates, who had been FBI station chief in London when Hollis was Director-General of MI5. The American intelligence experts testified unanimously against Hollis.[86]

With the end of the Cold War and the public release over the past decade of previously classified MI5 files, the debate about Hollis has resumed with renewed vigour.

In his 1984 book, *Too Secret Too Long*, the late Chapman Pincher had listed, in a chapter entitled 'The too incredible arm of coincidence', twenty-three serious anomalies in the life and career of Roger Hollis.[87] In the revised and expanded version of his final study of Hollis, *Treachery: Betrayals, Blunders and Cover-Ups: Six Decades of Espionage: The True Story of MI5*, published in 2012, the scroll of anomalies had more than doubled to fifty-six.[88]

Cambridge intelligence historian Christopher Andrew, in his authorised history of MI5, has dismissed Wright, Pincher and other Hollis critics as a 'disruptive minority' responsible for peddling 'intellectually threadbare conspiracy theories'.[89]

However, in December 2011, no less an authority than former senior CIA officer Hayden B. Peake, currently curator of the CIA's Historical Intelligence Collection, pointed out serious omissions in Andrew's authorised history and spoke highly of Pincher's study. He concluded:[90]

> The revised edition of *Treachery* does not resolve the Hollis dilemma, but it does refine the arguments while providing considerable material for counterintelligence scholars. The many questions it raises and the interpretation Pincher provides need to be resolved. This is the stuff of dissertations and should not be ignored.

In April 2015, the Washington-based Institute of World Politics (IWP) hosted a special conference on Roger Hollis, called 'British patriot or Soviet spy? Clarifying a major Cold War mystery'. The keynote speaker was Australia's Dr Paul Monk. Chairing the conference was John L. Wilhelm, a former U.S. Navy intelligence officer, who is currently completing a history of the GRU spy service.[91]

The public interest

It is clear from what we have seen in chapter 15 and 16 that there remain a lot of unanswered questions about the extent of Soviet penetration of ASIO and MI5.

Now, twenty-five years after the end of the Cold War, it is high time that certain previously classified material on secret intelligence should be made available to the public.

In particular, four items discussed in the book deserve to be released immediately:

1) **The 1965 Gray-Coyne inquiry into MI5**

   The U.S. government's Gray-Coyne inquiry of 1965, which reported adversely on the record of Britain's Security Service, MI5, and singled out Hollis for particular criticism, is of particular importance given Hollis' central role in setting up ASIO in 1949.

2) **Vasili Mikrokhin's archive on Australia and New Zealand**

   Former Soviet KGB officer Vasili Mikrokhin's so far suppressed archive on Australia and New Zealand, part of which prompted the Australian Federal Police in late 1992 to launch its probe into ASIO, would also help clear up many mysteries of the Cold War.

   The original intention of Major Mitrokhin, when he risked his life defecting to Britain in 1992, was for the material he brought with him to be published in full. This has not been done. As Mitrokhin reportedly told the British government's Intelligence and Security Committee, 'he wished that he had had full control over the handling of the material'.[92]

   Dr Paul Monk has added: 'The very least that should be done in Australia itself is now to insist on the declassification, without redaction, of the Mitrokhin documents on Australia, going all the way back to the 1930s.'[93]

3) Australian Federal Police's Operation Liver (1992/93)

As we have seen, the Keating Labor government in Australia, under pressure from the British and American security services, ordered an intensive investigation of ASIO in late 1992. The probe, which was carried out by the Australian Federal Police, was codenamed Operation Liver. To date, the results have been suppressed, but deserve to be made public.

4) The 1994 Cook Report

So sensational were the findings of the Operation Liver probe that the Keating government appointed senior intelligence specialist Michael Cook AO, to write a full report on the suspected Soviet penetration of ASIO. The review was completed in 1994, but its contents, like those of Operation Liver, have been suppressed for more than two decades.

Australia – and its British and American allies – should have nothing to fear and much to benefit from a full disclosure of Soviet espionage during the Cold War.

17

LOOKING TO THE FUTURE

National Socialism, Communism and Muslim extremism have all had similar beginnings, which are readily discernible to those who lived through and survived World War II.

We have seen the slow but determined progress by elements of certain countries laying 'foundations', backed by spreading political propaganda.

I saw this in Germany pre-war and well remember the very real anxiety expressed by many Germans. We all know only too well how National Socialism took hold. We also know the terrible war which was unleashed by Hitler and his regime.

Almost immediately after Hitler's defeat, Stalin emerged from the clouds of war victorious, his Red Army controlling half of Europe. He too felt he could show his muscle, though the world was staggered to learn of the horrific police-state oppression administered by the USSR's notorious spy agency, the NKVD, later known as the KGB, mentioned earlier.

Soviet spies were working overtime throughout Europe and beyond. Sinister tactics of using *rezidents* ('residents') proved most useful. The evil nature of communism became abundantly clear with the death toll of Soviet victims amounting to 30 million.

Many followers became ashamed and changed their views. After World War II, some famous disillusioned ex-communists, such as Arthur Koestler, Stephen Spender and Ignazio Silone, contributed essays to a famous book called *The God That Failed*. Other intellectuals, however, persisted with their faith and, strange as it may seem, communism received a new lease of life with the victory of Mao Zedong in China in 1949, of Fidel Castro in Cuba in 1959 and of Hugo Chavez in Venezuela, and a number of other unfortunate countries.

Now we face a new extremist threat – Muslim extremism – the hidden enemy, slowly but surely strengthening its hold in many cities across the civilised world.

The three ideologies listed above display similar danger signs which we cannot afford to overlook – premeditated and deliberate brutality, killing of the innocent, loss of human life on a vast scale, suppression of religious freedom and altogether the frightening prospect of terror, such as the beheadings of those who do not embrace the Muslim ideology and are seen as 'the infidels'.

How can imams and local preachers in the mosques espouse and speak of 'peace' under the circumstances we all fear and live with on a daily basis across the world? The Muslim community in each city and in every mosque must be made aware of the unspeakable barbarity that is being perpetrated both outside their country and, very sadly, recently within this peace-loving, democratic country of Australia which they have made their home.

People must all be protected from this scourge of extremists, not only in the Western democracies, but in countries where Muslim extremism is so evident – Afghanistan, Pakistan, Iraq, Syria, Nigeria and Guyana.

Can we now look forward to a respected ASIO with renewed energy and a confronted past? Such an important organisation on which so much responsibility rests today needs all the trust and respect of every Australian, particularly in our current, serious battles against militant fundamentalist Islamic terrorism.

It was my privilege to meet some outstanding personalities during my 30 years with ASIO. Some became life-long friends. When we meet, we enjoy reminiscing in the knowledge that the Organisation has developed over time along the hard road of trial and error.

May I wish the newly-appointed Director-General and all his staff every blessing and success in the arduous and difficult tasks with which they are confronted every day. They more than deserve all the respect this country can muster.

18

Judging cat shows from Melbourne to Moscow

When we arrived in Canberra in September 1969, our two Siamese cats went into a quarantine station at Abbotsford in Sydney, where they were to remain for three months after our arrival. They would be able to leave by Christmas. By 1970 I had become part of a team of Australian cat show judges, and by 1973 had travelled to every state of Australia judging at shows and meeting cats and their owners. It was a totally different scene from Europe. Across Australia were numerous 'cat fancy' clubs and bodies; but they operated without a unified purpose or discipline, resulting in vastly different standards across the continent of Australia. Each state and territory had different rules.

Gradually, we settled in Canberra where there was no official cat fancy or registration body. Pedigree cats in Canberra were registered in Sydney with the Royal Agricultural Society. There were a number of pedigree cats whose owners combined to form a small cat club. It was hard to believe we were living in a modern society, especially when I saw how expensive pedigree cats were housed and cared for. There was little or no guidance provided for the members of this club, and their meetings, which involved the members having a chat and a cup of coffee, were held spasmodically. It was far from inspiring for a serious cat lover.

After the first year and plenty of judging assignments interstate, I realised the many difficulties Australian breeders experienced. The quarantine laws that existed in those days often prevented the import of new bloodlines to improve the cat breeds. All breeds suffered and it was a rarity to find a truly 'best of show' of any breed. It was clear that much work needed to be done, starting with the study of genetics and pedigrees, an area largely unknown and untapped by most breeders in Australia at that time.

I was often shocked comparing a cat with its pedigree. In some instances, the two did not match. There were plenty of such occasions, which brought me to the horrendous discovery that some breeders were writing their own pedigrees. This, of course, led to grave errors all along the lines: good bloodlines were diluted. But, worst of all, a buyer was often disillusioned after having paid a substantial price for a breeding cat, which then failed to produce a kitten of the expected breed or quality. In every show there were genuine exhibitors, keen and willing to listen. Slowly but surely, more notice was taken of pedigrees, and irregularities were becoming harder to conceal. The larger clubs appointed 'registrars' to register kittens. Later, registration was automated and, as time went by, registrations became more and more reliable, real pedigrees were recognised and clubs were made responsible to their governing bodies.

A complete overhaul, nationwide, was highly desirable at this stage, largely to unify breed standards for the benefit of the true breeds. Any export or import would need to depend on this. The Kennel Club, which had been established for dogs, was a good example; but we had a long way to go to provide a similar facility for cats in Australia.

It always surprised me how advanced the New Zealand Cat Fancy was at that time. My first visit to it in 1971 was a welcome surprise, where both North and South Island cat shows were a pleasure to judge. It was interesting that many of the show winners in Australia had been imported from New Zealand and happily quarantine-free.

By 1972, together with Dr Michael Tait, a New Zealander and breeder of fine Birmans, we managed to assemble delegates from all over Australia at a meeting in Melbourne to endeavour to unify the cat fancy clubs and bodies for the benefit of all cats and fanciers. We had great support from the Royal Agricultural Society of Western Australia (RASWA), which generously supported our establishment and administration of a new Australian National Cat Federation, which later became the Australia Cat Federation (ACF).

In 1973 we introduced Madame Marguerite Ravel, a veteran cat fancy personality from France and founder of the *Fédération Internationale Féline* (FIFe) in Europe in 1949, together with its secretary, Brita Kastengren-Remborg from Sweden, to cat fanciers in Australia.

In 1974 we organised the first ACF international cat show in Canberra. Exhibitors from every state attended, making this the largest show of its kind ever held in Australia, with over 1,000 pedigree cats competing. Twelve FIFe judges from Europe officiated and bestowed the awards. It was an astounding success, but could not survive in Australia.

In 1977 we organised a fact-finding tour of Europe for twenty-five of our accredited ACF judges. They came from every state except News South Wales. Each of our touring judges was generously hosted by European *FIFe* breeders. The tour was intended to bring Australian judges up to date with other countries and their requirements, breeds and standards. Each judge had three assignments to undertake at European shows over a period of six weeks. They were required to base their judgements on *FIFe*-specified unified breed categories, and hence were judging under supervision. In Australia, at that time, each state was using its own standards, and the larger states had up to five different cat bodies with separate standards.

During our European tour, we travelled by rail, sea and bus, working six weekends. At that time, some international FIFe shows in Europe were held in huge venues, often with 1,200 to 1,500 exhibits. Many of the cats with their owners were flown in, not only from most of Europe's member-countries, but also from the United States of America. Such shows were staged in Amsterdam, Vienna, Paris, Lyon, Rome, Florence, Berlin, Wiesbaden, Oslo, Stockholm and Helsinki, among others. I have wonderful memories of two-day shows, usually attended by one or more local dignitaries. Nowadays, shows are essentially much smaller, but no less enjoyable for breeders and visitors.

Our first weekend was to cover a show in London organised by the United Kingdom's Governing Council of the Cat Fancy (GCCF). We were met at London's Heathrow Airport by our son John, at that time a senior captain with the British Overseas Airline Corporation (BOAC). Our welcome included lunch, after which we were taken by bus to our hotel near Marble Arch. Everyone was in high spirits and most opted to visit shops in Oxford Street. We all agreed to meet up again at 7:00 pm for dinner at our hotel, and parted company for four hours.

I remember we had a roll-call at the hotel at the scheduled time of 7:00 pm, only to find one judge absent. We all agreed to await her arrival, until the head waiter informed us that no dinner would be served after 10:00 pm; so we all trooped to our table and started our meal. Around 9:30 I was called to the phone and found myself speaking to the duty officer of the Marlborough police station. He asked me whether I knew a certain Australian woman whom they had arrested for causing a 'disturbance and affray' at Speakers' Corner, a famous free speech zone in London's Hyde Park, where crowds gather to listen to freelance speakers and agitators.

The police officer was concerned for the woman's safety, as the scene was getting very rough and out of hand. I was given to understand that I should come and collect her at the earliest possible opportunity, or else she would be charged and certainly detained overnight. I immediately agreed to come for her. I called a taxi and arrived shortly afterwards to find her waiting in the company of a policewoman who had given her a cup of soup. I kept the taxi waiting while a few official papers were signed.

We headed back to the hotel where she had a cold meal and a lot of questions from our group, which she refused blankly to answer. She certainly looked as though she had been through an unusual experience, and the next day there were some traces of blows around her face. The police certainly had a 'report of arrest' filed.

The policewoman told me what had occurred at Hyde Park Corner. She had advocated not only a republic for Australia, but one for England as well, at which the crowd suddenly erupted in fury, shouting and screaming abuse at her. She immediately shouted and screamed back at them. I listened with fascination as she described in vivid detail the unfolding drama. I don't think that she was aware of what the police had told me about her causing a 'disturbance and affray'. We never spoke about her special evening in London again. I doubt whether she told any of her fellow cat-judges, either. She was slight of build, dark-haired, sharp-featured and of fiery disposition. I certainly tried, with moderate success, to restrain her from quarrelling with others on the tour.

Back in Australia, the advancement we achieved in standards and our membership of the international body were not well received by all those in the cat world in Sydney, where an alternative group was set up under the title of the Cat Council of Australia. Its members were scattered, but some sort of unity was ultimately achieved, though each state still seemed to work as it chose.

In 1979 I disengaged from the ACF and concentrated on judging overseas, having been elected vice-president of FIFe, and subsequently president from 1988 to 1992. FIFe worked for the benefit of 39 member-countries at that time. I served on the International Committee of the Cat Fanciers Association of the USA for many years, and as vice-president of the New Zealand Siamese

Cat Association. During my fifty years as part of the cat fancy world, I held positions on the boards of local clubs; served as a judge, instructor and seminar organiser; ran courses; and managed shows. I am still involved as president of the Eastern Longhair and Semi-Longhair Club, which is affiliated to the UK's Governing Council of the Cat Fancy, and greatly enjoy keeping up with its activities.

While I was working in Canberra, from memory in 1973, there was a spate of 'cat-nabbing'; cats of all breeds were disappearing at an alarming rate from all the suburbs around the capital. Distressed owners were advertising and searching streets and gardens in search of their pets. It soon became a police matter. I received a call from the local RSPCA inspector with a request to assist him in identifying the many cat skins that had been confiscated by the police at the local market. This was not a very pleasant duty for me, but it was necessary. Next day I visited the RSPCA and was horrified to find many skins of family pets much missed and mourned by their owners. It was a most saddening duty to label each skin with a number and identify its breed. There was a large variety of skins from pedigree and domestic pet cats in excellent condition, as well as from obvious strays of lesser quality. There were skins of Rex cats (rare in those days), Abyssinians, Russian Blues, British Blues, Siamese and Long Hairs in various colours. The police launched an investigation into the matter, and organised night patrols to scour the streets in the suburbs.

Then came a further plea from distressed owners: could the police please investigate the inhabitants of the cat-section at the laboratories of the then Canberra Hospital? Schoolboys and young lads had been taking cats there for vivisection purposes and collecting five dollars per cat. It was alleged that these poor creatures had been snatched from gardens and neighbourhoods. The police granted permission for certain members of the public, who had reported the loss of their pets, to visit this lab. At least a dozen cats were thus identified and released from the lab to return to their happy and rightful owners.

Thereafter, the head of the laboratory agreed to refuse permission for any person under the age of eighteen years to deposit a cat. This was a happy outcome for the dozen lucky cats and satisfied owners. The police investigation continued for some time regarding the cat skins sold at the market, but the market vendor was nowhere to be found. The police thought he had gone interstate. Through my involvement with cats around the world, I met the best and the worst, the honest and the corrupt, the good, the bad, the indifferent, and plenty in between. I am happy to have no regrets, as I always put the cat first, with its health and welfare uppermost.

Hungary

I was invited to judge a two-day international cat show, held in April 1986 in Kaposvár, Hungary, then under communist rule. I travelled by train and, during my trip, was shocked at the poverty of the Hungarian population. On arrival, I was met by the president of the country's cat club, apparently a highly-placed official of the Hungarian Communist Party. He informed me there had been a serious nuclear explosion at Chernobyl, in Ukraine, which was not so far away from Hungary. I found a degree of panic in our hotel, which was a luxury holiday resort for senior Communist Party officials. The hotel management soon apologised that they had difficulty obtaining fresh fruit and vegetables uncontaminated by the radioactive fallout from Chernobyl, and we were told not to drink milk or water. There was much fear of contamination in Hungary.

The cat show itself was characterised by lively participation, much colour and flowers. Outside the show, however, abject poverty was clearly in evidence, with both cats and their owners clearly suffering malnutrition.

Despite the communist one-party rule they had been forced to endure since World War II, the Hungarian people refused to be downtrodden. They maintained their zest for life and their great love of their *czardas* music. I was enchanted by my experience of the country and its people during my entire stay.

The morning after the cat show, back at my hotel, I had a meagre breakfast of biscuits and packed Belgian cheese. By extraordinary coincidence, I spotted hanging on the dining-room wall a huge, larger-than-life picture of the then first secretary of the Hungarian embassy in Canberra.

The clean-up operations in the aftermath of the Chernobyl nuclear disaster would eventually involve 500,000 workers at a cost of 18 billion roubles over many years. On my return to London I underwent tests for radioactive contamination, which thankfully showed to be negative.

I returned to Hungary two years later and was once more impressed by the vibrancy, energy and interest displayed at the excellent cat show in progress. And some years later I again visited the beautiful capital city of Budapest, which I had previously visited as a little girl with my mother – and oh how I still enjoyed the *czardas* music.

Soviet Union

It was in October 1988, toward the end of the Cold War, when I received an invitation to judge the first official cat show to be held in communist Russia. The show, which was held in Moscow, was to be the showpiece prior to the official Russian application for membership of the *Fédération Internationale Féline*, an act which demanded a high standard of cats and their management. As president of the federation, I was invited to oversee, judge and report to the FIFe meeting on my findings and ensure a fair vote for endorsement to international membership. There appeared to be great excitement in anticipation of that occasion, and plenty of preparations were in progress. Everything had the official approval of the many government and civil authorities which were in some way connected in the USSR.

For me, things were somewhat more complicated crossing the 'Iron Curtain'. My previous occupation in secret intelligence would once have been a barrier to any travel to Europe's communist Eastern bloc. However, as I was now retired, this restriction no longer applied; so I accepted the invitation and preparations for my journey commenced. In mid-1989 I travelled to Austria and applied for my visa in Vienna. There were long queues at the Russian consulate with an assortment of travellers also seeking visas. At that time I held a San Marino diplomatic passport which I confidently produced to the Russian consulate official who seemed quite senior. Luckily for me, he stamped my passport with a large seal allowing a limited stay. I was rather surprised and relieved to see how easy it all was.

I packed my bag and caught a strange-looking Russian aircraft from Vienna to Moscow. The plane was old, the seating bare, and I was seriously concerned about its airworthiness. We took off and gradually gained height until we were flying at 30,000 feet. This was the first time in my life that I experienced the terror of flying! Never before, during my countless flights worldwide, had I experienced anything like it. Our landing in Moscow was bumpy and poorly executed; but the end result, thankfully, was that we had arrived safely. Very soon, I was walking through a packed lounge, consisting mainly of Japanese who, like me, were scurrying about looking for a currency-exchange booth. No such luck! However, in a very short time, I was accosted by five men offering me Russian roubles. I firmly declined their assistance and swiftly moved on, being aware that theirs was a well-known trick, at the time, to arrest people at the airport.

I soon met the familiar face of a club official I had met at our annual conference and was duly rescued from the crowded airport lounge. My escort accompanied me to the first floor of the Intourist Hotel, where a receptionist seated at a desk beside the elevator dealt with me, registered me and handed me the key to my room. We walked along a lengthy passage. My club official wanted to inspect my room to make sure I would be comfortable. It was clean and simply furnished with a clean bed. Overhead, suspended from the ceiling, was a huge complicated structure in the shape of a chandelier, much too high for me to examine! We said goodbye till next morning, when I was to be collected and escorted to the show hall in central Moscow, a cultural centre not far from the hotel. The club veterinary officer duly collected me in an old car which rattled down the cobble-stoned roads. On arrival we faced an enormous queue of hundreds of people waiting for admittance.

In 1988, Russia had applied for FIFe membership and I was supposed to determine whether the standard of cats, show management and caging of exhibits were up to FIFe standards. This was of course too much to expect to achieve at the first show. Many improvements and adjustments would need to be implemented before FIFe could grant Russia a licence to sponsor an international cat show.

At this Russian cat show, few genuine pedigree cats were on display. I did, however, judge all the exhibits. Awards were given and, with good language interpreters, much advice was passed on to interested and concerned owners at this show. I was amazed, surprised and delighted at the genuine interest and love shown by the proud owners I met that day. Sadly, it took several years for the Russian cat fancy to achieve the required overall standards, but it did catch up with Western European countries, and years later I gave many championships and grand championships awards to Russian exhibits, at cat shows in Moscow, St Petersburg and Samara (known from 1935 to 1991 as Kuybyshev).

On the last day of my stay in Moscow, I was packing my case, intending to write my report on the Russian show and be ready to be collected by a club official to catch my plane back to London that evening. A telephone caller interrupted my plan, inviting me downstairs for a 'tour of Moscow'. I was very surprised, as nobody in the club had mentioned this before. I went down and was met by a very smartly dressed man in a grey uniform. He addressed me in Russian with a big smile, took my arm and led me outside where a large, luxurious car was waiting with a second man at the wheel and an attractive young woman sitting in the back. She smilingly introduced herself as Karina from Intourist.

Little bells started ringing in my head and I was secretly concerned as to where I might be taken. The two men were talking and occasionally addressed Karina. Then she started speaking to me in fluent English. She asked me many personal questions, which I answered with due care. I felt I had better be complimentary about what I was about to see. They took me to some very beautiful churches and cathedrals, where I saw many people in deep prayer. Afterwards, I was taken to a luxurious American(!) restaurant which must have been extremely expensive for my Russian hosts.

The 'co-driver' who had collected me was clearly an official. He hosted the luncheon. Our conversation was measured but friendly. I was unobtrusively asked what my profession was. I was delighted to tell them I was a professional cat-breeder and was so pleased to have met Russian breeders. I doubt whether he believed me, but other questions followed about my family which I answered with caution.

The woman told me, when we visited the toilet, that she wanted to come to Australia, How could she get a visa? I remained quite official and referred her to the Australian embassy; there was no other way. Then she gave me a letter to deliver to an individual in Sydney, supposedly her uncle. I took the letter with great care and eventually delivered it to a certain address, on return to Australia.

After lunch we drove around the Kremlin and the notorious KGB headquarters in Lubyanka Square, in which I showed no overt interest.

The former KGB headquarters and prison at Lubyanka Square, Moscow, in its heyday

It was a dreary-looking place. It sickened me to think of the horrors that took place within its walls.

By 1600 hours I was returned to the hotel. What relief! No cat club member had arranged this tour or encounter, and all I planned to leave behind were my footprints.

19

COFFEE AND CAKE WITH MY INTERROGATOR

Communist East Germany

The infamous Berlin Wall – stark symbol of the postwar division of Europe between the free West and the communist Eastern bloc – was still standing in 1987, when I made an unexpected journey by car from Wiesbaden to West Berlin. This western part of the city was affiliated with, but physically not part of, the Federal Republic of Germany: it was a solitary free city, surrounded on all sides by communist East Germany.

A big international cat show was scheduled to be held there, so I brought with me in the car all the trophies and many files and documents I would need. My journey, however, necessitated my travelling via the dreaded communist-controlled East Zone Corridor that connected West Germany and West Berlin. This was fraught with risk as East Germany's secret police, the Stasi, were known to be both officious and brutal. I had high hopes that my diplomatic passport might give me a smooth passage, but the scene I encountered at the control post was quite different.

At least a dozen armed soldiers, some with fierce-looking Alsatian dogs, surrounded my car which, of course, bore a West German number plate. I presented the guard my diplomatic passport, hoping for a smooth clearance, but was surprised to be asked to alight and hand over my handbag, which the uniformed guard took into the customs shed. While I stood watching and worrying, three guards thoroughly searched the car, opening boxes and examining trophies, while two dogs were ordered to inspect under the car. Thankfully, the guards appeared fascinated rather than suspicious. They asked me questions in very poor English, to which I replied in good German, and a lively conversation on cat shows ensued.

All put together, however, this seriously worried the first guard who had taken my handbag. On his return he took me to see his chief in the office. They had found in my bag my two other passports, one British and the other Australian, which they considered demanded an interview if not an interrogation. This was a moment when I had to steel myself and show no fear. Secretly, I was wondering whether I would ever reach my destination, which was so close yet now seemed so far.

Two armed guards, one on either side of me, marched me into another office, where I felt many others before me had suffered the sort of anguish that was slowly creeping up on me; but I had to appear jovial and confident. This office was quite bare, just a desk, two chairs and one stool which was for me. The boss sat opposite and the armed guards stood behind me. My three passports were brought in by another guard and placed in front of the boss.

So I put on a big smile and spoke my best German and commented on the beautiful weather which greeted me in the Eastern Zone. It had been quite cold travelling. This really surprised the stocky, cheeky official whose intention it was to intimidate me. I went on to tell him of my previous trips to this part of Germany, relating some of my pre-war stays in Wernigerode Castle and climbing the Brocken Mountain. He listening carefully, while I thought to myself how Scheherazade had succeeded in saving her life with her gift for story-telling.

After about half an hour or so, he asked me how and why I possessed three passports. I gave him truthful answers. Then he questioned me on how I spoke such good German, which I obliged by quoting from Goethe and Heine from my German studies. This

The Berlin Wall, a barrier that divided the city from 1961 to 1989. The notice says: 'Caution! You are now leaving West Berlin.'

really impressed him, although I had been secretly hoping it would bore him. He suddenly gave me a big smile and ordered *Kaffee und Kuchen* ('coffee and cake')! I politely said that I did not take caffeine, but he insisted and I partook of the *Kuchen*.

Now, with his change of attitude towards me, I started to entertain other fears. All I wanted to do was to continue my journey! I politely indicated that my German hosts were expecting me, and I had been with customs for three hours already. His reply was thankfully interrupted by another poor traveller who was brought into the premises. I was politely released with a handshake and bidden *Auf Wiedersehen* ('until we see again'); but the latter was not my intention, nor was it in my travel plans.

A year later, I was invited to judge at the international cat show that was held in Leipzig (then still part of communist East Germany), and I accepted.

I travelled by train on the preceding Friday with a number of other passengers, and can vividly recollect a strange sensation provoked by some of them. Most were carrying large parcels and ragged-looking bags. They looked harassed and pale, probably scared and certainly underfed. The train was old, with wooden seats; and, to me, everyone looked suspicious. I was truly afraid to engage in conversation with any of my fellow passengers. Who were they? Would they be arrested between here and my destination? It was better therefore to avoid any contact with the unknown. After all this was a 'Russian train'!

I started reading and sensed an air of disquiet and anxiety in the carriage. Soon after approaching the border between West/East border, the train halted, the door of our carriage opened, and two guards came in, carrying small pistols. They hurried through and out of sight. As the train resumed its journey, an air of relief seemed to fill our carriage; but the underlying atmosphere of fear remained. I was not at all enjoying the trip, and was looking forward to when it would be over.

Dusk was falling and it would soon be dark. The train had few lights, so reading became impossible. I started to wonder how we would all fare at the Stasi control post, which I knew could not be far away. And where were those two guards who had whisked through the train? I tried to suppress any sense of concern, difficult though that increasingly became.

While I was turning things over in my mind, the train halted again, its brakes screeching noisily and with a background of dogs barking and women's loud shouts and screams. I could not figure out what was going on. We all waited in stunned silence. Minutes felt like hours. We had stopped at an almost uninhabited area. There were uniformed officials walking outside along the train. They were obviously searching for one or more passengers. Dogs were dispatched to scrutinise under the stationary carriages, while the officials were now entering from the back of the train and conducting a thorough search.

Suppressed panic was apparent, and passengers appeared worried about their bags and contents. I was dreading the inevitable search, even though I had nothing to hide. There remained, however, the possibility that the East German guards might have in their possession some spurious denunciation of me from some unknown source.

Suddenly, there erupted behind us a great noise and shouting. Our compartment door was flung open, and two men in handcuffs were pushed down the aisle by two guards. One of the prisoners had a bloodied face; the other was screaming, '*Ich bin unschuldig!*' ('I am innocent!'). However, neither of them lingered; there were large black boots waiting to keep them moving.

Four other guards followed, asking for our visas. I was ordered to stand up, and a guard searched my pockets and my handbag, removing my Australian and diplomatic-status passports, the latter holding my stamped visa. He scrutinised both, but did not return them. He asked me to follow him, then took my arm to escort me off the train. Not a pleasant experience when one fears the unknown! This was no doubt the doing of the Stasi, so I tried to be matter-of-fact and ready to answer any questions. I was taken into a bare room with a table and two chairs. I was left there for a while, experiencing a peculiar, pungent smell I could not identify. Was I being slowly poisoned? I had to wait and hope!

My fears on that score were allayed when a fat official entered, sat himself opposite me and prepared to interrogate me. All the signs were there and I had to conform. In very poor English he started by asking me for my full name, address and occupation, etc. Then I smiled and asked him not to struggle in English, as I spoke German. His facial expression changed and he tried to be more conciliatory. He complimented me on my hair and complexion. At this point, other fears came over me. So I tried to be very factual and cooperative in response to his questions.

I stated that I was a professional 'pedigree cat breeder', visiting East Germany to advise pedigree cat-owners on breeding to qualify for international recognition. I thereupon produced the letter inviting me to judge in Leipzig, signed by none other than the mayor of Leipzig himself. This almost ended my interrogation. The official stood up, took my hand and led me into his office, where he introduced me to his staff as a cat-breeder who was visiting Leipzig at the invitation of its mayor.

My two passports, which had been duly copied, were handed back to me in an envelop on which was written in German: 'The diplomatic cat lady'. I was politely escorted by two guards to my seat on the train. The two people who previously had sat opposite me in the coach were missing and did not return before the train rolled off into the dark.

After a while, we passed large blocks of flats, six to eight storeys high with very little light. It was hard to imagine how their residents could find their way around in them. Some time later, the train gradually slowed down and we drew into Leipzig railway station – a very dreary structure with unrepaired bomb-damage from the war still evident everywhere.

I was met by some local official, who was waiting at the platform, together with the president of the local cat club. They welcomed me with a small bunch of flowers, and we proceeded to an old Skoda car with a driver. They took me to my hotel on the city's main square. It was relatively luxurious in the circumstances, but was equally scarred by war and surrounded by houses and buildings similarly ravaged. Poverty was in evidence everywhere.

The international cat show in Leipzig was well organised, despite the hardships endured. Most breeders struggled to feed themselves and of course also their cats – a very sad state of affairs. All the cats were seriously malnourished.

During our lunch break I went outside into the square, which was a heart-breaking scene of human misery. There were numerous stalls run by desperate people, some weeping, who were trying to sell their last belongings to buy food. I was close to tears by what I saw in Leipzig, saddened at so much human and animal suffering.

Leipzig was just one of many, many, ruined and impoverished East German cities. The Stasi secret police were notorious for their brutality and their readiness to carry out grim tasks assigned to them by the Soviet KGB. I was grateful to leave East Germany after witnessing the large-scale suffering in a country, which had flourished before the war, but where Soviet communist police-state rule had brought Leipzig and other parts of East Germany to their knees.

In 1989, the Berlin Wall fell and communist East Germany was reunited with the Federal Republic of Germany. In 1993, I returned to Leipzig.

In comparison to a West Berlin cat show I had recently judged, the one in Leipzig was disgraceful. It is true that West German cat food companies provided much assistance, such as pet food and veterinary supplies, to cat-owners in the former communist east. Nonetheless, on its own, this could do little to offset the vast differences in living standards between the two parts of the now 'united' Germany. West Germany had promised to rebuild bombed cities, but above all to provide economic assistance to the East; but I saw no evidence of either. Four years after the collapse of the Berlin Wall, Leipzig was a sad reminder of the horror of Russian domination and communist misgovernment — an impoverished, badly damaged city with a disillusioned, unhappy, starving population.

I was so shocked at what I saw that I questioned many of the people I met, only to hear stories of closed factories, widespread unemployment and destitution, all very depressing. East Germany did have a terrible time under communist rule during the Cold War, and it was several years after German reunification that improvements slowly came for those living in the eastern zone.

Poland

Judging at shows in all countries in the former Soviet-controlled Eastern Europe made me realise the constant strain that the populations there lived under. It was often obvious in their guarded manner and behaviour. Some exhibitors would warn me there were 'police in the hall', which I readily believed.

I must admit, I was always on the alert in those countries and careful what I said and did – and always with a certain feeling of suspense. I had no doubt this feeling was shared with the local residents for whom there was little chance of escape. They just had to accept this mode of existence as a fact of life.

I judged in Warsaw on three occasions in the late 1980s and in the '90s. I always left base with coffee beans, cigarettes, bottles of whisky and tinned meats. There was much hardship in this country and silent poverty everywhere. Poland's cat fancy consisted of true cat-lovers, who succeeded in putting on a good show with well cared-for exhibits.

I much admired the tenacity of the Polish people, which shone through despite the many instances of hardship I witnessed. The shows I judged in Warsaw were always packed with visitors, with long queues of people waiting to catch a glimpse of the cats on exhibition. I remember the country always to be cold with snow and freezing winds. I understand that the cat fancy improved and grew with the years as did the hard-working nation which had suffered so much during the war.

I shall forever remember a very sad-looking old Polish woman coming up to me holding a basket covered in blue ribbons and lined with blue silk, containing a five-month-old male Blue Point Siamese. I had already judged and classified him – a dear little chap and alone in his class. After all the judging had been completed, this elderly lady came over to me weeping and with tears running down her cheeks telling me that her pet was the 'best kitten in the show'.

Sadly, this was not the case, as the award went to another kitten. Her disappointment was heart-rending and her tears kept coming, so she begged me to look at him again – perhaps I could change my mind! I had to explain how impossible that was once a decision had been made in a show. This was an unusual case of real grief. So, without breaking any rules, I came up with on the spot a prize that had not been listed in the programme catalogue: 'Best Blue Point Siamese Kitten'. Without letting her know, I quickly removed a ribbon from my bag and headed to the office of the secretariat (where all the prizes were sorted) and spoke to the show manager, who gladly added the award, certificate and ribbon to be given to the Polish woman's much-beloved kitten. Oh, the joy and tears that followed were well worth my trip to Poland!

(I was told later that this lady had been widowed and recently lost her only son).

Latvia and Estonia

These two attractive Baltic nations were, by their size and location, in some ways beholden to their mighty neighbour, Russia, and indeed were forcibly incorporated into the Soviet Union from World War II until 1991. Under Moscow's rule, these countries were more or less powerless politically and unable to make their own laws. I visited there much later, in 1996, a few years after the countries had finally achieved their independence.

Finland

This country had a thriving cat fancy, where I judged frequently over many years.

After World War II, Finland became essentially a junior trading partner with, and semi-satellite state of, the Soviet Union. Finnish scientists were working on scientific discoveries in the '80s, and I saw many Russian soldiers on recreation leave visiting Helsinki by the bus load. Despite everything, the Finns managed to do fairly well out of this liaison, and are now quite independent and thriving. They were charming people and excellent cat-breeders, who held superb cat shows.

Conclusion

I dealt with disciplinary matters connected with the international cat fancy and its many problems relating to national rules and regulations, show procedures, protocols, health and breeding, management and administration. Most importantly, however, I made life-long, wonderful friends whose friendship I still treasure.

The only unpleasant and most serious contingency I encountered and had to deal with was when I took over the presidency of FIFe in 1988. I experienced uneasy behaviour from the treasurer who had held the office since 1982. After scrutiny, it was established that there had been a very substantial unauthorised diversion of funds from the organisation's account. FIFe was incorporated in Switzerland, and I, together with FIFe's legal officer, took action to correct the situation, which involved the police, the Swiss and Austrian judiciaries and the bank. This investigation lasted for two years, resulting in the resignation of the treasurer and a rumpus at the second annual general assembly, which I closed prematurely with the support of the legal officer, because of illegal interferences from some members. After the meeting, I resigned from FIFe. My task was completed with the appointment of a new treasurer.

After fifty years of judging cats worldwide, I am now happily retired and look back with pride and gratitude at having handled, judged and awarded prizes to the world's finest feline exhibits. It has been a wonderful hobby for a true cat lover. Cats captured my heart many years ago, as did dogs, especially spaniels. Cats are clever and, if well treated and loved, will give their owner comfort, friendship, loyalty and trust. Each cat has its own unique personality and character. For me, cats are the perfect pet – gentle, sensitive, loving, always clean, graceful, stylish, fastidious and decorative. The ideal is to have a dog and a cat who get on well together in the family home.

20

THE MOST ANCIENT REPUBLIC OF SAN MARINO

Situated twelve miles inland from Rimini on the Adriatic coast, and often referred to as 'the Jewel in Italy's Crown', this beautiful old land can be traced back to the fourth century AD, when Marino, a stone-cutter from Arbe in Dalmatia, fled his land to escape the persecution of Christians by the Roman emperor Diocletian. He became a hermit and a holy man and founded a small community later named San Marino.

This historical peculiarity of San Marino is found in its ancient institutions, unique in the world, today. Its head of state is a dual one: it consists of two Captains Regent (*Capitani Reggenti*). The first pair were appointed in 1243, and this institution is still in force today. The Captains Regent remain in office for six months with equal powers. They are inaugurated every six months on April 1 and October 1, a strict protocol which has never changed over the centuries.

In 1861, Abraham Lincoln showed his friendship for San Marino by writing to the Captains Regent, 'Though your country is small, nevertheless it is one of the most honoured throughout history.' San Marino has a great tradition of hospitality, which was extended to Garibaldi and his men and later to the refugees who sheltered there during the World War II.

Queen Victoria visited San Marino during her reign and became a friend and admirer of the Republic and its people. A large portrait

The Republic of San Marino

of her still occupies a place of honour on a wall in the Government Palace in the capital.

The republic's capital, also called San Marino, is situated on Mount Titano, some 750 metres above sea level and is surrounded by nine muncipalities known as *castelli*. Three fortresses erected on the summit can be seen from many miles around. The Government Palace on Liberation Square is the traditional location of all government ceremonies and is one of the numerous beautiful old historical buildings, which also include the ancient church of St Francis dating back to the fourteenth century.

San Marino has sustained 1,830 years of independence, freedom and history. This is the oldest created republic, nestling in the heart of Italy. Over centuries, popes, potentates and even the French emperor Napoleon showed respect for the liberty of this country, which is today a fully-fledged member of the United Nations Organisation and the Council of Europe, as well as most other major organisations in which it strives to defend human rights and peace. It has also been declared a World Heritage Site.

During World War II, San Marino was accidentally bombed by an RAF plane, killing many people and demolishing some very old buildings. In 1946, the British Air Ministry expressed its profound regrets, providing a compensatory cheque. This was conveyed to San Marino by a special RAF delegation headed by a British army lieutenant-colonel and a Treasury official.

San Marino was severely impoverished during the war years. Heavy fighting took place all across Italy. But by being neutral, San Marino was able to offer a safe haven to many people fleeing the carnage. With its small population of approximately 26,000 inhabitants of its own, the Republic nonetheless managed to look after and house over 100,000 refugees.

After my retirement from ASIO in February 1983, I left Australia on a six-month assignment to the cat world in Europe in my capacity as vice-president of the *Fédération Internationale Féline* (FIFe), with its 39 member-countries. Based in the FIFe headquarters in Wiesbaden, Germany, I started by assisting the president and travelling each week on judging assignments all round Europe. I found this a wonderful change of occupation and loved every moment of it. I had dreaded the thought of retirement from ASIO, but this new career allowed me to throw off many shackles and work hard to overcome the many problems facing the cat fancy at that time. It also involved travelling to the United States and Canada and organising seminars and veterinary conferences. On the death of the president in 1988, I was elected to take over this position, so my return to Australia was delayed.

In the meantime, I had communication with friends in San Marino, and in 1984 was asked by its Foreign Minister to represent the Republic as its Consul-General in Australia, a task I accepted with enthusiasm. The exequatur came through early in 1985 and the consulate was opened on February 15 of that year. I was thrilled and delighted to have this new responsibility and to represent and promote this beautiful country in Australia. I enjoyed official visits to Queensland,

Captain Regent Enzo Columbini, right, commissioning the author as Honorary Consul in a ceremony held in San Marino's government palace (February 1985)

South Australia and Tasmania, meeting up with the Sammarinese who had settled there so happily and was able to assist them in different ways over the years, when needed. I also think that I contributed to bringing San Marino closer to the attention of the Australian public. Owing to official age regulations, I had to retire in 2010, but with many happy memories and many friends acquired over 25 years.

During my period as Consul-General, the Republic of San Marino signed a treaty with Australia establishing the extradition of individuals to face legal proceedings in either country, if requested. I recall a late-night visitor arriving at my front door at 2:30 am seeking 'asylum' in San Marino. He was agitated and fearful of being arrested and requested to be offered sanctuary. By this time he had his leg across the threshold preventing me from closing the door on him. I had little choice and allowed him in and agreed to listen to his story. He was adamant that he wanted to leave urgently for San Marino at the earliest opportunity. I explained the meaning of our recently promulgated treaty, which would not allow him to escape arrest in Australia or San Marino. Eventually, by 4:00 am, I was able to take him in my car to a relative of his. I notified the police of our encounter. He was known to them.

The consulate handled enquiries on many matters, including wills, weddings, the transfer of estates, and visits of both an official and personal nature. It was involved in the negotiations between the Bayside City Council, south-east of Melbourne, and the Republic's Tourism Ministry to establish a 'sister-city' relationship. That led to the participation of a famous Sammarinese chef in the Bayside Food and Wine Festival on two occasions. It also prompted the organisation of a week-long goodwill visit to San Marino by a group of twenty Bayside residents, which was an outstanding success. As I write, however, this 'sister-city' relationship is somewhat dormant.

On a lighter note, I recall a most embarrassing incident, which I experienced at a Government House function in Melbourne. It was an official Italian garden party where the *Banda Italiana* was assigned to supply the music on the day. I was a patron of this orchestra and had been invited to sit next to Victoria's then state governor, Sir James Augustine Gobbo. It was a beautiful, sunny afternoon, attended by a huge number of Australians with Italian connections. Towards the end of the function, words of thanks and appreciation were expressed to the official visitors and in this context I was presented with a huge bouquet of flowers, which I left my seat to receive. On my return to it, while carrying this beautiful floral arrangement, I caught my foot in the many wires connecting the audio system of the celebration, which were dangerously littering the ground. I flew up in the air only to land on Sir James's lap! I was, of course, mortified and tried to scramble to my feet with the assistance of the governor. Thankfully, this attracted good-natured laughter, including from Sir James and his wife.

21

Destiny turns up trumps again

After the death of my husband Robert in 1996, I experienced a great emptiness in my heart and life. We had been married for 49 years. The last twelve years involved my caring for Robert who had became increasingly unwell and immobile. The final two years were tragic and particularly difficult for him as a man who had previously enjoyed an energetic, active life. After a Service funeral with full RAF honours, he was cremated and his ashes interred in the family grave in the UK.

Being widowed created a very different lifestyle for me. I decided to offer my spare time and efforts to the Royal Air Force Association, which I had joined back in the UK in 1946. The Melbourne branch was urgently looking for a 'welfare officer' and, though I had no specific training for such a post, my services were gratefully accepted. My predecessor in the job, also an ex-RAF officer, had been forced to resign the previous year owing to poor health.

I found many members in great need of a visit and advice in areas affecting their well-being and entitlements. It discovered how few people, especially after bereavement, knew how to organise their affairs. Plenty of work was waiting to be done in all areas of Victoria, including assistance at funerals and on happier occasions. My involvement lasted four years. Regretfully, I had to resign as I was due to travel to the UK. My life was about to change completely. It all felt quite unreal.

Albert, with whom Robert and I had shared a house in Holland in the 1950s, with his lovely family, had since travelled the world with the Shell Company. His duties had taken him to South America, Indonesia, Nigeria, South Africa and other countries, from where he regularly kept in touch with us by mail. In 1977, he retired from his full-time employment with Shell but continued working as a consultant from his family residence in Carshalton Beeches in Surrey, southern England.

My frequent visits from Australia to Europe, mostly with Robert, provided many opportunities to make contact and keep the long friendship alive over time. In 1984 Robert suffered a stroke from which he was only slowly able to partly recover. We managed to organise a trip to the UK and Europe, during which I successfully completed my four-year assignment as president of FIFe (1988-1992), including in cat-judging, before returning to Melbourne in 1993. Slowly Robert's health deteriorated further, and he died in 1996. Albert's wife, Kay, who had suffered from diabetes and various serious complications, passed away in 1998. This was a sad blow to that close and loving family.

At the end of 1999, Albert visited his son, David, and his family who had lived in Australia since 1981, having transferred from South Africa where he had started his mining engineering career. David kindly included me in several family gatherings. Albert, ever the charmer, invited me out for walks, lunches and dinners, and we shared many happy memories of our earlier lives with family and friends. This situation lasted for some three months when he took his two elder grandsons with him on a tour of New Zealand. I learnt from the grandsons that they felt their grandfather 'had something on his mind' and was, at times, pensive and absent-minded.

We were all quite busy at the time, having recovered from the trauma of the predicted chaos of the 'Y2K' millennium bug that would supposedly disrupt computers worldwide with the introduction of the ciphers 2000 to the date. Fortunately, the feared breakdown never eventuated.

Then came Valentine's Day 2000. Albert dropped in for coffee, looking very serious. He took a seat on the sofa and said he had a statement to make. I was somewhat puzzled. Then followed a protracted telephone call from a friend seeking my help and advice on some matter. This went on for half an hour, during which the meeting paused and Albert twiddled his thumbs. The phone call finally came to an end, allowing Albert to continue, and, very romantically, propose marriage. I was totally dumbfounded.

Then a great happiness set in, a wonderful feeling embraced us both, with a new life opening up for us. We decided to announce our engagement by e-mailing all members of both our families. We were very happily surprised at the level of enthusiasm expressed in the replies we received. Albert brought me great happiness and peace. He was and is such joy to be with. Suddenly, there was so much to do, share and enjoy together. So we happily started planning the new century with our wedding and the years to come.

Albert's family home in Carshalton Beeches awaited our arrival in England, where we would plan our wedding date to enable most of the family to attend. I had left my house in Melbourne in the hands of friends from Brisbane, and joined Albert who had flown to London a few weeks earlier. We were to have a spring wedding to inaugurate the new millennium. All guests were advised of the date, and a wedding luncheon at the Lensbury Club, in Teddington, south-west London, was arranged to follow a wedding ceremony at Sutton. We invited fifty guests: family and close friends only. Our church wedding followed on return to Melbourne.

It was a joyous day. My nephew Gordon and his wife Kathy gave us a great surprise by collecting and delivering us to the registry in Sutton, and afterwards to Lensbury, in his 1923 Rolls Royce. What a treat! It was good to have almost all the family, many of whom had travelled from far distant parts of the world, there together. Kind and lovely words were spoken, particularly by Henry, Albert's younger brother. He expressed his happiness at our union, noting that his mother would have been particularly delighted. I had met their mother many times, first at family gatherings at Scheveningen and later in her retirement flat in Brussels. I had often visited there during my many duty visits, back in the days of my work in The Hague, to the Australian embassy in Brussels.

Since that happy day, now over 15 years ago, we have enjoyed so many wonderful things together. With our main residence in London, we have travelled the world, each year spending one half, the local summer and autumn, in London and Europe, and the other half in Melbourne in our respective homes. In both cities we acquired new residences. The one in Melbourne was purchased on a sudden urge, at a house auction that we happened to be present at. It is situated in Hampton, close to the road that follows the eastern shore of Port Phillip Bay. To symbolise the joy it generated, the house was christened with the name of Shangri-La after the legendary kingdom of that name, made famous by British novelist James Hilton in his 1933 novel, *Lost Horizon*. In the UK we sold Albert's family home that needed modernisation and, after a disappointing experience, we found and acquired a cosy apartment on the River Thames at Teddington.

While in Europe I am always struck with the deterioration of the European summers compared with my recollection of what they were like when I lived there half a century before. But we thoroughly enjoy all the activities that are still much in evidence and maintain contact with the very many relatives and friends we have in Western Europe, and en route, in North America. My duties and visits to San Marino are now much reduced from the annual attendance that was previously required. But we still visit there in memory of old times.

The joy of travelling has always intrigued us, and we are so fortunate that we both enjoy doing so many things together, particularly seeing new places and sharing time with our mutual friends of many years' standing.

My husband Albert is an extraordinary, interesting and witty individual, always friendly and polite, kind, ever helpful and patient and with the rare gift of being able to repair a great many gadgets that break down in the home. I happily award him full marks towards 'husband of the year'! He turned my life around, bringing a new perspective into daily living. We enjoy life, despite getting older, and we understand and avoid what we cannot do, occupying ourselves with useful and pleasant pastimes.

We have travelled, and greatly enjoyed, the many cruises we have taken, including to some of the Pacific Islands, New Zealand, Alaska, the Far East, China and Japan, and around Britain, and look forward to many more to come. We have taken advantage of the fact that our daughter's husband has served as Canada's Ambassador and High Commissioner to many countries. This has allowed us to visit places such as Romania, Pakistan, Malaysia and parts of Africa.

However, the place that takes the prize is Kenya, where we spent several unforgettable weeks on safari, two years running, acquainting ourselves with this intriguing country, its people and its wonderful wildlife. We witnessed, unfortunately, much poverty, but took heart at many signs of improvements.

I was particularly touched by my four visits to Dame Daphne Sheldrick's elephant orphanage and nursery outside Nairobi, where I 'adopted' two orphaned baby elephants, Kaipuki and Sities, aged two and four months respectively. This refuge has done much to alleviate the intense suffering of baby elephants, left behind by the death of their mother at the hands of wicked poachers hunting for ivory. These poor traumatised and grief-stricken babies are left to wander and cannot fend for themselves. Milk-dependent for three years and motherless, they stray and become targets for hungry predators such as lions, hyenas and cheetahs.

The Sheldrick nursery will rescue any lost baby elephant found or reported in any area. An aircraft is sent to the location, and a team consisting of a veterinary surgeon and keepers will collect the baby who will then be given both veterinary and loving care to assist recovery and help rehabilitation. Sadly, some do not survive, but most do respond to the loving treatment they receive. They are soon able to communicate and mix with the older elephants who come in from the wild and who will eventually accept these youngsters once they are old and strong enough to join a herd. It is a remarkable method of rescuing young elephants who are so sensitive and to whom it is all-important to be part of a herd. They are highly intelligent animals, and 'family life' is truly part of their existence.

At the close of this book I must recollect some memories from my last overseas trip, which started in Western America. The breathtaking and unforgettable train journey across the Canadian Rockies from Vancouver, and a brief exploration of the Rockies around Banff and Lake Louise, must surely count among some of the most unforgettable experiences on earth. We stayed at the Fairmont Chateau Lake Louise, a huge comfortable hotel with every luxury available. We had a lovely room overlooking the lake, gardens and a majestic snow-capped mountain as a backdrop, with its reflection in the waters of the lake. This surely equalled paradise. An atmosphere of peace, beauty and tranquillity was everywhere.

Our next stop was Toronto, where Albert caught up with his old university pal and close friend, Sidney, as well as his family. This turned out to be most timely as Sid passed away a few months later. Our stay in Toronto was followed by a visit to Smiths Falls, a country town near Ottawa. Smiths Falls is where my stepson Christopher and his family have been living since his retirement from the Canadian Civil Aviation Authority where he had served as a pilot and senior captain for over thirty years. We spent happy times reminiscing.

As one grows older, so does one grow in appreciation of family and good friends, of kindness and concern, all having been shown and shared so readily and generously. Also one continues to appreciate

The author with her beloved Albert

the intense beauty of nature: the wonders of animal and bird life, the flowers and trees. Yes, and the soul-stirring power of beautiful music, all of which surrounds us so richly. How great is life before us, every day!

Albert and I are now both over ninety and each day is precious to us, but so are the many memories of happy times in a full life lived in many places.

NOTES AND REFERENCES

Introduction
1. David Horner, *The Spy Catchers: The Official History of ASIO, 1949-1963* (Sydney: Allen & Unwin, 2014).

Chapter 1: Growing up between the wars
1. First recorded in Anna Eliza Bray, *Traditions, Legends, Superstitions and Sketches of Devonshire*, 3 vols (London: John Murray, 1838), Vol. II, pp. 287-288, and collected by James Orchard Halliwell in the mid-nineteenth century.
2. *Front Line 1940-41: The Official Story of the Civil Defence of Britain* (London: HMSO 1942).

Chapter 5: On assignment for British secret intelligence
1. Roy Rutter, "Russia's mystery space man is working for us", *The People* (UK), January 25, 1959.
2. Robert Conquest, *The Nation Killers: The Soviet Deportation of Nationalities* (London: Macmillan, 1970).
3. Nigel West, *A Matter of Trust: MI5 1945-72* (London: Hodder & Stoughton, 1983), p.41.
4. Grigori A. Tokaev, *Stalin Means War* (London: Weidenfeld & Nicolson, 1951).
— *The Betrayal of an Ideal* (London: Harvill Press, 1954).
— *Comrade X* (London: Harvill Press, 1956).

Chapter 6: Britain rocked by treachery of the Cambridge spies
1. Christopher Andrew, *The Defence of the Realm: The Authorized History of MI5* (London: Penguin Books, updated 2010), p. 420.
2. Christopher Andrew and Vasili Mitrokhin, *The Mitrokhin Archive I: The KGB in Europe and the West* (London: Allen Lane The Penguin Press, 1999), p. 73.
3. Richard C.S. Trahair and Robert L. Miller, *Encyclopedia of Cold War Espionage, Spies, and Secret Operations* (New York: Enigma Books, 3rd revised edition, 2012), pp. 107-108.

4. Andrew, *The Defence of the Realm*, p. 173.
5. Christopher Andrew and Oleg Gordievsky, *KGB: The Inside Story of its Foreign Operations from Lenin to Gorbachev* (London: Hodder & Stoughton, 1990), pp. 159-161.
6. Philby, quoted in Andrew, *The Defence of the Realm*, p. 171.
7. Andrew, *The Defence of the Realm*, p. 180.
8. Andrew and Gordievsky, *op. cit.*, p. 155.
9. Andrew and Mitrokhin, *op. cit.*, p. 76.
10. Ibid., p. 76.
    Ben Macintyre, *A Spy Among Friends: Kim Philby and the Great Betrayal* (London: Bloomsbury, 2014), pp. 37-38.
11. Andrew and Mitrokhin, *op. cit.*, p. 76.
    Andrew, *The Defence of the Realm*, p. 169.
12. Andrew, *The Defence of the Realm*, p. 169.
13. Deutsch, quoted in Andrew, *The Defence of the Realm*, p. 171.
14. Kim Philby, *My Secret War: The Autobiography of a Spy* (London: MacGibbon & Kee, 1968), p. xix, quoted in Robert Cecil, "The Cambridge Comintern", in Christopher Andrew and David Dilks (eds), *The Missing Dimension: Governments and Intelligence Communities in the Twentieth Century* (London: Macmillan, 1984), p. 172.
15. Andrew, *The Defence of the Realm*, p. 172.
16. Ibid., p. 169.
17. Andrew and Mitrokhin, *op. cit.*, p. 76.
    Andrew, *The Defence of the* Realm, p. 169.
18. Trahair and Miller, *op. cit.*, p. 418.
19. Cecil, "The Cambridge Comintern", *op. cit.*, p. 179.
20. Ben Macintyre, *A Spy Among Friends: Kim Philby and the Great Betrayal* (London: Bloomsbury, 2014), p. 90.
21. Bruce Page, David Leitch and Phillip Knightley, *Philby: The Spy Who Betrayed a Generation* (London: André Deutsch, 1968), p. 139.
22. Macintyre, *op. cit.*, p. 29.
23. Ibid., p. 29.
24. Ibid., p. 18.

25. Ibid., p. 102.
26. Trahair and Miller, *op. cit.*, p. 418.
    Andrew, *The Defence of the Realm*, p. 422.
27. Robert J. Lamphere and Tom Shachtman, *The FBI-KGB War: A Special Agent's Story* [1986] (Macon, Georgia: Mercer University Press, revised edition, 1995), p. 246.
28. Lamphere and Shachtman, *op. cit.*, p. 238.
    Andrew and Gordievsky, *op. cit.*, pp. 321-322.
    Yuri Modin, *My Five Cambridge Friends: Burgess, Maclean, Philby, Blunt and Cairncross by their KGB Controller*, English trans. (New York: Farrar Straus Giroux, 1994), pp. 186-187.
    Macintyre, *op. cit.*, pp. 115-116, 123-125, 127-129, 135-137.
29. Modin, *op. cit.*, pp. 186-187.
30. Andrew and Gordievsky, *op. cit.*, p. 321.
31. Macintyre, *op. cit.*, p. 137.
32. Ibid., pp. 77-78, 83, 86-87.
33. Andrew and Gordievsky, *op. cit.*, p. 167.
34. Robert Cecil, *A Divided Life: A Personal Portrait of the Spy Donald Maclean* (London: The Bodley Head, 1988), p. 30.
35. Cecil, *A Divided Life*, p. 26.
36. Andrew and Gordievsky, *op. cit.*, p. 169.
37. Andrew and Mitrokhin, *op. cit.*, p. 79.
38. Trahair and Miller, *op. cit.*, p. 302.
39. Cecil, *A Divided Life*, p. 42.
40. Andrew and Gordievsky, *op. cit.*, p. 170.
41. Page, Leitch and Knightley, *op. cit.*, pp. 33, 81, 83, 99.
    Trahair and Miller, *op. cit.*, pp. 302-303.
42. Modin, *op. cit.*, p. 101.
43. Andrew and Gordievsky, *op. cit.*, pp. 260-261.
    Trahair and Miller, *op. cit.*, p. 303.
44. Cecil, *A Divided Life*, p. 74.

45. Ibid., p. 74.
46. Hugh Trevor-Roper, *The Wartime Journals*, edited by Richard Davenport-Hines (London: I.B. Taurus, new paperback edition, 2015), p. 90, footnote 31.
47. Cecil, *A Divided Life*, pp. 102-104.
48. Andrew and Gordievsky, *op. cit.*, p. 325.
    Trahair and Miller, *op. cit.*, p. 304.
49. Andrew, *The Defence of the Realm*, p. 422.
50. Robert Cecil, *The Times* (London), January 2, 1981, quoted in Andrew and Gordievsky, *op. cit.*, p. 325.
51. Andrew and Mitrokhin, *op. cit.*, p. 79.
52. Andrew and Gordievsky, *op. cit.*, p. 161.
53. Page, Leitch and Knightley, *op. cit.*, p. 70.
    Andrew and Gordievsky, *op. cit.*, p. 170.
54. Anthony Blunt, quoted in Peter Wright, with Paul Greengrass, *Spycatcher: The Candid Autobiography of a Senior Intelligence Officer* (Melbourne: William Heinemann Australia, 1988), pp. 242-243.
55. Trahair and Miller, *op. cit.*, p. 61.
56. Ibid., p. 61.
57. Quoted in Andrew and Gordievsky, *op. cit.*, p. 323.
58. Andrew and Gordievsky, *op. cit.*, p. 324.
59. Page, Leitch and Knightley, *op. cit.*, pp. 75-76, 213.
60. Andrew and Gordievsky, *op. cit.*, p. 324.
61. Trahair and Miller, *op. cit.*, p. 61.
62. Lamphere and Shachtman, *op. cit.*, p. 230.
63. Andrew, *The Defence of the Realm*, p. 424.
64. David Martin, *The Web of Disinformation: Churchill's Yugoslav Blunder* (San Diego: Harcourt Brace Jovanovich, 1990), pp. 3-4.
65. Andrew and Gordievsky, *op. cit.*, p. 167.
66. Andrew and Mitrokhin, *op. cit.*, p. 82.
67. Martin, *op. cit.*, pp. 1, 4.
68. Quoted in Martin, *op. cit.*, p. 7.

69. Martin, *op. cit.*, p. xix.
70. Peter Batty, *Hoodwinking Churchill: Tito's Great Confidence Trick* (London: Shepheard-Walwyn, 2011), pp. 158-159.
71. Batty, *op. cit.*, pp. ix, 167.
72. Max Hastings, *Winston's War: Churchill, 1940-1945* (New York: Alfred A. Knopf, 2010), pp. 377, 379.
73. Ibid., p. 378.
    Batty, *op. cit.*, pp. 178-179.
74. Martin, *op. cit.*, pp. 23-24, 252, 256.
75. Ibid., p. 89, 227-228. See particularly chapters 15 and 28.
76. Quoted in Hastings, *op. cit.*, p. 379.
77. Martin, *op. cit.*, pp. 272-273.
    Batty, *op. cit.*, pp. 257, 346.
78. Martin, *op. cit.*, p. 27.
79. Batty, *op. cit.*, p. 252.
80. Martin, *op. cit.*, p. 274.
    Batty, *op. cit.*, p. 264.
81. Martin, *op. cit.*, pp. 239-240.
    Batty, *op. cit.*, p. 64.
82. Batty, *op. cit.*, p. 252.
83. Quoted in Martin, *op. cit.*, p. 6.
84. Andrew and Mitrokhin, *op. cit.*, p. 464.
85. Andrew, *The Defence of the Realm*, p. 404.
86. Andrew and Gordievsky, *op. cit.*, pp. 164-165.
87. Trahair and Miller, *op. cit.*, p. 50.
88. Andrew, *The Defence of the Realm*, p. 268.
89. Andrew and Mitrokhin, *op. cit.*, pp. 83-84.
90. Andrew and Gordievsky, *op. cit.*, p. 242.
91. Andrew, *The Defence of the Realm*, pp. 269-270.
92. Quoted in Andrew, *The Defence of the Realm*, p. 270.
93. Andrew and Gordievskly, *op. cit.*, pp. 243-244.

94. Modin, *op. cit.*, p. 163.
95. Cecil, "The Cambridge Comintern", *op. cit.*, p. 178.
96. Andrew and Gordievsky, *op. cit.*, p. 244.
    Modin, *op. cit.*, p. 92.
97. Andrew and Mitrokhin, *op. cit.*, p. 167.
98. Andrew, *The Defence of the Realm*, pp. 289-292.
99. Trahair and Miller, *op. cit.*, p. 51.
100. Miriam L. Wharton, *The Development of Security Intelligence in New Zealand, 1945-1957*, a thesis presented in partial fulfilment of the requirements for the degree of Master of Defence Studies (Manawatu, New Zealand: Massey University, 2012), p. 49.
     URL: http://mro.massey.ac.nz/bitstream/handle/10179/4251/02_whole.pdf?sequence=1
101. Ian McGibbon, "Desmond Patrick Costello: 1912-1964", *Dictionary of New Zealand Biography*, Vol. 5, 2000, reproduced in *Te Ara Encyclopedia of New Zealand*.
     URL: www.teara.govt.nz/en/biographies/5c37/costello-desmond-patrick
102. Andrew and Mitrokhin, *op. cit.*, p. 864, note 73.
103. Ibid., p. 534.
104. Andrew and Gordievsky, *op. cit.*, pp. 366-367.
105. Andrew, *The Defence of the Realm*, p.438.
106. Andrew and Mitrokhin, *op. cit.*, pp. 84–85.
107. Stephen Roskill, *Hankey: Man of Secrets*, 3 vols (London: Collins, 1970-74).
108. Modin, *op. cit.*, p. 109.
109. Ibid., p. 109.
110. Andrew and Gordievsky, *op. cit.*, pp. 247-248.
111. Quoted in Ronald Lewin, *Ultra Goes to War: The Secret Story* [1978] (London: Grafton Books, 1988), p. 183.
112. Tom Bower, "Obituary: John Cairncross", *The Independent* (UK), October 10, 1995.
     URL: www.independent.co.uk/news/people/obituaries-john-cairncross-1576877.html
113. Nigel West and Oleg Tsarev, *The Crown Jewels: The British Secrets at the Heart of the KGB Archives* (HarperCollins / Yale University Press, 1999), p. 134.

114. Andrew and Gordievsky, *op. cit.*, p. 175.
West and Tsarev, *op. cit.*, p. 134.
115. Trahair and Miller, *op. cit.*, pp. 267-270.
116. Ibid., p. 19.
117. Andrew, *The Defence of the Realm*, pp. 265-267, 341.
118. Trahair and Miller, *op. cit.*, p. 269.
119. Andrew and Mitrokhin, *op. cit.*, p. 167.
Batty, *op. cit.*, p. 89.
M. Stanton Evans and Herbert Romerstein, *Stalin's Secret Agents: The Subversion of Roosevelt's Government* (New York: Threshold Editions, 2013), pp. 161-162.
120. Andrew, *The Defence of the Realm*, pp. 342-343.
Trahair and Miller, *op. cit.*, pp. 518-520.
121. Andrew, *The Defence of the Realm*, pp. 375, 420, 423-426.
122. Ibid., pp. 430-431.
123. Ibid., pp. 435-436.
124. Ibid., pp. 436-437.
125. Lord Clifford of Chudleigh, "Subversive and extremist elements", *House of Lords: Hansard*, Vol. 357, February 26, 1975.
URL: http://hansard.millbanksystems.com/lords/1975/feb/26/subversive-and-extremist-elements
Martin, *op. cit.*, p. 4.
126. Martin, *op. cit.*
127. Batty, *op. cit.*
128. Chapman Pincher, *Their Trade is Treachery* (London: Sidgwick & Jackson, 1981), pp. 126-131, 187.
129. *House of Commons: Hansard*, November 9, 1981, col. 40, quoted in Chapman Pincher, *Too Secret Too Long: The Great Betrayal of Britain's Crucial Secrets and the Cover-Up* (London: Sidgwick & Jackson, 1984), pp. 378 and 611 note.
130. Andrew and Gordievsky, *op. cit.*
131. Andrew, *The Defence of the Realm*, pp. 489-491, 537-538.

Roger Hermiston, *The Greatest Traitor: The Secret Lives of George Blake* (London: Aurum Press, 2014).

Tom Parfitt and Justin Huggler, "Revealed: Grim fate of the MI6 agents betrayed by George Blake", *The Telegraph* (UK), March 14, 2015. URL: www.telegraph.co.uk/news/worldnews/europe/russia/11472573/Revealed-Grim-fate-of-the-MI6-agents-betrayed-by-George-Blake.html

132. Hermiston, *op. cit.*, p. 159
133. Hermiston, *op. cit.*, pp. 155-158.
134. Andrew, *The Defence of the Realm*, p. 490.
135. Hermiston, *op. cit.*, pp. 295, 305-311.

Chapter 7: Air photographic intelligence during the Cold War

1. Taylor Downing, *Spies in the Sky: The Secret Battle for Aerial Intelligence During World War II* (London: Abacus, 2012), pp. 9-10.
2. Ibid., pp. 86 and 130.
3. Ibid., pp. 88-89.
4. Ibid., p. 229.
5. Ibid., pp. 302-303, 346.
6. Christine Halsall, *Women of Intelligence: Winning the Second World War with Air Photos* (Stroud, Gloucestershire, UK: The History Press, 2012), p. 179.
7. Downing, *op. cit.*, p. 290.
8. Ibid., pp. 292, 299-300.
9. Ibid., pp. 299-300.
10. Ibid., p. 285
11. Constance Babington Smith, *Evidence in Camera: The Story of Photographic Intelligence in World War II* (London: Chatto & Windus, 1958), pp. 208, 221-223.
    Downing, *op. cit.*, pp. 286, 290, 294-295.
12. Downing, *op. cit.*, p. 295.
13. Babington Smith, *op. cit.*, p. 225.
    Downing, *op. cit.*, pp. 288-289.
14. Downing, *op. cit.*, pp. 344-345.

Kevin Wright and Peter Jefferies, *Looking Down the Corridors: Allied Aerial Espionage over East Germany and Berlin 1945-1990* (Stroud, Gloucestershire, UK: The History Press, 2015).

Chapter 8: Working with Dutch counter-espionage

1. Peter Wright, with Paul Greengrass, *Spycatcher: The Candid Autobiography of a Senior Intelligence Officer* (Melbourne: William Heinemann Australia, 1988), pp. 325-330.

Chapter 10: A special invitation from an eminent Australian

1. *Report of the Australian Royal Commission on Espionage* ["Petrov Royal Commission"] (Sydney, NSW: Government Printer), published August 22, 1955.
2. David Horner, *The Spy Catchers: The Official History of ASIO, 1949-1963* (Sydney: Allen & Unwin, 2014).
3. "I, Spry: the rise and fall of a master spy", Australian Broadcasting Corporation (ABC) television documentary, broadcast on November 4, 2010.
4. Anthony McAdam, "Why does the ABC treat Charles Spry so shabbily?", *The Spectator* (Australian edition), November 13, 2010.
   URL: www.spectator.co.uk/australia/6457198/part_4/why-does-the-abc-treat-charles-spry-so-shabbily.thtml

   "ABC denigrates former ASIO director-general", *News Weekly* (Australia), November 27, 2010.
   URL: www.newsweekly.com.au/article.php?id=4649

   "How the ABC maligned former ASIO director-general Sir Charles Spry", *National Observer: Australia and World Affairs*, Issue 84, 2011.
   URL: www.nationalobserver.net/2011/84-3-charles-spry-asio-abc.htm
5. Justice Robert Hope, *Royal Commission on Australia's Security and Intelligence Agencies* (Canberra: Australian Commonwealth Government, 1986).

Chapter 12: Heroes, has-beens, bunglers, spies

1. Edward Woodward, *One Brief Interval: A Memoir* (Melbourne: Miegunyah Press, 2005), pp. 156-157.

2. From an unpublished manuscript by a former senior ASIO officer.
3. Larry Pickering, "Kooks and spooks", *The Pickering Post*, August 17, 2014.
   URL: http://pickeringpost.com/story/kooks-and-spooks/3673
4. Justice Robert Hope, *Royal Commission into Intelligence and Security* (Canberra: Australian Commonwealth Government, 1977).
5. David Lague, "The spy who wasn't", *Sydney Morning Herald*, February 18, 1995.
   URL: www.canberraremovalist.com.au/canberra-removalist-articles/1995/2/18/the-spy-who-wasnt/
6. David Horner, *The Spy Catchers: The Official History of ASIO, 1949-1963* (Sydney: Allen & Unwin, 2014), p. 269.
7. Lague, *op. cit.*
   Horner, *op. cit.*, p. 269.
8. Lague, *op. cit.*
9. Cameron Stewart, "The KGB spy who came in from the heat", *The Australian*, November 8, 2014.
   URL: www.theaustralian.com.au/news/features/the-kgb-spy-who-came-in-from-the-heat/story-e6frg6z6-1227116368736
10. Lague, *op. cit.*
11. Discussed at length in edited transcript of interview with Michael Boyle, ASIO first assistant director-general (1991-1993), *Four Corners*, Australian Broadcasting Corporation (ABC) television, November 1, 2004.
    URL: www.abc.net.au/4corners/content/2004/s1231975.htm
12. Lague, *op. cit.*
    Andrew Fowler, "Trust and betrayal", *Four Corners*, Australian Broadcasting Corporation (ABC) television, November 2, 2004.
    URL: www.abc.net.au/4corners/content/2004/s1232663.htm
    Horner, *op. cit.*, p. 269.
13. An edited transcript of an interview with Tanya Smith, George Sadil's sister and a former ASIO employee, *Four Corners*, Australian Broadcasting Corporation (ABC) television, November 1, 2004.
    URL: www.abc.net.au/4corners/content/2004/s1232724.htm
14. Horner, *op. cit.*, pp. 519-520.

Chapter 13: ASIO's national headquarters in Melbourne

1. Christopher Andrew and Vasili Mitrokhin, *The Mitrokhin Archive I: The KGB in Europe and the West* (London: Allen Lane The Penguin Press, 1999), pp. 316-317, 512-513.
2. Job advertisement to recruit intelligence officers for ASIO, in *The Australian*, January 31, 2015.

Chapter 14: Soviet penetration of Australian security: the evidence

1. Speech attributed to Cicero, quoted in Taylor Caldwell, *A Pillar of Iron: A Novel About Cicero and the Rome He Tried to Save* (New York: Doubleday & Company, Inc., 1965), p. 556.
2. Richard C.S. Trahair and Robert L. Miller, *Encyclopedia of Cold War Espionage, Spies, and Secret Operations* (New York: Enigma Books, 3rd revised edition, 2012), pp. 511-513.
3. Richard J. Aldrich, *GCHQ: The Uncensored Story of Britain's Most Secret Intelligence Agency* (London: Harper Press, 2011), p. 86.
4. Desmond Ball and David Horner, *Breaking the Codes: Australia's KGB Network, 1944-1950* (Sydney: Allen & Unwin, 1998), p. 205.
5. Nigel West, *Venona: The Greatest Secret of the Cold War* (London: HarperCollins, 1999), p. 112.
6. Aldrich, *op. cit.* p. 87.
7. Identities of these spies, together with their Soviet codenames, are listed in David Horner, *The Spy Catchers: The Official History of ASIO, 1949-1963* (Sydney: Allen & Unwin, 2014), pp.486-487.
8. Aldrich, *op. cit.* pp. 86-87.
9. David Humphries, "The spy who came in from the cold after his death", *Sydney Morning Herald*, June 26, 2010.
   URL: www.smh.com.au/national/the-spy-who-came-in-from-the-cold-after-his-death-20100625-z9s3.html

   Horner, *op. cit.*, pp. 471-475.
10. Trahair and Miller, *op. cit*, pp. 319-321.
11. Horner, *op. cit.* pp. 55-56, 142.
12. Ibid., p. 413.

13. Trahair and Miller, *op. cit.*, p. 201.
14. Horner, *op. cit.*, pp. 142-144.
15. John McNair, "Visiting the future: Australian (fellow)-travellers in Soviet Russia", *Australian Journal of Politics and History*, Vol. 46, No. 4, December 2000, p. 468, note 30.
16. Andrew A. Campbell, "Dr H.V. Evatt – Part II: the question of loyalty", *National Observer: Australia and World Affairs*, No. 76, March-May 2008, pp. 36-37.
   URL: www.nationalobserver.net/pdf/evatt_part2_natobs76.pdf
17. Horner, *op. cit.*, pp. 491-492.
18. Ibid., pp. 495-496.
19. Phillip Adams interviews John Burton on ABC Radio National's *Late Night Live* programme (Australian Broadcasting Corporation), 2004.
   URL: www.abc.net.au/radionational/programs/latenightlive/john-burton/3415784
20. Geoffrey Bolton, *Paul Hasluck: A Life* (Perth: UWA Publishing, 2014), p. 177.
21. Robert O'Neill, "Coral Bell AO 1923-2012: A balanced, independent, realist-minded scholar of world politics", *The Interpreter* (Lowy Institute, Australia), October 3, 2012.
   URL: www.lowyinterpreter.org/post/2012/10/03/Coral-Bell-AO-1923-2012-a-balanced-independent-realist-minded-scholar-of-world-politics.aspx
22. Desmond Ball, "Soviet spies had protection in very high places", *The Australian*, January 14, 2011.
   URL: www.theaustralian.com.au/news/features/soviet-spies-had-protection-in-very-high-places/story-e6frg6z6-1226243892165
23. Ibid.
24. Ibid.
25. Campbell, *op. cit.*, p.39.
26. Richard Whyment, *Stalin's Spy: Richard Sorge and the Tokyo Espionage Ring* (London: I.B. Taurus, 1996), p. 299.
27. Campbell, *op. cit.*, p. 39.
28. Rob Foot, "The curious case of Dr John Burton: Soviet agent or useful idiot?", *Quadrant*, Vol. 57, No. 11, November 2013, p. 53.

29. Andrew A. Campbell, "Dr H.V. Evatt – Part 1: a question of sanity", *National Observer: Australia and World Affairs*, No. 73, June-August 2007, pp. 25-39.
   URL: www.nationalobserver.net/pdf/evatt_part1_natobs73.pdf
   —, "Dr H.V. Evatt – Part II: the question of loyalty", *National Observer: Australia and World Affairs*, No. 76, March-May 2008, pp. 33-55.
   URL: www.nationalobserver.net/pdf/evatt_part2_natobs76.pdf
30. Campbell, "Dr H.V. Evatt – Part II: the question of loyalty", *op. cit.*, pp. 33-35.
31. Ibid., pp. 35-37.
32. Paul Hasluck, *Diplomatic Witness: Australian Foreign Affairs 1941-1947* (Melbourne: Melbourne University Press, 1980), p. 196, quoted in Campbell, "Dr H.V. Evatt – Part II: the question of loyalty", *op. cit.*, p. 42.
33. Ball and Horner, *op. cit.*, p. 177.
   Campbell, "Dr H.V. Evatt – Part II: the question of loyalty", *op. cit.*, pp. 36, 52.
   Horner, *op. cit.*, pp. 486-497.
34. Campbell, "Dr H.V. Evatt – Part II: the question of loyalty", *op. cit.*, pp. 50-51.
35. Gavan Duffy, *Demons and Democrats: 1950s Labor at the Crossroads* (Melbourne: Freedom Publishing Co., 2002), pp. 81-82.
36. Robert Manne, *The Petrov Affair* [1987] (Melbourne: Text Publishing, revised edition, 2004), pp. 82-83.
37. Ibid., pp. 116-117.
38. Ibid., pp. 110-116.
39. Ibid., pp. 87-88, 95-99, 123-125, 133-135, 177-179, 183-184, 198-199, 225-227.
40. Ibid., pp. 280-281.
41. Bob Carr, "Sleeping with the enemy", *The Spectator* (UK), July 17, 2010.
   URL: www.spectator.co.uk/australia/6163653/sleeping-with-the-enemy/
42. Bill Hayden, *Hayden: An Autobiography* (Sydney: Angus & Robertson, 1996), p. 91.
43. John Ballantyne, "Australia's Dr Jim Cairns and the Soviet KGB", *National*

Observer: Australia and World Affairs, No. 64, March-May 2005, pp.52-63.
URL: www.nationalobserver.net/2005_autumn_109.htm

44. Ibid.

45. Dr J.F. Cairns speech on South Vietnam, *House of Representatives: Hansard* (Commonwealth Parliament, Canberra), April 8, 1975, p. 1248.

46. Hal G.P. Colebatch, "The Whitlam government and the betrayal of the South Vietnamese", *Quadrant*, Vol. 58, No. 6, June 2014.
URL: https://quadrant.org.au/magazine/2014/06/whitlam-government-betrayal-south-vietnamese/

47. John Barron and Anthony Paul, *Murder of a Gentle Land: The Untold Story of Communist Genocide in Cambodia* (New York: Reader's Digest Press, 1977).

    Jean-Louis Margolin, "Cambodia: the country of disconcerting crimes", in Stéphane Courtois (ed.), *The Black Book of Communism: Crimes, Terror, Repression* (Cambridge, Massachusetts: Harvard University Press, 1999), Part IV, Chapter 4.

48. Carr, *op. cit.*

49. "Mitrokhin's KGB archive opens to public", Archives Centre, Churchill College, University of Cambridge, July 7, 2014.
URL: www.chu.cam.ac.uk/news/2014/jul/7/mitrokhins-kgb-archive-opens/

    Philip Dorling, "Agent Albert: MP listed as secret KGB informant in Russian archives", *Sydney Morning Herald*, August 11, 2014.
URL: www.smh.com.au/national/agent-albert-mp-listed-as-secret-kgb-informant-in-russian-archives-20140810-102jtm.html

50. Ibid.

51. Rick Morton, "Influential Labor man and alleged communist Arthur Gietzelt dies", *The Australian*, January 8, 2014.
URL: www.theaustralian.com.au/national-affairs/influential-labor-man-and-alleged-communist/story-fn59niix-1226796868369

52. Jenny Hocking, *Lionel Murphy: A Political Biography* (Cambridge UK: Cambridge University Press, 2000), p. 49.

53. Stephen Loosley, *Machine Rules: A Political Primer* (Melbourne University Press, 2015), quoted in Troy Bramston, "Arthur Gietzelt a communist, ALP man Stephen Loosley claims", *The Australian*, July 18, 2015.

URL: www.theaustralian.com.au/national-affairs/arthur-gietzelt-a-communist-alp-man-stephen-loosley-claims/story-fn59niix-1227446411687

54. Troy Bramston, "Paper trail leaves red prints on Labor's past", *The Australian*, November 13, 2010.
URL: www.theaustralian.com.au/news/features/paper-trail-leaves-red-prints-on-labors-past/story-e6frg6z6-1225952472147

55. Troy Bramston, "Truth about Communist Party infiltrator Arthur Gietzelt still not officially out there", *The Australian*, August 9, 2014.
URL: www.theaustralian.com.au/opinion/columnists/truth-about-communist-party-infiltrator-arthur-gietzelt-still-not-officially-out-there/story-fnbcok0h-1227018460443

56. Arthur Gietzelt, *Nation Review* (Australia), January 11-17, 1974, quoted in James Curran, *Unholy Fury: Whitlam and Nixon at War* (Melbourne University Publishing, 2015), p. 178.

57. Morton, *op. cit.*

58. "Gietzelt, Arthur Thomas", *Australian Honours Roll* (Canberra: Australian Government, 1992).
URL: www.itsanhonour.gov.au/honours/honour_roll/search.cfm?aus_award_id=884414&search_type=simple&showInd=true

59. Carr, *op. cit.*

60. Christian Kerr, "Secret past of Greens senator Lee Rhiannon", *The Australian*, January 28, 2012.
URL: www.theaustralian.com.au/news/features/secret-past-of-greens-senator-lee-rhiannon/story-e6frg6z6-1226255689458

61. Mark Aarons, "Comment: The Greens and fundamentalism", *The Monthly* (Australia), May 2011.
URL: www.themonthly.com.au/issue/2011/may/1307065885/mark-aarons/comment

62. Ibid.

63. Kerr, *op. cit.*

64. Mark Aarons, *The Family File* (Melbourne: Black Inc., 2010), quoted in an opinion piece by an unnamed retired ASIO officer: "Aunty's sneering aside, ASIO effectively kept communists in check", *The Australian*, November 13, 2010.

URL: www.theaustralian.com.au/news/features/auntys-sneering-aside-asio-effectively-kept-communists-in-check/story-e6frg6z6-1225952473981

65. Philip Dorling, "Spies, lies and archives", *Sydney Morning Herald*, April 23, 2011.
URL: www.smh.com.au/national/spies-lies-and-archives-20110422-1drfm.html

66. Philip Dorling, "KGB 'recruited' two politicians as agents", *Sydney Morning Herald*, October 14, 2013.
URL: www.smh.com.au/federal-politics/political-news/kgb-recruited-two-politicians-as-agents-20131013-2vgtp.html

67. Ibid.

68. Ibid.

69. Ibid.

70. David Lague, "The spy who wasn't", *Sydney Morning Herald*, February 18, 1995.
URL: www.canberraremovalist.com.au/canberra-removalist-articles/1995/2/18/the-spy-who-wasnt/

71. Dorling, "KGB 'recruited' two politicians as agents", *op. cit.*

72. Andrew Fowler, "Trust and betrayal", *Four Corners*, Australian Broadcasting Corporation (ABC) television, November 2, 2004.
URL: www.abc.net.au/4corners/content/2004/s1232663.htm

73. George Leggett, *The Cheka: Lenin's Political Police* (Oxford University Press, 1981).

74. Robert Conquest, *Harvest of Sorrow: Soviet Collectivisation and the Terror-Famine* (London : Hutchinson, 1986).

—, *The Great Terror: A Reassessment* (New York: Oxford University Press, 1990).

R.J. Rummel, *Lethal Politics: Soviet Genocide and Mass Murder since 1917* (New Brunswick: Transaction Publishers, 1990).

Stéphane Courtois (ed.), *The Black Book of Communism: Crimes, Terror, Repression* (Cambridge, Massachusetts: Harvard University Press, 1999).

75. Aleksandr Solzhenitsyn, *The Gulag Archipelago* (3 vols), English translation (London: Collins, 1974-1978).

76. "Jaundiced view of ASIO history", *The Australian*, November 5, 2010.

URL: www.theaustralian.com.au/opinion/editorials/jaundiced-view-of-asio-history/story-e6frg71x-1225948014378

77. Cameron Stewart, "ASIO fears its historians will shed too much light on dark past of Soviet infiltration", *The Australian*, December 27, 2014. URL: www.theaustralian.com.au/national-affairs/asio-worried-its-historians-will-shed-too-much-light-on-dark-soviet-past/story-fn59niix-1227167397275

78. Quoted in Christopher Andrew, *The Defence of the Realm: The Authorized History of MI5* (London: Penguin Books, updated 2010), p. 861.

Chapter 15: The last secrets of the Cold War

1. Herbert Butterfield, *History and Human Relations* (London: Collins, 1951), p. 186.
2. Andrew Fowler, "Trust and betrayal", *Four Corners*, Australian Broadcasting Corporation (ABC) television, November 2, 2004.
   URL: www.abc.net.au/4corners/content/2004/s1232663.htm
3. Oleg Kalugin and Fen Montaigne, *SpyMaster: My 32 Years in Intelligence and Espionage Against the West* (London: Smith Gryphon, 1994).
4. Fowler, "Trust and betrayal", *op. cit.*
5. Christopher Andrew and Oleg Gordievsky, *KGB: The Inside Story of its Foreign Operations from Lenin to Gorbachev* (London: Hodder & Stoughton, 1990).
6. Oleg Gordievsky, *Next Stop Execution: The Autobiography of Oleg Gordievsky* (London: Macmillan, 1995), pp. 365-367.
7. Ibid., p. 365.
   "NZ soft spying target for KGB", *New Zealand Herald*, June 30, 2000.
   URL: www.nzherald.co.nz/nz/news/article.cfm?c_id=1&objectid=128345
   See especially: Bernard Moran and Trevor Loudon, "The untold story behind New Zealand's ANZUS breakdown", *National Observer: Australia and World Affairs*, No. 74, March-May 2007, pp. 21-36.
   URL: www.nationalobserver.net/2007_spring_toc.htm
8. Christopher Andrew and Vasili Mitrokhin, *The Mitrokhin Archive I: The KGB in Europe and the West* (London: Allen Lane, 1999), pp. 1, 9-16.
9. "Obituary: Vasili Mitrokhin", *The Telegraph* (UK), February 2, 2004.

URL: www.telegraph.co.uk/news/obituaries/1453209/Vasili-Mitrokhin.html
10. Andrew and Mitrokhin, *The Mitrokhin Archive I*, pp. 1, 9-16.
11. Christopher Andrew and Vasili Mitrokhin, *The Mitrokhin Archive II: The KGB and the World* (London: Allen Lane, 2005), p. xxiii.
12. "Obituary: Vasili Mitrokhin", *op. cit.*
13. Andrew and Mitrokhin, *The Mitrokhin Archive I*, p. 1.
14. Andrew and Mitrokhin, *The Mitrokhin Archive II*, p. xxiv.
15. Christopher Andrew and Vasili Mitrokhin, *The Mitrokhin Archive I: The KGB in Europe and the West* (London: Allen Lane, 1999).

    Christopher Andrew and Vasili Mitrokhin, *The Mitrokhin Archive II: The KGB and the World* (London: Allen Lane, 2005).
16. "Mitrokhin's KGB archive opens to public", Archives Centre, Churchill College, University of Cambridge, July 7, 2014.
    URL: www.chu.cam.ac.uk/news/2014/jul/7/mitrokhins-kgb-archive-opens/
17. Philip Dorling, "Agent Albert: MP listed as secret KGB informant in Russian archives", *Sydney Morning Herald*, August 11, 2014.
    URL: www.smh.com.au/national/agent-albert-mp-listed-as-secret-kgb-informant-in-russian-archives-20140810-102jtm.html
18. Phil Kitchin, "Fresh twist in 40-year-old Cold War spy mystery", *Dominion Post* (Wellington, New Zealand), August 11, 2014.
    URL: www.stuff.co.nz/dominion-post/news/10369208/Fresh-twist-in-40-year-old-Cold-War-spy-mystery

    Alex Fensome, "Sutch spy allegations rocked New Zealand", *Dominion Post*, March 20, 2015.
    URL: www.stuff.co.nz/dominion-post/capital-life/67451537/Sutch-spy-allegations-rocked-New-Zealand
19. Intelligence and Security Committee, *The Mitrokhin Inquiry Report* (London: UK Government), June 2000: *Annex E – Details of Events*, para 3.
20. *Australian Federal Police: The First Thirty Years* (Canberra: The AFP Historical Project, 2009), p. 101.
    URL: www.afp.gov.au/~/media/afp/pdf/a/afp-the-first-thirty-years.pdf
21. Fowler, "Trust and betrayal", *op. cit.*

22. Canberra Observed column, "Spy scandal throws spotlight on intelligence community", *News Weekly* (National Civic Council, Melbourne), June 5, 1999, pp. 8–9.
23. Laurie Oakes, "KGB cover-up spooks security alliance", *The Bulletin* (Sydney), June 15, 1999, p. 58.

Chapter 16: MI5's Roger Hollis and the founding of ASIO

1. David Horner, *The Spy Catchers: The Official History of ASIO, 1949-1963* (Sydney: Allen & Unwin, 2014), chapters 3 and 4.
2. Ibid.,, pp. 56-57.

    Miriam L. Wharton, *The Development of Security Intelligence in New Zealand, 1945-1957*, a thesis presented in partial fulfilment of the requirements for the degree of Master of Defence Studies (Manawatu, New Zealand: Massey University, 2012), p. 19, note 5, and p.127.
    URL: http://mro.massey.ac.nz/bitstream/handle/10179/4251/02_whole.pdf?sequence=1

3. Horner, *op. cit.*, pp. 56-57
4. Christopher Andrew, *The Defence of the Realm: The Authorized History of MI5* (London: Penguin Books, updated 2010), pp. 370, 763.

    Horner, *op. cit.*, p. 96.

5. Horner, *op. cit.*, p. 91.
6. Andrew, *The Defence of the Realm*, p. 370.

    Horner, *op. cit.*, p. 91.

7. Chapman Pincher, *Their Trade is Treachery* (London: Sidgwick & Jackson, 1981).
8. Rt Hon. Margaret Thatcher, *House of Commons: Hansard* (UK), March 26, 1981, quoted in Chapman Pincher, *Too Secret Too Long: The Great Betrayal of Britain's Crucial Secrets and the Cover-Up* (London: Sidgwick & Jackson, 1984), Appendix B, p. 629.
9. Peter Wright, with Paul Greengrass, *Spycatcher: The Candid Autobiography of a Senior Intelligence Officer* (Melbourne: William Heinemann Australia, 1988).
10. Tom Bower, *The Perfect English Spy: Sir Dick White and the Secret War 1935-90* (London: William Heinemann, 1995), p. 54.

Chapman Pincher, *Treachery: Betrayals, Blunders and Cover-Ups: Six Decades of Espionage: The True Story of MI5* [2009] (Edinburgh: Mainstream Publishing, 2nd updated and expanded edition, 2012), p. 38.

11. Pincher, *Treachery*, pp. 35-40.
12. Bower, *op. cit.*, p. 54.

Pincher, *Treachery*, p. 41.

13. Pincher, *Treachery*, pp. 36, 43-44.
14. Pincher, *Too Secret Too Long*, pp. 10, 18, 20-21, 29, 41, 43, 130, 431, 481, 501.

    David P. Hornstein, *Arthur Ewert: A Life for the Comintern* (Lanham, Maryland: University Press of America, 1993), pp. 135-139.

15. Letter from Rewi Alley to Chapman Pincher, quoted in Pincher, *Too Secret Too Long*, pp. 12, 18 and 589: note 15.
16. Hornstein, *op. cit.*, pp. 9, 137.
17. Wright and Greengrass, *op. cit.*, p. 289.

    Hornstein, *op. cit.*, pp. 135-136.

    Pincher, *Treachery*, p. 48.

18. Robert Whyment, *Stalin's Spy: Richard Sorge and the Tokyo Espionage Ring* (London: I.B. Taurus, 1996), pp. 29-32.

    Ruth Price, *The Lives of Agnes Smedley* (New York: Oxford University Press, 2005), pp. 197-201.

19. Einar Sanden, *An Estonian Saga* (London: Boreas Publishing House, 1996), pp. 173-176, 179-182, 184-186, 195-196, 366-367, 371-373.
20. Price, *op. cit.*, p. 231.
21. Sanden, *op. cit.*

    Hollis's alleged affair with Luise Klas and possible recruitment by the GRU is discussed extensively in Pincher, *Treachery*, chapters 82 and 83.

22. Anthony Glees, *The Secrets of the Service: A Story of Soviet Subversion of Western Intelligence* (London: Jonathan Cape, 1987), pp. 384-385.

    Pincher, *Treachery*, pp. 49-50.

23. Pincher, *Treachery*, pp. 50-51.
24. Pincher, *Treachery*, p. 52.
25. Glees, *op. cit.*, p. 370.

    Pincher, *Treachery*, pp. 61-65.

26. Pincher, *Too Secret Too Long*, p. 41.
27. Pincher, *Treachery*, p. 47.
28. Benjamin B. Fischer, "Farewell to Sonia, the spy who haunted Britain", *International Journal of Intelligence and CounterIntelligence* (Washington, DC), Vol. 15, No. 1, January 2002, pp. 67-68.
29. Pincher, *Too Secret Too Long*, p. 57.
    Fischer, *op. cit.*, pp. 68-69.
30. Ruth Werner [pen-name of Ursula Ruth Kuczynski], *Sonya's Report: The Fascinating Autobiography of One of Russia's Most Remarkable Secret Agents* [1977], Renate Simpson trans. (London: Chatto & Windus, 1991), p. 221.
31. Andrew, *The Defence of the* Realm, pp. 231-232.
32. Werner, *op. cit.*, pp. 232-234.
    Pincher, *Too Secret Too Long*, pp. 58 & 60.
33. Pincher, *Too Secret Too Long*, pp. 60-65, including map on page 63.
34. Fischer, *op. cit.*, p. 65.
35. Andrew and Mitrokhin, *The Mitrokhin Archive I*, pp. 151-152, 167-168.
36. Fischer, *op. cit.*, pp. 69-70.
    Richard C.S. Trahair and Robert L. Miller, *Encyclopedia of Cold War Espionage, Spies, and Secret Operations* (New York: Enigma Books, 3rd revised edition, 2012), pp. 148-149.
37. Fischer, *op. cit.*, p. 70.
38. Andrew and Mitrokhin, *The Mitrokhin Archive I*, p.153.
39. Ibid., p. 152.
40. V. Bochkarev and I.A. Kolpakidi, *Superfrau iz GRU* [*Superfrau in the GRU*] (Moscow: Olma Press, 2002), quoted in Pincher, *Treachery*, pp. 15-19, 115, 184-187, 597-598, 650.
41. Andrew and Mitrokhin, *The Mitrokhin Archive I*, p. 152.
    Fischer, *op. cit.*, p. 62.
    Pincher, *Treachery*, p. 592.
42. Pincher, *Treachery*, pp. 15, 597.
43. Fisher, *op. cit.*, p. 63.
44. Pincher, *Treachery*, p. 85.

45. David Burke, *The Lawn Road Flats: Spies, Writers and Artists* (Woodbridge, Suffolk, UK: The Boydell Press, 2014), p. 162.
46. Sir Dick White's entry for Roger Hollis in the *Dictionary of National Biography* (1986), quoted in Glees, *op. cit.*, p. 179.
    Pincher, *Treachery*, pp. 145-147.
47. John C. Curry, *The Security Service 1908-1945: The Official History* [1946] (Kew, Surrey, UK: Public Record Office, 2nd edition 1999), Appendix II: Organisational Charts (April 1943).
48. Pincher, *Treachery*, p. 147.
49. Kim Philby, *My Secret War: The Autobiography of a Spy* (London: MacGibbon & Kee, 1968), p. 125.
50. Robert Cecil, "The Cambridge Comintern", in Christopher Andrew and David Dilks (eds), *The Missing Dimension: Governments and Intelligence Communities in the Twentieth Century* (London: Macmillan, 1984), p. 179.
51. Curry, *op. cit.*, p. 358.
52. Pincher, *Treachery*.
53. Ibid., pp. 140-141.
54. Ibid., pp. 87-88, 309.
55. Ibid., pp. 196-197.
56. Ibid., pp. 307, 343.
57. Bower, *op. cit.*, pp. 93-94.
    Pincher, *Treachery*, pp. 307, 343, 624: note 25.
58. Pincher, *Treachery*, p. 209.
59. Ibid., pp. 231, 315.
60. David Burke, *The Spy Who Came in from the Co-op: Melita Norwood and the Ending of Cold War Espionage* (Woodbridge, Suffolk, UK: The Boydell Press, 2008), p. 153.
61. Fischer, *op. cit.*, p. 73
62. Andrew, *The Defence of the* Realm, pp. 389-391.
63. Burke, *The Spy Who Came in from the Co-op*, pp. 13, 15.
64. Ibid., p. 174.
65. John Earl Haynes, Harvey Klehr and Alexander Vassiliev, *Spies: The Rise and*

Fall of the KGB in America (New Haven, Connecticut: Yale University Press, 2009), pp. 64-68, 94-95, 117, 143.

66. Ben Macintyre, "The spy who started the Cold War", *The Times* (London), June 10, 2009.
URL: www.thetimes.co.uk/tto/news/politics/article2028586.ece

67. Pincher, *Treachery*, pp. 305, 613.

68. Paul Monk, "The strange case of Roger Hollis", *Quadrant* (Australia), Vol. 54, No. 4, April 2010.
URL: http://quadrant.org.au/magazine/2010/04/christopher-andrew-and-the-strange-case-of-roger-hollis/

69. Trahair and Miller, *op. cit.*, p. 167.

70. Pincher, *Treachery*, p. 215.

71. Glees, *op. cit.*, pp. 310-311.

72. Pincher, *Treachery*, pp. 243-244.

73. Pincher, *Too Secret Too Long*, pp. 623-627: Appendix A: Igor Gouzenko's memorandum to the Royal Canadian Mounted Police (RCMP), May 6, 1952.

74. Ibid., p. 625.

75. Christopher Hollis, *Along the Road to Frome* (London: Harrap, 1958), quoted in Chapman Pincher, *Treachery*, p. 30.

76. Nigel West, *Molehunt: The Full Story of the MI5 Spy in MI5* (London: Hodder & Stoughton, 1987), p. 229.

77. Nigel West, "Cold War intelligence defectors", in Loch K. Johnson (ed.), *Handbook of Intelligence Studies* (Oxford: Routledge, 2007), pp. 232-233.

78. Bower, *op. cit.*, p. 331.

79. Bower, *op. cit.*, p. 338.

80. Chapman Pincher, *Their Trade is Treachery* (London: Sidgwick & Jackson, 1981).

81. Rt Hon. Margaret Thatcher, *House of Commons: Hansard* (UK), March 26, 1981, quoted in Chapman Pincher, *Too Secret Too Long* (London: Sidgwick & Jackson, 1984), Appendix B, p. 629.

82. Wright and Greengrass, *op. cit.*, p. 54.

83. UK Government Publication, *MI5: The Security Service* (London: Her

Majesty's Stationery Office [HMSO], 3rd edition, 1998), quoted at: URL: www.mi5.com/security/mi5org/spycatcher.htm

84. Oleg Gordievsky, *Next Stop Execution: The Autobiography of Oleg Gordievsky* (London: Macmillan, 1995), pp. 255-256.

85. Glees, *op. cit.*, chapters 8 and 9.

86. Pincher, *Treachery*, pp. 435-436, 611-612.

87. Pincher, *Too Secret Too* Long, p. 479.

88. Chapman Pincher, *Treachery: Betrayals, Blunders and Cover-Ups: Six Decades of Espionage: The True Story of MI5* [2009] (Edinburgh: Mainstream Publishing, 2nd updated and expanded edition, 2012), pp. 622-628: "Appendix: The scroll of anomalies".

89. Andrew, *The Defence of the* Realm, p. 520.

90. Hayden Peake's review of Chapman Pincher's book, *Treachery* (updated and expanded edition, 2011), in *Studies in Intelligence* (Washington, DC: Center for the Study of Intelligence, CIA), Vol. 55, No. 4, December 2011.
URL: www.cia.gov/library/center-for-the-study-of-intelligence/csi-publications/csi-studies/studies/vol.-55-no.-4/intelligence-officer2019s-bookshelf.html#intelligence-abroad

91. "British patriot or Soviet spy? Clarifying a major Cold War mystery", a presentation analysing whether former MI5 Director-General, Sir Roger Hollis, was or was not a Soviet agent, hosted by the Institute of World Politics (IWP), in Washington, DC, on April 10, 2015.
URL: www.iwp.edu/events/detail/british-patriot-or-soviet-spy-clarifying-a-major-cold-war-mystery

92. Intelligence and Security Committee (UK) report, p.20, quoted in Burke, *The Spy Who Came in from the Co-op*, pp. 165-167.

93. Paul Monk, *op. cit.*

Bibliography

Books

Aarons, Mark. *The Family File* (Melbourne: Black Inc., 2010).

Aldrich, Richard J. *GCHQ: The Uncensored Story of Britain's Most Secret Intelligence Agency* (London: Harper Press, 2011).

Andrew, Christopher, and Dilks, David (eds). *The Missing Dimension: Governments and Intelligence Communities in the Twentieth Century* (London: Macmillan, 1984).

Andrew, Christopher, and Gordievsky, Oleg. *KGB: The Inside Story of its Foreign Operations from Lenin to Gorbachev* (London: Hodder & Stoughton, 1990).

Andrew, Christopher, and Mitrokhin, Vasili. *The Mitrokhin Archive I: The KGB in Europe and the West* (London: Allen Lane The Penguin Press, 1999).

Andrew, Christopher, and Mitrokhin, Vasili. *The Mitrokhin Archive II: The KGB and the World* (London: Allen Lane, 2005).

Andrew, Christopher. *The Defence of the Realm: The Authorized History of MI5* (London: Penguin Books, updated 2010).

Australian Federal Police: The First Thirty Years (Canberra: The AFP Historical Project, 2009). URL: www.afp.gov.au/~/media/afp/pdf/a/afp-the-first-thirty-years.pdf

Australian Government. *Report of the Australian Royal Commission on Espionage* ["Petrov Royal Commission"] (Sydney, NSW: Government Printer), published August 22, 1955.

Babington Smith, Constance. *Evidence in Camera: The Story of Photographic Intelligence in World War II* (London: Chatto & Windus, 1958).

Ball, Desmond, and Horner, David. *Breaking the Codes: Australia's KGB Network, 1944-1950* (Sydney: Allen & Unwin, 1998).

Barron, John, and Paul, Anthony. *Murder of a Gentle Land: The Untold Story of Communist Genocide in Cambodia* (New York: Reader's Digest Press, 1977).

Batty, Peter. *Hoodwinking Churchill: Tito's Great Confidence Trick* (London: Shepheard-Walwyn, 2011).

Bochkarev, V., and Kolpakidi, I.A. *Superfrau iz GRU* [*Superfrau in the GRU*] (Moscow: Olma Press, 2002).

Bolton, Geoffrey. *Paul Hasluck: A Life* (Perth: UWA Publishing, 2014).

Bower, Tom. *The Perfect English Spy: Sir Dick White and the Secret War 1935-90* (London: William Heinemann, 1995).

Bray, Anna Eliza. *Traditions, Legends, Superstitions and Sketches of Devonshire*, 3 vols (London: John Murray, 1838), Vol. II.

Burke, David. *The Spy Who Came in from the Co-op: Melita Norwood and the Ending of Cold War Espionage* (Woodbridge, Suffolk, UK: The Boydell Press, 2008).

Burke, David. *The Lawn Road Flats: Spies, Writers and Artists* (Woodbridge, Suffolk, UK: The Boydell Press, 2014).

Butterfield, Herbert. *History and Human Relations* (London: Collins, 1951).

Caldwell, Taylor. *A Pillar of Iron: A Novel About Cicero and the Rome He Tried to Save* (New York: Doubleday & Company, Inc., 1965).

Cecil, Robert. "The Cambridge Comintern", in Andrew, Christopher, and Dilks, David (eds). *The Missing Dimension: Governments and Intelligence Communities in the Twentieth Century* (London: Macmillan, 1984).

Cecil, Robert. *A Divided Life: A Personal Portrait of the Spy Donald Maclean* (London: The Bodley Head, 1988).

Conquest, Robert. *The Nation Killers: The Soviet Deportation of Nationalities* (London: Macmillan, 1970).

Conquest, Robert. *Harvest of Sorrow: Soviet Collectivisation and the Terror-Famine* (London : Hutchinson, 1986).

Conquest, Robert. *The Great Terror: A Reassessment* (New York: Oxford University Press, 1990).

Courtois, Stéphane (ed.). *The Black Book of Communism: Crimes, Terror, Repression* (Cambridge, Massachusetts: Harvard University Press, 1999).

Curran, James. *Unholy Fury: Whitlam and Nixon at War* (Melbourne University Publishing, 2015).

Curry, John C. *The Security Service 1908-1945: The Official History* [1946] (Kew, Surrey, UK: Public Record Office, 2nd edition 1999).

Downing, Taylor. *Spies in the Sky: The Secret Battle for Aerial Intelligence During World War II* (London: Abacus, 2012).

Duffy, Gavan. *Demons and Democrats: 1950s Labor at the Crossroads* (Melbourne: Freedom Publishing Co., 2002).

Evans, M. Stanton, and Romerstein, Herbert. *Stalin's Secret Agents: The Subversion of Roosevelt's Government* (New York: Threshold Editions, 2013).

Glees, Anthony. *The Secrets of the Service: A Story of Soviet Subversion of Western Intelligence* (London: Jonathan Cape, 1987).

Gordievsky, Oleg. *Next Stop Execution: The Autobiography of Oleg Gordievsky* (London: Macmillan, 1995).

Halsall, Christine. *Women of Intelligence: Winning the Second World War with Air Photos* (Stroud, Gloucestershire, UK: The History Press, 2012).

Hasluck, Paul. *Diplomatic Witness: Australian Foreign Affairs 1941-1947* (Melbourne: Melbourne University Press, 1980).

Hastings, Max. *Winston's War: Churchill, 1940-1945* (New York: Alfred A. Knopf, 2010).

Hayden, Bill. *Hayden: An Autobiography* (Sydney: Angus & Robertson, 1996).

Haynes, John Earl, Klehr, Harvey, and Vassiliev, Alexander. *Spies: The Rise and Fall of the KGB in America* (New Haven, Connecticut: Yale University Press, 2009).

Hermiston, Roger. *The Greatest Traitor: The Secret Lives of George Blake* (London: Aurum Press, 2014).

Hocking, Jenny. *Lionel Murphy: A Political Biography* (Cambridge UK: Cambridge University Press, 2000).

Hollis, Christopher. *Along the Road to Frome* (London: Harrap, 1958).

Hope. Justice Robert. *Royal Commission into Intelligence and Security* (Canberra: Australian Commonwealth Government, 1977).

Hope. Justice Robert. *Royal Commission on Australia's Security and Intelligence Agencies* (Canberra: Australian Commonwealth Government, 1986).

Horner, David. *The Spy Catchers: The Official History of ASIO, 1949-1963* (Sydney: Allen & Unwin, 2014).

Hornstein, David P. *Arthur Ewert: A Life for the Comintern* (Lanham, Maryland: University Press of America, 1993).

Johnson, Loch K. (ed.). *Handbook of Intelligence Studies* (Oxford: Routledge, 2007).

Kalugin, Oleg, and Montaigne, Fen. *SpyMaster: My 32 Years in Intelligence and Espionage Against the West* (London: Smith Gryphon, 1994).

Lamphere, Robert J., and Shachtman, Tom. *The FBI-KGB War: A Special Agent's Story* [1986] (Macon, Georgia: Mercer University Press, revised edition, 1995).

Leggett, George. *The Cheka: Lenin's Political Police* (Oxford University Press, 1981).

Lewin, Ronald. *Ultra Goes to War: The Secret Story* [1978] (London: Grafton Books, 1988).

Loosley, Stephen. *Machine Rules: A Political Primer* (Melbourne University Press, 2015).

Macintyre, Ben. *A Spy Among Friends: Kim Philby and the Great Betrayal* (London: Bloomsbury, 2014).

McGibbon, Ian. "Desmond Patrick Costello: 1912-1964", *Dictionary of New Zealand Biography*, Vol. 5, 2000, reproduced in *Te Ara Encyclopedia of New Zealand*. URL: www.teara.govt.nz/en/biographies/5c37/costello-desmond-patrick

Manne, Robert. *The Petrov Affair* [1987] (Melbourne: Text Publishing, revised edition, 2004).

Margolin, Jean-Louis. "Cambodia: the country of disconcerting crimes", in Stéphane Courtois (ed.). *The Black Book of Communism: Crimes, Terror, Repression* (Cambridge, Massachusetts: Harvard University Press, 1999), Part IV, Chapter 4.

Martin, David. *The Web of Disinformation: Churchill's Yugoslav Blunder* (San Diego: Harcourt Brace Jovanovich, 1990).

Modin, Yuri. *My Five Cambridge Friends: Burgess, Maclean, Philby, Blunt and Cairncross by their KGB Controller*, English trans. (New York: Farrar Straus Giroux, 1994).

Page, Bruce, Leitch, David, and Knightley, Phillip. *Philby: The Spy Who Betrayed a Generation* (London: André Deutsch, 1968).

Philby, Kim. *My Secret War: The Autobiography of a Spy* (London: MacGibbon & Kee, 1968).

Pincher, Chapman. *Their Trade is Treachery* (London: Sidgwick & Jackson, 1981).

Pincher, Chapman. *Too Secret Too Long: The Great Betrayal of Britain's Crucial Secrets and the Cover-Up* (London: Sidgwick & Jackson, 1984).

Pincher, Chapman. *Treachery: Betrayals, Blunders and Cover-Ups: Six Decades of Espionage: The True Story of MI5* [2009] (Edinburgh: Mainstream Publishing, 2nd updated and expanded edition, 2012).

Price, Ruth. *The Lives of Agnes Smedley* (New York: Oxford University Press, 2005).

Roskill, Stephen. *Hankey: Man of Secrets*, 3 vols (London: Collins, 1970-74).

Rummel, R.J. *Lethal Politics: Soviet Genocide and Mass Murder since 1917* (New Brunswick: Transaction Publishers, 1990).

Sanden, Einar. *An Estonian Saga* (London: Boreas Publishing House, 1996).

Solzhenitsyn, Aleksandr. *The Gulag Archipelago* (3 vols), English translation (London: Collins, 1974-1978).

Tokaev, Grigori A. *Stalin Means War* (London: Weidenfeld & Nicolson, 1951).

Tokaev, Grigori A. *The Betrayal of an Ideal* (London: Harvill Press, 1954).

Tokaev, Grigori A. *Comrade X* (London: Harvill Press, 1956).

Trahair, Richard C.S., and Miller, Robert L. *Encyclopedia of Cold War Espionage, Spies, and Secret Operations* (New York: Enigma Books, 3rd revised edition, 2012).

Trevor-Roper, Hugh. *The Wartime Journals*, edited by Richard Davenport-Hines (London: I.B. Taurus, new paperback edition, 2015).

Werner, Ruth [pen-name of Ursula Ruth Kuczynski]. *Sonya's Report: The Fascinating Autobiography of One of Russia's Most Remarkable Secret Agents* [1977], Renate Simpson trans. (London: Chatto & Windus, 1991).

West, Nigel. *A Matter of Trust: MI5 1945-72* (London: Hodder & Stoughton, 1983).

West, Nigel. *Molehunt: The Full Story of the MI5 Spy in MI5* (London: Hodder & Stoughton, 1987).

West, Nigel. *Venona: The Greatest Secret of the Cold War* (London: HarperCollins, 1999).

West, Nigel. "Cold War intelligence defectors", in Loch K. Johnson (ed.), *Handbook of Intelligence Studies* (Oxford: Routledge, 2007).

West, Nigel, and Tsarev, Oleg. *The Crown Jewels: The British Secrets at the Heart of the KGB Archives* (HarperCollins / Yale University Press, 1999).

Wharton, Miriam L. *The Development of Security Intelligence in New Zealand, 1945-1957*, a thesis presented in partial fulfilment of the requirements for the degree of Master of Defence Studies (Manawatu, New Zealand: Massey University, 2012). URL: http://mro.massey.ac.nz/bitstream/handle/10179/4251/02_whole.pdf?sequence=1

Whyment, Richard. *Stalin's Spy: Richard Sorge and the Tokyo Espionage Ring* (London: I.B. Taurus, 1996).

Woodward, Edward. *One Brief Interval: A Memoir* (Melbourne: Miegunyah Press, 2005).

Wright, Kevin, and Jefferies, Peter. *Looking Down the Corridors: Allied Aerial Espionage over East Germany and Berlin 1945-1990* (Stroud, Gloucestershire, UK: The History Press, 2015).

Wright, Peter, with Greengrass, Paul. *Spycatcher: The Candid Autobiography of a Senior Intelligence Officer* (Melbourne: William Heinemann Australia, 1988).

UK Government. *Front Line 1940-41: The Official Story of the Civil Defence of Britain* (London: HMSO 1942).

UK Government. *MI5: The Security Service* (London: Her Majesty's Stationery Office [HMSO], 3rd edition, 1998).

UK Government. Intelligence and Security Committee, *The Mitrokhin Inquiry Report* (London: UK Government), June 2000.

Articles and speeches

Aarons, Mark. "Comment: The Greens and fundamentalism", *The Monthly* (Australia), May 2011. URL: www.themonthly.com.au/issue/2011/may/1307065885/mark-aarons/comment

Ball, Desmond. "Soviet spies had protection in very high places", *The Australian*, January 14, 2011. URL: www.theaustralian.com.au/news/features/soviet-spies-had-protection-in-very-high-places/story-e6frg6z6-1226243892165

Ballantyne, John. "Australia's Dr Jim Cairns and the Soviet KGB", *National Observer: Australia and World Affairs*, No. 64, March-May 2005, pp.52-63. URL: www.nationalobserver.net/2005_autumn_109.htm

Bower, Tom. "Obituary: John Cairncross", *The Independent* (UK), October 10, 1995. URL: www.independent.co.uk/news/people/obituaries-john-cairncross-1576877.html

Bramston, Troy. "Paper trail leaves red prints on Labor's past", *The Australian*, November 13, 2010. URL: www.theaustralian.com.au/news/features/paper-trail-leaves-red-prints-on-labors-past/story-e6frg6z6-1225952472147

Bramston, Troy. "Truth about Communist Party infiltrator Arthur Gietzelt still not officially out there", *The Australian*, August 9, 2014. URL: www.

theaustralian.com.au/opinion/columnists/truth-about-communist-party-infiltrator-arthur-gietzelt-still-not-officially-out-there/story-fnbcok0h-1227018460443

Bramston, Troy. "Arthur Gietzelt a communist, ALP man Stephen Loosley claims", *The Australian*, July 18, 2015. URL: www.theaustralian.com.au/national-affairs/arthur-gietzelt-a-communist-alp-man-stephen-loosley-claims/story-fn59niix-1227446411687

Cairns, Dr J.F. Speech on South Vietnam, *House of Representatives: Hansard* (Commonwealth Parliament, Canberra), April 8, 1975.

Campbell, Andrew A. "Dr H.V. Evatt – Part 1: a question of sanity", *National Observer: Australia and World Affairs*, No. 73, June-August 2007, pp. 25-39. URL: www.nationalobserver.net/pdf/evatt_part1_natobs73.pdf

Campbell, Andrew A. "Dr H.V. Evatt – Part II: the question of loyalty", *National Observer: Australia and World Affairs*, No. 76, March-May 2008, pp. 33-55. URL: www.nationalobserver.net/pdf/evatt_part2_natobs76.pdf

Canberra Observed column. "Spy scandal throws spotlight on intelligence community", *News Weekly* (National Civic Council, Melbourne), June 5, 1999, pp. 8–9.

Carr, Bob. "Sleeping with the enemy", *The Spectator* (UK), July 17, 2010. URL: www.spectator.co.uk/australia/6163653/sleeping-with-the-enemy/

Clifford of Chudleigh, Lord. "Subversive and extremist elements", *House of Lords: Hansard*, Vol. 357, February 26, 1975. URL: http://hansard.millbanksystems.com/lords/1975/feb/26/subversive-and-extremist-elements

Colebatch, Hal G.P. "The Whitlam government and the betrayal of the South Vietnamese", *Quadrant*, Vol. 58, No. 6, June 2014. URL: https://quadrant.org.au/magazine/2014/06/whitlam-government-betrayal-south-vietnamese/

Dorling, Philip. "Spies, lies and archives", *Sydney Morning Herald*, April 23, 2011. URL: www.smh.com.au/national/spies-lies-and-archives-20110422-1drfm.html

Dorling, Philip. "KGB 'recruited' two politicians as agents", *Sydney Morning Herald*, October 14, 2013. URL: www.smh.com.au/federal-politics/political-news/kgb-recruited-two-politicians-as-agents-20131013-2vgtp.html

Dorling, Philip. "Agent Albert: MP listed as secret KGB informant in Russian archives", *Sydney Morning Herald*, August 11, 2014. URL: www.smh.com.

au/national/agent-albert-mp-listed-as-secret-kgb-informant-in-russian-archives-20140810-102jtm.html

Fensome, Alex. "Sutch spy allegations rocked New Zealand", *Dominion Post*, March 20, 2015. URL: www.stuff.co.nz/dominion-post/capital-life/67451537/Sutch-spy-allegations-rocked-New-Zealand

Fischer, Benjamin B. "Farewell to Sonia, the spy who haunted Britain", *International Journal of Intelligence and CounterIntelligence* (Washington, DC), Vol. 15, No. 1, January 2002.

Foot, Rob. "The curious case of Dr John Burton: Soviet agent or useful idiot?", *Quadrant*, Vol. 57, No. 11, November 2013.

Fowler, Andrew. "Trust and betrayal", *Four Corners*, Australian Broadcasting Corporation (ABC) television, November 2, 2004. URL: www.abc.net.au/4corners/content/2004/s1232663.htm

Humphries, David. "The spy who came in from the cold after his death", *Sydney Morning Herald*, June 26, 2010. URL: www.smh.com.au/national/the-spy-who-came-in-from-the-cold-after-his-death-20100625-z9s3.html

Kerr, Christian. "Secret past of Greens senator Lee Rhiannon", *The Australian*, January 28, 2012. URL: www.theaustralian.com.au/news/features/secret-past-of-greens-senator-lee-rhiannon/story-e6frg6z6-1226255689458

Kitchin, Phil. "Fresh twist in 40-year-old Cold War spy mystery", *Dominion Post* (Wellington, New Zealand), August 11, 2014. URL: www.stuff.co.nz/dominion-post/news/10369208/Fresh-twist-in-40-year-old-Cold-War-spy-mystery

Lague, David. "The spy who wasn't", *Sydney Morning Herald*, February 18, 1995. URL: www.canberraremovalist.com.au/canberra-removalist-articles/1995/2/18/the-spy-who-wasnt/

Macintyre, Ben. "The spy who started the Cold War", *The Times* (London), June 10, 2009. URL: www.thetimes.co.uk/tto/news/politics/article2028586.ece

McAdam, Anthony. "Why does the ABC treat Charles Spry so shabbily?", *The Spectator* (Australian edition), November 13, 2010. URL: www.spectator.co.uk/australia/6457198/part_4/why-does-the-abc-treat-charles-spry-so-shabbily.thtml

McNair, John. "Visiting the future: Australian (fellow)-travellers in Soviet Russia", *Australian Journal of Politics and History*, Vol. 46, No. 4, December 2000.

Monk, Paul. "The strange case of Roger Hollis", *Quadrant* (Australia), Vol. 54, No. 4, April 2010. URL: http://quadrant.org.au/magazine/2010/04/christopher-andrew-and-the-strange-case-of-roger-hollis/

Monk, Paul, *et alia*."British patriot or Soviet spy? Clarifying a major Cold War mystery", a presentation analysing whether former MI5 Director-General, Sir Roger Hollis, was or was not a Soviet agent, hosted by the Institute of World Politics (IWP), in Washington, DC, on April 10, 2015. URL: www.iwp.edu/events/detail/british-patriot-or-soviet-spy-clarifying-a-major-cold-war-mystery

Moran, Bernard, and Loudon, Trevor. "The untold story behind New Zealand's ANZUS breakdown", *National Observer: Australia and World Affairs*, No. 74, March-May 2007, pp. 21-36. URL: www.nationalobserver.net/2007_spring_toc.htm

Morton, Rick. "Influential Labor man and alleged communist Arthur Gietzelt dies", *The Australian*, January 8, 2014. URL: www.theaustralian.com.au/national-affairs/influential-labor-man-and-alleged-communist/story-fn59niix-1226796868369

Oakes, Laurie. "KGB cover-up spooks security alliance", *The Bulletin* (Sydney), June 15, 1999, p. 58.

O'Neill, Robert. "Coral Bell AO 1923-2012: A balanced, independent, realist-minded scholar of world politics", *The Interpreter* (Lowy Institute, Australia), October 3, 2012. URL: www.lowyinterpreter.org/post/2012/10/03/Coral-Bell-AO-1923-2012-a-balanced-independent-realist-minded-scholar-of-world-politics.aspx

Parfitt, Tom, and Huggler, Justin. "Revealed: Grim fate of the MI6 agents betrayed by George Blake", *The Telegraph* (UK), March 14, 2015. URL: www.telegraph.co.uk/news/worldnews/europe/russia/11472573/Revealed-Grim-fate-of-the-MI6-agents-betrayed-by-George-Blake.html

Peake, Hayden. Review of Chapman Pincher's book, *Treachery* (updated and expanded edition, 2011), in *Studies in Intelligence* (Washington, DC: Center for the Study of Intelligence, CIA), Vol. 55, No. 4, December 2011. URL: www.cia.gov/library/center-for-the-study-of-intelligence/csi-publications/csi-studies/studies/vol.-55-no.-4/intelligence-officer2019s-bookshelf.html#intelligence-abroad

Pickering, Larry. "Kooks and spooks", *The Pickering Post*, August 17, 2014. URL: http://pickeringpost.com/story/kooks-and-spooks/3673

Rutter, Roy. "Russia's mystery space man is working for us", *The People* (UK), January 25, 1959.

Stewart, Cameron. "The KGB spy who came in from the heat", *The Australian*, November 8, 2014. URL: www.theaustralian.com.au/news/features/the-kgb-spy-who-came-in-from-the-heat/story-e6frg6z6-1227116368736

Stewart, Cameron. "ASIO fears its historians will shed too much light on dark past of Soviet infiltration", *The Australian*, December 27, 2014. URL: www.theaustralian.com.au/national-affairs/asio-worried-its-historians-will-shed-too-much-light-on-dark-soviet-past/story-fn59niix-1227167397275

Unnamed retired ASIO officer. "Aunty's sneering aside, ASIO effectively kept communists in check", *The Australian*, November 13, 2010. URL: www.theaustralian.com.au/news/features/auntys-sneering-aside-asio-effectively-kept-communists-in-check/story-e6frg6z6-1225952473981

"ABC denigrates former ASIO director-general", *News Weekly* (Australia), November 27, 2010. URL: www.newsweekly.com.au/article.php?id=4649

"Gietzelt, Arthur Thomas", *Australian Honours Roll* (Canberra: Australian Government, 1992). URL: www.itsanhonour.gov.au/honours/honour_roll/search.cfm?aus_award_id=884414&search_type=simple&showInd=true

"How the ABC maligned former ASIO director-general Sir Charles Spry", *National Observer: Australia and World Affairs*, Issue 84, 2011. URL: www.nationalobserver.net/2011/84-3-charles-spry-asio-abc.htm

"Jaundiced view of ASIO history", *The Australian*, November 5, 2010. URL: www.theaustralian.com.au/opinion/editorials/jaundiced-view-of-asio-history/story-e6frg71x-1225948014378

Job advertisement to recruit intelligence officers for ASIO, in *The Australian*, January 31, 2015.

"Mitrokhin's KGB archive opens to public", Archives Centre, Churchill College, University of Cambridge, July 7, 2014. URL: www.chu.cam.ac.uk/news/2014/jul/7/mitrokhins-kgb-archive-opens/

"NZ soft spying target for KGB", *New Zealand Herald*, June 30, 2000. URL: www.nzherald.co.nz/nz/news/article.cfm?c_id=1&objectid=128345

"Obituary: Vasili Mitrokhin", *The Telegraph* (UK), February 2, 2004. URL: www.telegraph.co.uk/news/obituaries/1453209/Vasili-Mitrokhin.html

Broadcast media

Adams, Phillips. John Burton interviewed on ABC Radio National's *Late Night Live* programme (Australian Broadcasting Corporation), 2004. URL: www.abc.net.au/radionational/programs/latenightlive/john-burton/3415784

Boyle, Michael. Edited transcript of interview with Michael Boyle, ASIO first assistant director-general (1991-1993), *Four Corners*, Australian Broadcasting Corporation (ABC) television, November 1, 2004. URL: www.abc.net.au/4corners/content/2004/s1231975.htm

Smith, Tanya. Edited transcript of an interview with Tanya Smith, George Sadil's sister and a former ASIO employee, *Four Corners*, Australian Broadcasting Corporation (ABC) television, November 1, 2004. URL: www.abc.net.au/4corners/content/2004/s1232724.htm

"I, Spry: the rise and fall of a master spy", Australian Broadcasting Corporation (ABC) television documentary, broadcast on November 4, 2010.

INDEX

Aarons, Laurie 196
Aarons, Mark 194-196
Academy of Music, London 17-18
Adams, Phillip 178-179
Aldrich, Richard J. 173-174
Alekseev, Vladimir A. 194, 197
Alley, Rewi 219
Allied Military Government for Occupied Territories 26
Andover, RAF Station 57
Andrew, Christopher x, 62, 73, 84, 210, 216, 223, 233
Angleton, James Jesus 74-75
Archer (née Sissmore), Mrs Jane 85
Attlee, Clement 52, 216, 228
Australian Broadcasting Corporation (ABC) xi, xvii, 133-134
Australian Constitution 195-196
Australian Federal Police (AFP) x, xviii, 141, 155, 205, 212, 234-235
Australian Security Intelligence Organisation (ASIO) ix-xii, xvii-xix, 91, 104-106, 119, 126, 129, 136-140, 142-144, 149-171, 173, 191-199, 201-208, 211-215, 233-238, 264
Australian-Soviet Friendship Society 195
AVH (communist Hungary's secret police) 111, 164-166

Babington Smith, Constance 94-95
Ball, Desmond 173-174, 181
Barbour, Peter 146-147, 152
Bates, Charles 232
Batty, Peter 89
Behm, Jack 128
Bell, Coral 179-181
Bentley, Elizabeth 60
Bergen-Belsen, German concentration camp 32
Berlin Blockade and Airlift (1948/49) 60
Berlin Wall 251-253, 257
Bernie, Frances 183
Beurton, Len 221
Beurton, Ursula Ruth (*see* Kuczynski, Ursula Ruth)
Bevin, Ernest 52-53
Blake, George 89-91
Bletchley Park 64, 84, 92, 173
Blunt, Anthony 78-81
Blunt, Wilfred 79-80, 84, 87-89, 91
Bonaparte, Napoleon 263
Brezhnev, Leonid 195
Broda, Engelbert 228-229
Brown, Bill and Freda 194
Brown, Major Colin 128, 139, 150, 159
Brown, Lee (*see* Rhiannon, Lee)

Burgess, Guy 61, 66, 68, 71-75, 78-80, 84, 86-88
Burke, David 228
Burley Griffin, Walter 138, 143
Burton, Dr John W. 178-183
Butterfield, Sir Herbert 204
BVD (Dutch Domestic Security Service) 105, 109-111, 116-122, 131

Cadogan, Sir Alexander 55
Cairncross, John 79, 82-84, 89
Cairns, Dr Jim 187-190, 194-195
Cameron, Clyde 186
Campbell, Dr Andrew 182-184
Campbell, Sir Roderick 70-71
Carr, Bob 187, 190, 193
Castro, Fidel 237
Cecil, Robert 66-67, 69, 72, 80-81, 225
Central Intelligence Agency (CIA) x, 65, 67-68, 74, 90, 131, 191, 202, 207, 209, 213, 230
Chambers, Whittaker 60
Chavez, Hugo 237
Chernobyl nuclear disaster (1986) 245-246
Chetniks, Serbian 76-78, 85, 88-89
Chifley, Ben 172-173, 175, 182-183, 216-217
Churchill, Clarissa 73
Churchill, Winston 52, 55, 59, 73, 76-78, 81, 203, 224

Cicero, Marcus Tullius 172
Clayton, Walter 174-177
Clifford of Chudleigh, Lord 88
Cline, Ray 232
Cockburn, Claud 218, 220
Cohen, Morris and Lona 82
Colebatch, Dr Hal G.P. 189-190
Coleman, Peter ix-xii
Colombini, Captain Regent Enzo 265
Combe, David 157
Communist Party of Australia (CPA) 192-196
Cook AO, Michael x, 212, 214, 235
Costello, Desmond Patrick 'Paddy' 79, 81-82
Cowgill, Felix 66
Coyne, J. Patrick 230, 234
Cram, Cleveland 230
Cranbourne, Lord 182
Cuban missile crisis (1962) 114, 165
Curry, John 225
Curtin, John 179, 182

Dalziel, Allan 183, 186
Davis, Commissioner Jack 152
Day-Lewis, Cecil 218
Democratic Labor Party (DLP) 186
Deutsch, Dr Arnold 62-66, 69, 72-73, 75, 80-81, 83
Dies Committee (U.S.) 85

Dorling, Philip 191, 210-211
Downing, Taylor 92-93

Eden, Sir Anthony (Lord Avon) 73, 76-78, 182
Einthoven, Colonel Louis 109, 118, 121-122
Eisenhower, General Dwight 77, 93, 230
Ekimenko, Alexander 191
Elliott, John C. 139-140, 149, 158-159, 197
Elliott, Nicholas 68-69, 87-88
Ellis, Captain Charles 'Dick' 106
Evatt, Dr Herbert V. 'Bert' 106, 128, 178-187, 191
Ewert, Arthur 218-220

Federal Bureau of Investigation (FBI) x, 65, 67-68, 207, 209, 226, 232
Fédération Internationale Féline (FIFe) xviii, 241-248, 260-261, 264
Fischer, Benjamin 222
Foot, Rob 181
Fowler, Andrew 158, 198-199, 205, 212
Fraser, Malcolm 147, 193
Freedom for the Moluccas Movement 112
Fuchs, Klaus 60, 222-223, 227

GCHQ (UK Government Communications Headquarters) 173
Gerbrands, Pieter 110, 116-123
Gietzelt AO, Arthur 192-194
Gillis QC, Bernard 232
Glees, Anthony 232
Gobbo, Sir James A. 266
Goebbels, Dr Joseph 94
Gordievsky, Oleg ix, 73, 84, 89, 205, 207-208, 232
Gordon-Oliver, Robert 36-43, 97, 101-107, 115-117, 121, 135-138, 162-163, 267-268
Gorton, John 191
Gouzenko, Igor 60, 229-230
Governing Council of the Cat Fancy (GCCF) 242
Gray, Gordon 230, 234
Gray, Olga 64
Greene, Graham 67
Greenless, Major Kenneth 76
Greens Party (Australia) 195
GRU (Soviet Military Intelligence) 46, 60-61, 85, 91, 106, 109, 120, 142-144, 149, 159, 198, 201, 219-232
Grundeman, Albert 183, 186

Halifax, Lord 70
Halperin, Israel 227
Halsall, Christine 93-94

Hamburger, Rudolf 'Rolf' 221
Hamburger, Ursula Ruth (*see* Kuczynski, Ursula Ruth)
Hankey, Maurice (Lord) 83
Hartley, Christopher 47
Harvey, Bill and Libby 74-75
Hasluck, Paul 179, 182
Hawke, Bob 157-158, 167, 192-193, 208
Hawkinge, RAF Station 56-57
Hayden, Bill 187
Hill, Jim 176-177
Hill, Ted 176-177, 180
Hilton, James 270
Holdich, Roger 169
Hollis, Sir Roger xi, 91, 215-235
Hope, Justice Robert xi, 134, 153, 156-158, 162, 201
Horner, David xi, 128, 173-174, 216-217

Institute of World Politics 217, 233
International Ladies' College, The Hague 12-17
Islamic extremism 236-238
Ivanov, Valery 157

James, Albert 'Bert' 190-191, 194-195, 211
Joint Air Photographic Intelligence Centre (JAPIC) 95-100

Kalugin, Oleg ix, 205-208
Kastengren-Remborg, Brita 241
Keating, Paul x, 192, 235
Kennedy, President John F. 115
Kerr, Christian 195
KGB (Soviet Committee for State Security) ix, 46, 55, 61-63, 71, 90-91, 105-106, 109, 117-122, 142-144, 155, 164, 191, 194, 197-201, 205-213, 222, 236
KGB headquarters, Moscow 249-250
Khrushchev, Nikita 61, 114-115
Kisch, Egon 182
Kitchin, Phil 211
Klas, Luise 219
Klugmann, Norman John 'James' 71, 75-78, 83, 85-89
Koestler, Arthur 236
Kondrashev, Sergei 90
Korean civilian airliner shot down (1983) 164-165
Korean War (1950-53) 60, 72, 74, 90
Kosov, Nikolai 117-122
Krivitsky, Walter 85
Kuczynski, Brigitte 226
Kuczynski, Jürgen 226
Kuczynski, Robert 'René' 224, 226
Kuczynski, Ursula Ruth 219-228

Labor Party split (Australia, 1954) 186
Lague, David 156
Lamphere, Robert 67, 75, 232

Lange, David 208
Lazovik, Geronty P. 197
Lenin, Vladimir, I. 199
Leydin, Reginald 185
Lincoln, Abraham 262
Lippe, Baron von 33-34
Lives of Others, The (2006 German film) ix
Lloyd George, David 83
Long, Leo 79, 84, 89
Loosley AM, Stephen 192
Lyalin, Oleg 230
Lyons, Joseph 182

McAdam, Anthony 133
McCarthy, U.S. Senator Joseph 200
McIntosh, Alister 81
Macintyre, Ben 67-68
Maclean, Donald 61, 63, 66, 68-75, 78, 83-88, 173
Maclean, Melinda 70
Macmillan, Harold 87
McNamara, Captain 'Jack' 73
Manne, Robert 184
Manusama, Dr Johannes 112
Martin, David 75-77, 88
May, Alan Nunn 229
Medmenham, RAF Station 92-95
Menzies, Robert 127, 129, 175, 183, 185-186
MI-14 (Britain's Directorate of Military Intelligence) 84

MI5 (Britain's Security Service) xi, 44, 64, 85, 89, 91, 126, 130-131, 207, 211, 216, 220, 224-234
MI6 (Britain's Secret Intelligence Service) x, 44-46, 62, 64-69, 86, 89-91, 207, 209, 211, 225-226
Mihailovich, General Draza 76-78, 85, 88-89
Miller, Robert L. 81
Mills, AFP Commander Alan 212
Milner, Dr Ian 175-176
Milte, Kerry 152
Minh, Ho Chi 189
Mitchell, Graham 230
Mitrokhin, Vasili ix, xvii, 191, 205, 207-211, 214, 234
Modin, Yuri 68, 80, 83
Molody, Konon 82
Molotov, Vyacheslav 182, 186-187
Monk, Dr Paul 217, 228, 233-234
Murphy QC, Lionel 151-153
Mussert, Anton 127

National Socialism (Nazism) 236-238
Nayanov, Gennadiy 197
Negus, George 152
Netherlands flood disaster (1953) 98-99
Nienaber, Blair 128
North Atlantic Treaty Organisation (NATO) 60
Norwood, Melita 223, 228

Nuneham Park, RAF Station 92, 95-100

Oakes, Laurie 213
Office of National Assessments (ONA) x, 160, 182, 212
O'Leary, Des 128, 152
Operation Liver x, 205, 212, 214, 234-235
O'Sullivan, Fergan 183-184

Partisans, Yugoslav communist 76-78, 85-86, 111-112
Peake, Hayden B. 233
Peter the Great, tsar of Russia 230
Petrov, Vladimir ix, 105-106, 126-127, 143, 184-187
Petrov, Vladimir von 106
Petrova, Evdokia ix, 105-106, 126-127, 143, 184-187
Philby, Aileen 74-75
Philby (née Kohlmann), Alice 'Litzi' 65
Philby, H.A.R. 'Kim' 62-75, 78, 83-88, 91, 106, 173, 223-226, 229, 232
Phillips, Max 105, 126
Pickering, Larry 152
Pincher, Chapman 89, 217-233
Pontecorvo, Bruno 227-228
Portland Spy Ring 82
Prague Spring (1968) 194

Prichard, Katharine Susannah 176-178, 182
Putin, Vladimir 202, 224
Putron, Owen W. de 43

Quebec Agreement (August 1943) 224

Rado, Alexander 221
Radio Security Service (RSS) 226
Rank, Arthur 55
Ravel, Marguerite 241
Reed, Justice Geoffrey 129, 217
Rees, Goronwy 74
Reid, Alan 152
Rhiannon (née Brown), Lee 194-195, 197
Richards, Ron 128
Richardson, Maurice 218
Rimm, Karl 219
Rooney, Frank 183-184
Roosevelt, President Franklin D. 224
Rose, Alan 204-206
Rose, Fred (Australian public servant) 180
Rose, Fred (Canadian parliamentarian) 229
Rosenberg, Julius and Ethel 82
Royal Society for the Prevention of Cruelty to Animals (RSPCA) 244

Sadil, George 154-159, 204-206

San Marino, Republic of xix, 247, 262-266
Sasson, Albert 107, 268-273
Schramm, David 140-141
Seton-Watson, Hugh 78
Sheldrick, Dame Daphne 271
Silone, Ignazio 236
Sillitoe, Sir Percy 216
Skripov, Ivan 152
Smedley, Agnes 218-220
Smith, Keith 113
Smith (née Sadil), Tanya 157-158
Socialist Party of Australia (SPA) 194-196
Society of British Aircraft Constructors 57
Solzhenitsyn, Aleksandr 200
'Sonia' (*see* Kuczynski, Ursula Ruth)
Sorge, Richard 181, 219-220
Spanish Civil War 66
Special Operations Executive (SOE) 64, 66, 76-78
Spender, Stephen 236
Spry, Brigadier Sir Charles v, xi-xii, xvii, 105, 109, 119, 126-134, 136-139, 142, 147, 153, 168, 170, 173, 175
Stables, Captain Tony 219
Stalin, Joseph 45, 48, 52, 188, 199-200, 236
Stanley, Colonel Roy 93, 95

Stasi (communist East Germany's secret police) ix, 251, 254, 257
Stenin, Ivan 194, 197
Stepanenko, Yuriy S. 198
Stewart, Cameron 203
Straight, Michael 88
Stupin, Leonid 210
Susemihl, Igor 120, 123
Sutch, William 211
SVR 62-63, 156

Tait, Dr Michael 240
Tasoev, Yuri 48-50
Tatarinov, Vyacheslav, V. 156
Thatcher, Margaret 89, 217, 231
Thomson, Dr Lloyd 116
Throssell, Hugo 'Jim' 177
Throssell, Richard 'Ric' 177-178, 180-181
Thwaites, Michael 127
Tito, Josip Broz 76-78, 85, 88, 111
Tokaev (Tokaty), Grigori and Aza 45-56, 108-109, 122, 230
Toynbee, Arnold 180
Toynbee, Philip 72
Trahair, Richard C.S. 81
Truman, Harry 59, 77
Tulayev, Vladimir Y. 197
Turnbull QC, Malcolm 231

V-1 flying bomb 94-95

Van Druten, John 98
Venona Project 87, 127, 173-174, 182
Victoria, Queen 262
Victory in Europe (V-E) Day, 1945 31
Vietnam War 188
Volkov, Igor 159
Volkov, Konstantin 86-87
Waterman, Ted 113
West, Nigel 230
West Drayton, RAF Station 46
White, Dick 80, 218
Whitlam, Gough 147, 152-153, 189 189, 193, 198

Wilhelm, John L. 233
Wilhelmina, Dutch Queen Mother 106-107
Wilmslow, RAF Station 21
Woodward, Justice Sir Edward 147, 153, 162, 201
World Peace Council 188-189
World War II 17-31
Wright, Peter 217, 231-233

Yugoslavia 75-78, 85

Zaitsev, Viktor S. 181
Zedong, Mao 60, 237

www.ingramcontent.com/pod-product-compliance
Lightning Source LLC
Chambersburg PA
CBHW052051230426
43671CB00011B/1867